LADIES COURTING
TROUBLE

Also by
Dolores Stewart Riccio

THE DIVINE CIRCLE OF
LADIES MAKING MISCHIEF

CHARMED CIRCLE

CIRCLE OF FIVE

LADIES COURTING TROUBLE

DOLORES STEWART RICCIO

KENSINGTON BOOKS
http://www.kensingtonbooks.com

To Nancy Erikson and her girls—

"We'll take a cup of kindness yet
For auld lang syne . . ."

ACKNOWLEDGMENTS

With warmest thanks to some very special people . . .

To my wonderful husband, Rick, who has encouraged and counseled me in all my writing through the years.

To my daughter, Lucy, for sharing her computer wisdom, and other special knowledge, and to my son, Charlie, for his own unique contribution to my world.

To all the dear friends and family who have formed my ideal of friendship over the years.

To my editor at Kensington, Audrey LaFehr, whose continued guidance and enthusiasm have meant so much, and to copy editor, Margaret Jarpey, for her care, thoroughness, and kind words.

Bright Blessings to all!

Chapter One

"Double, double, toil and trouble..." Phillipa grinned wickedly as she lay down the tenth card from the Rider-Waite deck, last of the layout; it was called *The Moon*. "I wouldn't take on any new crusades if I were you, Cass. From start to finish, this reading counsels you to watch your step." She leaned over the layout, dark wings of her hair falling forward, her expression disapproving, like a garage mechanic sizing up a faulty carburetor.

A bunch of swords and wands in my cards, so what? I was beginning to be sorry that I'd asked her to read the tarot for me. Three phases of the moon looking down upon a howling wolf and a smiling dog—what was so bad about that?

"It's a card of hidden foes and unforeseen perils. The wolf, now—that's a symbol of untamed creation. The dog, on the other hand, adapts to mankind insofar as it suits his own interests, sort of like your dog, Scruffy. And see this rugged path through hostile country? Not to mention this crayfish popping out from the pool of the Cosmic Mind." Phillipa's blunt fingernail pointed to various pictorial elements. "What did you tell me you were doing this Samhain? I mean, apart from our own circle ceremony."

"Church. I've been invited to give a talk at the Garden of

Gethsemane Ladies' League on the origins of Halloween in our Samhain. I really loathe giving speeches, but I feel I ought to represent Wicca in a favorable light whenever I have the chance."

"'Fire burn, and cauldron bubble,'" my hostess intoned, giving a quick stir to the pot of pear and mango chutney simmering on her Viking range, wafting the spicy aroma throughout the room. I thought there must be extra calories in the very air of Phillipa's state-of-the-art kitchen. Not to mention the "Fall Fruit Breads" we were sampling with our tea, the theme of her next bimonthly cable cooking show, *Kitchen Magic*. As Colette wrote, and Phillipa was fond of quoting on and off the air, "'If you aren't up to a little magic, you shouldn't waste your time trying to cook.'"

Phillipa returned to the long marble table and gave my cards another gloomy look before gathering them up. "Five of wands, seven of swords. Maybe the Gethsemane Ladies are planning an exorcism or something. Rid you of the cursed demons that possess you, my dear."

"Not at all," I said. "The Reverend Peacedale couldn't be more ecumenical-minded. I suspect he's quite interested in the mystic experience per se. My clairvoyant episodes, I mean. And he understands that the ancient nature religions predate the advent of Satan and therefore have nothing devilish about them."

"Well, don't say you weren't warned."

Which is what I thought about later, while having my stomach pumped out at Jordan Hospital. The Ladies' League Hospitality Hour had been as disastrous as my lugubrious friend possibly could have predicted. Only the strong hands of my bridegroom, Joe Ulysses, holding me back by one shoulder, and those of a robust nurse on the other side had kept me from pulling the gagging, scratching tube out of my throat and to hell with it. Probably one of the worst hours of my life. I really was tempted to call up a few impish entities I'd read about to avenge my misery, but I am pledged to work on the white side of Wicca.

I wasn't the only one enduring the unendurable. Several members of the League and the minister's wife were also at the hospital, and as I learned later, one of the older spinsters, whose passion was chocolate—Lydia Craig—wouldn't be making it to the All Saints' Day service on November first. Poison hemlock causes weakness, nausea, vomiting, difficulty in breathing, and, if enough of it is ingested, paralysis and death. And those mystery brownies had been cleverly laced with the stuff. It was almost enough to turn a gal off chocolate forever.

I recalled how Mrs. Peacedale—Patty—had made a face when she nibbled at her brownie, muttering that the baking soda had not been properly sifted into the flour. I too had thought they were rather musty or mousy-tasting despite a liberal dose of vanilla. But any brownies would suffer in comparison to Phillipa's.

Then, when everyone began to feel ill, the herbal lore in my brain clicked in. I guessed immediately what we'd eaten and told the paramedics. "I'm certain it was poison hemlock—that mousy aftertaste," I'd said weakly. Due to my conviction, we all got our stomachs pumped out immediately, while I was mentally kicking myself for my stupidity. I'd eaten one too many bites of that fetid brownie, purely out of politeness.

As the endless day at Jordan Hospital wore on, and it was obvious that I would never eat again, I urged Joe to go home to feed himself and Scruffy. "Don't worry about me," I said faintly, laying on the guilt. "You two have a good meal."

His Aegean blue eyes looked worried and somewhat reproachful. "How could this happen? And at a church social, for God's sake? Can't you go anywhere without being drawn into danger?"

"Is this the pot calling the kettle *black ass?*" I suggested. As a ship's engineer for Greenpeace, Joe continually sails into his own share of perilous misadventures.

"And I thought that once we were married you'd be happy to stay at home and tend to the weaving," he complained, grinning sheepishly. After a few restorative kisses, he left, with touching reluctance, and the evening nurse appeared.

"Hi. My name is Brenda. Are we feeling better now, Mrs. Ulysses?" she inquired briskly while she took my blood pressure.

Although assuming an air of motherly authority, she was at least ten years younger than I, a pale girl with slightly protruding eyes and fine brown hair falling out of its coil. "You were lucky, you know, honey. You didn't eat too much, and it didn't get too far. Was that your husband who just left? Nice tan for this time of year. Tanning salon?"

"No, Greenpeace. He travels the world in search of environmental hazards, often in tropical climes. And it's *Ms.* Shipton," I mumbled. My throat was still sore. "My good luck was being the guest speaker at the League. People kept asking me questions, so I was delayed in getting to the hospitality table until after almost everyone else. And I didn't finish my brownie, which didn't taste very good."

She checked my bracelet I.D. "Oh, yes. Shipton. I see. I wouldn't mind being a Mrs. myself, but that's just me. What was the talk about, honey?"

"Nature spirituality religions in pagan times. The origins of Halloween. And modern-day Wicca."

"Is that, like, witches, curses, and all?" Nurse Brenda glanced at my face again as if she might have missed some telltale sign, such as green skin or a wart on my nose. Soon she'd connect "Shipton" with our circle's notoriety in becoming involved in local crimes.

Speaking of which, any minute now the circle would be alerted. Phillipa would probably hear the news first and call Fiona, Heather, and Deidre. The circle would be swarming in here, bringing their various healing arts, none of which would include anything as cursed as gastric lavage, ugh. A few stomach-calming herbs, a little white light, a homey lecture from Fiona.

"Not witches. Wiccans, actually," I corrected Brenda. "So, have they discovered who brought the lethal brownies to the Ladies' League yet?"

"I can't imagine *who* would try to poison a nice group of church ladies. Two detectives are working their way down the hall right now, questioning the victims who are well enough to provide information. They'll get to you pretty soon, and you can ask them if an arrest is imminent." Brenda cast a calculating look my way. Perhaps I had made her personal list of suspects—either because of the Wiccan connection or my herbal business, Cassandra Shipton, Earthlore Herbal Preparations and Cruelty-Free Cosmetics.

Besides "whodunit?" the other big question on my mind, which I did not voice aloud, was how a person with clairvoyant skills like myself could munch up a poisoned brownie without a clue. Admittedly, I could hardly ever summon up my visions at will. They came and went by their own mysterious plan, hardly ever with glad tidings or a winning lottery number.

I was relieved to see it was Stone Stern and his partner, Billy Mann, who arrived at my room soon after Brenda bustled away. Phillipa's husband is a tall, scholarly looking man, surprisingly gentle for one in his profession. "Cass, what in the world?" Stone took my hand and squeezed it gently. There was real warmth in those gray eyes behind oval, metal-framed glasses. "I don't mean to scold you when you're in a weakened state, but why do I always find you in the midst of mayhem and murder?"

"Same question Joe often asks me. Obviously, it's my karma. Does Mrs. Peacedale know who donated the hemlock treats? Did Bevvy Besant eat the damned things? She's the hospitality chairperson, so she might have an idea who brought them. And how many victims were there, anyway?"

"Relax, Cass. Mundane as my talents may be, I'll do the investigating. But no, the minister's wife doesn't know who donated the brownies to the hospitality table. And yes, Mrs. Besant is here in the hospital but indisposed at the moment. Thirteen persons in all were admitted to the hospital, including a teenage boy delivering office supplies who copped a brownie out of the church kitchen. Tough on him, but a good thing, actually. Narrowed the poison field down to the brownies, although you helped with that, too, so I heard. Nevertheless, every item served will be tested."

"Uh oh—Bevvy's getting pumped, the poor baby," I murmured. "And what about poor Lydia Craig? She seemed like a sprightly old lady. The poison took her rather fast, didn't it? Has her family arrived?"

"Yes, it was all over quickly. Speedier than Socrates, in fact. But relatively painless as poisons go. The ancient Greeks considered it a humane method of execution. Weakness of the limbs, followed by paralysis of the breathing apparatus. She must have eaten quite a few of those brownies, although all the survivors mentioned a kind of 'musty' or 'bitter' flavor. Apparently, the Craig woman was known to have a big yen for chocolate." Turning to his partner, Stern said, "Have the Craig family members been notified yet, Billy?"

Billy, a beefy, red-cheeked guy who looked as if he'd been sent down from Central Casting to play an Irish cop, had been leaning on the door frame, studying his notes with a puzzled frown. At the mention of his name, however, he looked up and grinned. "Hey, Cass. How ya doing? Reverend Peacedale and a uniform are breaking the news to the Craigs. I understand the old lady was a spinster, no immediate family, but some nephews and a niece who are local."

"So, Cass," Stone continued, "can *you* shed any light at all on the poisonings?"

"Did the incident have anything to do with your being the guest of honor?" Billy asked. He removed a pencil stump wedged behind his ear and poised it above his notebook.

I hadn't thought of that. Could anyone be crazy enough to register their protest to Wicca by poisoning the brownies? "Maybe. But I don't really feel that was the motive. And beyond that, I haven't a clue. Sorry." And I was sorry. I really wanted to help Stone. What I needed here was a helpful little vision showing me why, when, and, above all, who. "Maybe something will come to me later."

"No one seems to know anything," Billy complained. "We can pair up every single one of those sweets with a church member *except* the brownies. They simply appeared out of nowhere in the kitchen, and the coffee-hour hostesses set them out on the buffet."

"Like magic." Stone winked at me, squeezed my hand again, then stepped back to allow my so-called dinner tray to be placed in front of me. After the orderly left, Stone said, "Before you eat any of that stuff, I should warn you that Phil's on her way." Then he and Billy departed to see if Bevvy was talking yet.

"Drink it, you mean," I muttered to myself, eyeing my tray. Insipid broth, industrial tea, pale apple juice, and some kind of weird gelatin, Laboratory Lime perhaps.

My next visitor was Selwyn ("call me Wyn") Peacedale, pastor of the Garden of Gethsemane Presbyterian Church of Plymouth, which was located just around the corner from my house, an antique saltbox overlooking the Atlantic. I've always thought Wyn resembles a heavenly cherub who has aged a bit, but today his round cheeks and dimples were lost in grief. He took my hand in a pastoral way; his was feverishly damp, mine icy cold. "How're you doing, Cass? What a terrible thing this is! I'm so sorry that you were a victim in this vicious attack on the church. As it happened, I had to leave to attend to some pressing parish matters right after your most informative talk, or I probably would have been poisoned myself. I love chocolate stuff, you know. But you . . . your first time as a visitor to Gethsemane. . . ."

"Not exactly the first time. I attended the Donahue funeral—standing room only at that one. Anyway, I'm alive—that's the main thing. Poor Lydia Craig. It must have been terrible telling her family. And how's Patty?"

"Patty's doing well physically, I believe. Like you, she's been treated, had her whiffs of oxygen, and now she's having a little liquid supper. But she's very upset about what happened, just to think that one of our own may have done something like this. There are always some disagreements and strained relations, of course, but . . ." He sighed heavily. "As for counseling the Craigs, I've visited the niece and nephew who are living here in Plymouth.

There's another nephew in Marshfield. The niece offered to notify him and various cousins." He sighed again and flushed slightly. "I believe Lydia's left the church quite a bit of money. At least that's what she told me last Christmas when I was seeking contributions towards some renovations. I could hardly believe it, given her usual modest donations, but she said it was a fait accompli, and I would be mighty surprised, but not to call the contractors just yet, as she intended to live a good long while. Well, well . . . poor Lydia. *'Tomorrow is promised to no one,'* as they say. Such a cruel end to her expectations." He was quiet then, looking out the window at the October darkness, lips moving silently. For a moment, he seemed to have forgotten where he was. Then a look of apprehension crossed his face, and he remembered he'd been talking to me. "I trust this bequest won't cause a problem. With the relatives, that is."

"From what I've seen of inheritance procedures, I would say, steel yourself, Wyn." It still hurt me to speak, so I said no more.

"Patty and I will pray about it. And for you, too, Cass, may the Lord bless and keep you." He trudged out with steps quite disconsolate for a pastor who'd just got a fortune to spend on his church. Right in the vestibule, exhibited on an easel, I'd seen an architect's drawing of a grand new entrance and an addition. Wyn called it his "heart's wish made visible," and I'd said that's a magic visualization, same as we do.

As predicted, the circle descended en masse a few minutes later, bringing a discernible wave of warmth and energy into my room.

"Don't touch that slop," Phillipa commanded immediately, unpacking the small hamper she carried on her arm. "I've brought you a thermos of my own double chicken-beef herbed broth, jellied pomegranate juice with a touch of port wine, and some Assam tea."

"What, no calf's-foot jelly?" I whined. The broth smelled heavenly rich.

"Phil finds it really hard to get decent calves' feet these days." Tall, lithe Heather Devlin pushed past Phillipa to give me a hug, her long bronze braid swinging halfway down the back of her khaki jacket, like some modern-day Maid Marian. "Look, I've brought you one of my best candles. Light this, my dear, and you'll breathe in the ocean's healing power."

The candle was greenish and looked like a tide pool, being filled with tiny crustaceans and shells coated with barnacles. If I lit the thing, in a thrice Brenda would be rushing into my room with a fire extinguisher. But it's the thought that counts. "Thoughts are things," was my grandma's favorite saying, and it's become one of my guiding lights.

"And *I've* brought you an amulet, a little gargoyle to frighten away the bad vibes." Deidre Ryan was trying to lean over me and fasten her handiwork to one of my bed's white enamel posts, but she's a petite gal and was having to stand on her tiptoes.

Heather took the ghoulish artifact out of Deidre's hand and tied it up above the nurse's buzzer. "Nice eyes," she commented. "I like that angry red glare."

"Now, girls," Fiona Ritchie took over the room with her new wisewoman glamour. In the slight shift of perception caused by the glamour, her normally plump, rather frumpish self had metamorphosed into a regal, Minerva-like person to whom anyone would want to listen attentively. It was an enviable talent.

"How does she do that?" Deidre whispered in my ear.

"I think it's akin to *presence*, the kind of aura that some actors are able to project," I whispered back.

"If you had dowsed your food, as I taught you to do, you would have detected the poison," Fiona scolded.

"Fiona, it was a church social! How would it have looked if I took out a pendulum and let it swing over the cookies?"

"Exceptional people have to learn to tolerate some puzzlement among the mundanes. Do you know," Fiona continued, "that there are some religious sects that claim their true believers can handle snakes or drink poison without harm? In ancient times, priestesses of the Great Mother, too, were snake handlers. No, no—don't look so alarmed. It's not a test I want us to try. From my studies, I think harmony is the key, and disharmony equals dis-ease. No lectures today, however." Her deep, warm hug was like medicine itself, and I basked in it. "But on Samhain, we'll talk of this again. Meanwhile"—out of the pocket of her coat sweater of many colors, Fiona fished a Walkman CD player— "here are some magical tunes to help restore the harmony. Play it later, when you're alone. I want to see you dancing out of here by tomorrow."

Dancing after hemlock poisoning? Sure, why not. Just don't ask me to make friends with snakes.

The "magic tunes" turned out to be a tract of medieval music played at my wedding to Joe last Yule. And bringing with it memories of our enchanted honeymoon in New Zealand, it did indeed make me feel like dancing.

Chapter Two

"I'm trying to get it out of my head that this calamity was Mrs. Pynchon's doing, because she herself is such a poisonous individual." Patty Peacedale confided to me over a cup of my stomach-soothing triple mint-and-chamomile tea. It was several days after the hemlock incident. Thanks to fast action at the hospital, we'd all recovered well enough, except for poor Lydia Craig, of course. Her funeral, just yesterday, had been one of the best attended since the Donahues' (a double murder two years ago that had packed the church to standing room only). "That miserable woman has been the bane of my existence ever since Wyn took over Gethsemane."

"I suspect there's one like her in every church." I passed Patty a plate of lemon cookies. Normally, I might have offered cheering chocolate, but I'd lost my taste for that treat, however it might perk up one's brain chemistry. I suspected that Patty felt the same.

Lying under the kitchen table, my dog, Scruffy, sighed heavily to remind me that he hadn't as yet had as much as a crumb of cookie. *A bite of sweet stuff hones my superior senses, Toots. Your pal, now, smells lost and sad to my sensitive olfactory system, like she can't remember where the good bones are buried.* Scruffy has his own way of communicating, and somehow I always hear what he's thinking.

"This is Wyn's third church, and believe me, Pynchon's unique in our experience." Patty gazed out my kitchen window. "It's nice here. If I had this view of the ocean to look at every day, I'd never get anything else done. So, what do you think, Cass? I mean, vibe-wise."

"Vibe-wise, I don't believe that the poisoner was motivated by hate, meanness, or church politics. More than that, I can't say. My first instinct, however, is to rule out the ladies of the League. I'm familiar with *Conium maculatum*. It's the black sheep of the parsley, parsnip, and carrot family, and anyone who set out to harvest poison hemlock would have to be as knowledgeable as myself and wear protective clothing as well," I mused. "I must tell Stone to watch out for someone with a case of dermatitis."

"Well, I definitely suspect Mrs. Pynchon myself. I don't suppose you could . . ." Patty reached in her knitting bag, took out a blue object, either a sleeve or a wind sock, I couldn't tell which, and began to complete it. She kept her eyes on the work.

"No fortune-telling, no hexes, no potions," I interrupted, not wanting my guest to suggest a Pynchon-remedy she'd regret later. Basically, Patty Peacedale was a good soul. With her heart-shaped face and tiny, pointed chin, she would have been cute, although well past the age for it, if her hazel eyes hadn't been filled with anxiety and her hair limp from general exhaustion. She dressed as one who wanted above all to avoid notice: a powder blue cardigan, a matching blouse with a silver circle pin at the neck, and a navy skirt of the classic just-below-the-knee length. Her shoes were navy blue comfort moccasins, and the matching handbag was slightly scuffed leather. A single brown curl fell in an oily swirl over her broad, fair forehead.

When Patty had first begun to confide the problems of being a pastor's wife to me, she'd said it was because I was unconnected in any way to her husband's parish. *Unlikely to judge or to blab*, I thought. Rather like a priest, or more aptly, a priestess. Thus I had come to know a great deal about Mrs. Pynchon's iron grip on her church. At least once a year the woman convened some committee or other to talk about booting out the Peacedales. She fought any innovative idea with tooth and claw, grumbled about every expenditure, ferreted out everyone's secret vice, and used it as food for gossip. In her spare time, she complained about Patty's lack of Christian spirit and housekeeping skills. She even blamed Patty for being childless. The congregation had invested substantially in a four-bedroom parsonage, she'd declared in Patty's hearing, to house a pastor's growing family. Instead, there were only Wyn and Patty rambling around in all that expensive space. Patty's hobby room and her own personal office should properly be used as children's rooms, Mrs. Pynchon had asserted. But was she the poisoner? Somehow, I didn't think so, much as Patty would have liked to see her persecutor dragged away in handcuffs to the local jail.

"She told everyone in the church that she drew a cross in the dust on my tier table and three days later it was still there." The knitting needles clicked angrily.

"Oh, Patty, a little dust is so unimportant in the larger scheme of things!" At least I hoped so. Looking around, I wondered when the last time was that I'd slicked up the tops of things. "Why is it that women can always be made to feel guilty about housework? A home needs to be a place of comfort, creativity, and a touch of beauty—not operating-room sterile. Especially if you live with animals."

We canines prefer dirt floors—cool in summer, warm in winter. Scruffy yawned, stretched, and came out from under the table. *Need to pee now, Toots.*

"Hold it a minute, Sport," I said. Patty looked at me strangely. "Talking to the dog," I explained, going to the stove to fetch the kettle and refill the teapot with dried mint leaves and boiling water. Making herb tea is something I do on automatic pilot, so I paused to gaze dreamily out the window where the lowering sun was gilding the little houses along the curving shore, and I noted the way the gulls were lifting and gliding in the golden rays. As sometimes happens when I get rapt by light, I began to get that slightly nauseous feeling that precedes a vision. I sat down quickly in a kitchen chair.

From what seemed like a long distance away, I could hear Patty saying, "Cass . . . Cass, are you all right?" Then the kitchen faded from view, and I saw a pair of hands protected by work gloves. A shiny red-handled knife unfolded. A rutted field between two stands of pine, and, growing in that field, a weed that looked like Queen Anne's Lace, wild carrot. The hands, using tiny steel scissors to snip away at the herb, stashed the fresh green stalks in a canvas bag. An overcast, grisly day, and someone was collecting hemlock. I could see everything except the face and figure of the person harvesting the poison.

The scene faded, and I found myself back in my own kitchen. Scruffy was nosing my leg in a concerned way. *Hey, Toots . . . you're dragging your tail. Maybe you'd better lap up some cold water.* And Patty was leaning over me, slapping at my wrist. She waved a small, open bottle under my nose. A more than bracing odor hit my brain.

"Smelling salts?" I murmured.

"Never leave home without it," Patty said. "You had yourself a little transient episode of some kind, dear. Should I call your doctor?"

"Thanks, but I'm fine. The episode was clairvoyant. That's how it strikes me."

Patty clapped her hands, her melancholia having evaporated into a pleased smile. "Oh, Wyn will be so interested that I've observed you in action, so to speak. Did you see who did it? *The murderer?*" she whispered.

I sighed. It wasn't easy to explain about the gaping holes in clairvoyance. I described the hands, the knife, the scissors, the field, the harvesting of herbs on a raw day. "I think it must have been September, because the plants had not yet dried on the stalk. Someone planned ahead, I'd say. But I did not see a face, nor even enough to guess if it was a man or a woman. Still, maybe

I'll see that same field somewhere around Plymouth and we'll at least have a location, a place to start."

"The scissors, now. I've seen those on a Swiss Army knife." Patty began to clear the table, motioning me to sit where I was, and, in truth, I did feel a bit weak. "I believe they fold up inside the pocket knife with several other useful tools. Will you tell all this to Detective Stern?"

"Of course, but it's not much to go on. If I were Stern, I'd put my money on forensics, maybe some fingerprints on that plastic dish that held the brownies."

"Well, that's that, then," Patty said, dusting a few cookie crumbs off her hands. "I have to get back to the parish for a committee meeting. The Christmas Bazaar, you know. Wyn always says I don't have to be part of every committee. 'My job description doesn't include an indentured wife,' he declares to the church governing board from time to time. But you know it's expected, especially by Mrs. P. I just wish our living room wasn't considered the parish club, if you know what I mean. And they notice every flaw. If only Mrs. Pynchon . . . Will you be all right now, Cass, here by yourself?"

Apparently this dumb dame hasn't noticed that you're watched over by a superior companion animal. Scruffy sighed, muttered, and walked to the door to speed the departing visitor.

"I'll be fine. Scruffy considers himself an excellent nurse and guard dog, rather like Nana in *Peter Pan*," I said. "And Joe will be home soon, laden with do-it-yourself supplies from Home Warehouse." Joe's projects around the house were nearly always interrupted by his Greenpeace assignments, so he tended to work at a feverish pitch between expeditions. Any day now, I expected him to fly off to parts unknown, abandoning the latest home improvement, a terrific array of skunk-deterrent floodlights strung from tree to tree, lighting up our backyard like Massasoit Mall.

As she opened the kitchen door that led to our architecturally incorrect back porch, Patty looked perkier than she had when she arrived. "If you have another vision, please do give us a call. It's *so* interesting."

Perhaps it was a trick of sun and shadow through the trees, but suddenly I seemed to see her in double exposure, one form erect and smiling, the other bent over in anguish.

"Patty . . . when you have these committee meetings, are refreshments served?"

"Of course, but I only have to manage the tea and coffee. People usually bring baked goods." She stopped stock-still and put her hand over her mouth. "Oh, my good heavens!"

"You need to be super careful that you know who brought what from now on. Like the airlines, you need to connect each offering with a person who is present among you. No mystery snacks. Promise?"

"You don't think . . . the poison person will try again?"

"I do have that notion. I hope I'm wrong."

"Well, this certainly has been enlightening. I'll have such a lot to share with Wyn. Thank you, Cass."

Scruffy scooted by Patty and hit the nearest tree with a sigh of relief. Patty turned and waved again as she got into her car, a black Buick Regal.

"I like Patty," I said to Scruffy. "She's rather a dear person."

Yeah, but she has the manners of a poodle—hogged all the cookies herself and never dropped a bite. What's for supper, Toots?

"What would you say to a nice beef stew with dumplings?" Already my head was in the refrigerator, taking out beef, carrots, celery. I wished I had the moral courage to be a vegetarian, but having a robust man to feed was a good excuse to ignore the issue. "At least it's free-range, organic beef," I justified myself to the dog. "And we won't tell Joe that I picked these mushrooms myself in Jenkins Park. It makes him so nervous, poor darling."

Chapter Three

Joe keeps his cell phone at the ready day and night, a minor annoyance. The major pain is when it rings, because its chief purpose is to connect with Greenpeace for yet another summons to an environmental challenge. All right, I have to admit, it's his job, but Greenpeace takes him away from me at short notice and for weeks at a time. As a Libran, I do like to live a well-balanced life. Of course, Joe would complain that I throw my own life out of whack when I embark on a crime-solving spree. Phillipa says we're both crusaders and will just have to put up with each other's quests.

At least it wasn't the Pategonian toothfish emergency this time. It's really demoralizing to be abandoned to my fate by someone intent on saving an endangered fish. This newest call had come just as we were relaxing with a favorite old film—*Ladyhawk*—and a bowl of popcorn.

"I'll have to leave tomorrow," he said with a rueful smile. I didn't have to be a clairvoyant to see that gleam of anticipation lighting up his blue eyes. "I'm shipping on the *Esperanza* to Miami. You remember that Greenpeace is being brought up on charges for boarding a ship transporting illegally harvested mahogany from Brazil to the United States?"

"They arrested the activists instead of checking out the illegal cargo?"

"Yeah, and all we were going to do was to hang a banner, 'Mr. President, stop illegal logging.'"

"Well, sure—you dummies had to bring in the president."

"It's called the right of free speech and peaceful protest. Anyway, we're making another run at the scene of the crime to see what happens."

"Throw your hats in the door, so to speak?"

"In the port. Probably the worst thing will be a media feeding frenzy."

"You hope."

"The case against Greenpeace hangs on a hundred-year-old law called 'sailor-mongering.'"

"I don't even want to know what *that* is."

"It's what you think—a law against boarding a ship that's entering the harbor with the intention of accosting the crew. Pimps used to row out to arriving ships and proposition the guys, take them to shore, and after some revelry with the girls, relieve them of their money. Not exactly applicable to Greenpeace. And sympathetic public opinion, I admit, may make a difference, possibly get the charge thrown out of court."

"So the feeding frenzy is okay by you?"

"Right."

"You might even, if necessary, stir up the media a little?"

Joe merely smiled, a male version of Mona Lisa's inscrutable smirk. "It's all just part of the job, ma'am."

"So, let's see. It's almost Samhain now. Think you'll be out of jail by Thanksgiving?"

"If this is still a free country."

"Or at least by Yule?"

"Our first anniversary! Would I miss that?"

That called for a kiss, and the kiss led to a prolonged farewell in the warm, cushioned nest of our bedroom. As always, his compact muscular body and spicy scent were irresistibly sexy. And I was addicted to the gentle strength of his touch. Perhaps the honeymoon is never over for sailor's wives.

"Do you think that poison is a woman's weapon?" I asked Phillipa. We were in her spacious kitchen, where she was putting the finishing touches on the fruit breads for the TV show. These were the perfect creations she would display on a buffet at the end of the show, not the ones haphazardly mixed on camera and baked during the taping.

"Hmmm," she replied, realigning a candied fruit decoration.

"Phil, it's perfection. Stop messing around, and answer me."

"Well, it would be my weapon of choice, that's for sure. Such a simple thing to do, if you know your herbs—right, dear? My personal favorite would be the Destroying Angel mushroom. But, unfortunately, I don't know a toadstool from a puffball."

"*Amanita*. I learned all about mushrooms at my grandma's knee, so I could teach you, if you like. My experience has been that if you're not trained in foraging as a child, you'll never be a confident forager later. No wonder poison as a weapon comes to mind for you, since you're a professional cook. But what about other women, regular women . . ."

". . . who spend a good portion of their lives in kitchens, preparing foods for unappreciative men to consume? If time's no object, and a wife can afford a leisurely pace, it could be done simply by loading up the husband with salt, sugar, and saturated fats. Women do that all the time. Perhaps that's why we have so many merry widows."

"I had no idea you harbored these murderous impulses."

"Not at all. And especially not toward my own lean and lovely husband. You asked me a question, and I replied with a creative scenario. The bottom line is, yes, poison is a woman's weapon. Same as a medical worker's first choice might be drugs, and good old boys favor guns."

"But not *necessarily* a woman's weapon."

"*Especially* if you wanted to make it look like a woman's work."

"So I'm back to square one."

"No, because you're a clairvoyant. You've already seen where the poison hemlock grows. It's only a matter of time before you see who's been harvesting it."

"If I find that stand of hemlock, I'll root out every bit of it. Before there are any more deaths. It's a mercy, though, that this criminal herbalist didn't use water hemlock instead of plain old poison hemlock."

"What's the difference? Poison's poison." Phillipa busied herself making cappuccino for two.

"Water hemlock is a root, also known as cowbane. It's even more painful and deadly. Supposing you survive the convulsions, there's still liable to be heart damage. And it tastes better, sort of like parsnips, to which it's related. Poison hemlock is ferny, works more slowly, and tastes fetid. Thankfully. Because that's why I ate only half of that brownie."

"Many people don't have a finely honed sense of taste." Phillipa held a metal pitcher under the steamer nozzle to froth the milk. "If I were to use poison hemlock, I'd double up on the vanilla, maybe throw in a shot or two of crème de cacao."

"Now that you mention it, there was a stronger taste of vanilla than is usual with brownies. I wonder if we should warn people about the taste of hemlock, maybe write a letter to the *Pilgrim Times*."

"Don't be a fool. The public will be lynching self-confessed herbalists like you if this poison gambit continues, as I guess you believe it will. You think the poisoner will strike again." She handed me my cup of cinnamon-scented cappuccino. "And here I thought this was a one-time hit. Some disgruntled parishioner holding a grudge against the church. Drummed out of the choir perhaps, or she found one of Peacedale's sermons personally libelous."

"I feel this isn't the end of our troubles. More I don't know." I took a sip. Perfection!

"Well, I can't see how *we* would be involved again. There, how do these look?" Phillipa had arranged her breads on a large wooden cutting board and surrounded them with fake fall leaves.

"Superb. When's the taping?"

"Tonight, actually. Live audience, too. Want to come?"

"Thanks, but I'm expecting a call from Joe. They've reached Miami, and as soon as they've docked and made their point, he'll be on his way home. And I can't very well bring my cell phone to your taping."

"All right, loyal helpmate, false friend. Stay home and pine away if you wish. Just remember that Joe's probably out carousing with the crew in Miami's hotspots."

I sighed. "Maybe. Okay. What time?"

"Oh, good. Five-thirty sharp. Bring the Wagoneer, will you. I hate transporting food in my BMW. So messy."

So there I was, in the studios of WSOS-TV, the South Shore's community access cable station where Phillipa tapes *Kitchen Magic*. The show was aired on various PBS channels, and sometimes on the Food Network at odd hours of the night. The taping's small but appreciative audience included the Myles Standish Free Library's Cookbook Club, some members of the Sizzling Seniors with their chaperone, Patty Peacedale, who waved to me gaily, and a cooking class from one of the local schools with their pink-cheeked teacher, Miss Synge. When the taping was over, the breads were cut up and passed around among the audience, who had clapped madly whenever prompted to do so. Pumpkin Cranberry, Ginger Pear, and Spicy Brandied Apple. Lucky me, all I got was a taste of the Ginger Pear, because I really couldn't have stood another round with the stomach pump.

The Pumpkin Cranberry Bread was strongly flavored with spices, which must have masked any odd flavor. As we learned later, some common but highly poisonous berries had been tossed in among the dried cranberries that wound up in the bread. The poison-laced loaf was the last one that Phillipa had mixed on camera. By the time that one came out of the oven, warm and aromatic, the audience had petered away. So the camera crew, Gus and Greg, decided that demolishing the pumpkin bread was a legitimate part of cleaning up. Shortly thereafter, the two guys had been in severe gastrointestinal distress. After the incident at the church, Phillipa lost no time in calling 911 and her husband.

We raced after Gus and Greg in my Wagoneer to Jordan Hospital, where we met Stone. Our favorite detective was pacing the hall while his partner leaned against the wall making notes. The dose had been small, gastric lavage had been swiftly administered, and the crew's recovery seemed assured before we left them.

The studio with the kitchen set used by Phillipa was duly locked up and designated a crime scene, a major inconvenience to other cooking shows taped at WSOS. Stone ordered all foods on the premises to be analyzed. Privet berries were found in the bag of dried cranberries in the off-the-set real kitchen—a converted storage room really—where the ingredients were measured out by Junie Hershey, a production assistant. A few members of the audience, Junie didn't remember exactly who, had popped in to watch her at work. Later Junie had set up the elegant dining table and placed the finished breads among decorative gourds and fall leaves.

Three loaves of each bread had been prepared. The first group had been perfectly garnished in Phillipa's own kitchen for the on-camera buffet. The second, also precooked at Phillipa's, was ready for her to remove from the oven as if freshly baked. The final trio of breads was mixed on the set and placed in the oven to bake in real time, simply not to waste them. In this latter group, only the Pumpkin Cranberry contained a poisonous substance, ligustrin, found in all parts of privet hedge.

"To think we were just discussing poisons!" Phillipa wailed to me on the phone the next day. "This may be the end of *Kitchen Magic*, you know, if the cameramen decide to sue. Public broadcasting's budget is not what I would call 'deep pockets.'"

I was in my cellar workroom, formerly a cold room where my grandma used to store preserves and home-canned foods. The pine shelves were perfect for stocking the supplies to fill herbal orders. I'd left Scruffy upstairs, in case the odd field mouse might have found its way in through the ancient stone foundation. My dog could never rest once he caught that scent but would paw at the shelves, destroying carefully stacked bags of herbs, until he found and dispatched the culprit with a single canine wallop—no feline games for him!

With the phone held in the crook of my neck, I kept on working. "No one died, or even sustained permanent injuries," I countered. "And none of the audience ate the poisoned bread. They'd all left before that last Pumpkin Cranberry was even out of the oven. And it isn't as if you have sponsors who will cancel."

"You're *such* a comfort, Cass. Say, you don't suppose someone really is targeting *you*, do you? At this point, you're the only common denominator between the two poisonings."

"Not unless the poisoner has prescience. No one, not even myself, expected me to be at your taping. On the other hand, we're both Wiccans. Could that be the link? No, I really think that's unlikely, don't you? By the way, Phil, you were wonderful. I don't know how you talk off-the-cuff that way, so smooth and coherent, while whipping up beautiful foods."

The phone had become uncomfortable, so I stopped trying to fill dream pillows and sat in my old cane chair. A green-shaded lamp hung over the gateleg table that was missing its gate leaf but was a good sturdy work surface. Cobwebs in the corners added to the mysterious ambience.

Phillipa seemed to perk up a bit at the praise. "It's not difficult to talk if you know your material."

"I find it difficult. My talk on Samhain and Wicca at the Ladies' League sounded really stilted to my own ears. But back to the poisonings. It's hard to imagine what the common denominator can be." The green lamp began to swing back and forth of its own volition, like a pendulum. I watched it idly as we talked, realizing that the cellar was fading away. At that point, I must have dropped the phone.

Suddenly I was in the Peacedale kitchen, a room I had barely glimpsed before, although I had been in their parlor and Wyn's study several times. Now I could see the counters—rather messy, with cereal boxes not put away and dishes still in the sink. The refrigerator was open. Someone, I couldn't quite see who, was pulling out a crisper drawer, opening a package of salad greens. Looked like baby lettuces. The scene faded. Like all visions, it had a timeless quality. I never know how long in real time I'm traveling that astral plane, unless someone else who is present tells me. I just know I found myself at the cellar table again, feeling nauseated and disoriented as usual.

I picked up the phone. "Hello," I said in a weak voice. No answer. I hung up, thinking I'd better call her back as soon as I got my wits together. Then I went upstairs to fix myself a bracing cup of Assam tea, a welcome-home-from-the-hospital gift from Phillipa. I'd need to decide what this vision meant and what I should do about it.

Before the kettle had boiled, Phillipa was at my back door pounding on the wooden frame of its glass panel. The Sterns live less than a mile down the road, with Jenkins Woods between us. Although it's called Jenkins Park now, since we saved it from developers and their seaside condominiums by establishing the place as a wetland and bald eagle preserve. My friend's face looked pale and anxious as I unlocked and opened the door.

"You're just in time for tea," I said.

"Sweet Isis, Cass—I thought you'd had a stroke or something. What happened?"

"What usually happens to me? Psychically speaking, I was having a look around the Peacedale kitchen. Take down the cups, will you? I think I'd better call Patty. What I saw was rather peculiar."

I punched in the parsonage's number. She answered at once. "Hell-o," in a musical two syllables. "Patty Peacedale here."

"Patty! I hope you won't think this bizarre, but I've just had a glimpse of your kitchen. Well, it was more like a vision. And I saw something that worried me."

"Oh, lovely!" she caroled.

"Patty, this isn't an epiphany. Would you look in the crisper drawers in your refrigerator and tell me what you find there?"

"*So exciting!* Just give me a minute, Cass—I'm in my little office. I'll pick this up on the kitchen phone." A few moments passed, and Patty spoke again. "Gosh, Cass—not much. Three onions on one side, and a few Granny Smiths on the other. Wyn does love a cold, juicy apple when he's composing a sermon."

Phillipa, who was shamelessly listening in over my shoulder, muttered, "Onions? In the refrigerator?"

"Hush! No, not you, Patty. No salads, then?"

"Well, you see, Cass, we're scheduled for some dinner function or other every night this week, so I haven't bothered with any grocery shopping."

"I don't mean to intrude, Patty, but as you look at your counters, are there any open boxes of cereal standing there?"

"Oh, dear. This is a bit like having a surveillance camera in one's kitchen, isn't it? No cereal boxes right now, Cass, but it has been known."

"Okay, don't give it another thought. But when you do go grocery shopping, be especially careful about salads, will you? A whole head of lettuce is your best bet, maybe a few tomatoes."

"Iceberg, no doubt. Ugh, boring," whispered Phillipa.

"But wholesome," I said when I'd finally got a chance to hang up on Patty's enthusiastic curiosity.

Chapter Four

"The mundanes do tend to panic when their sixth sense kicks in," Fiona said abstractedly, apropos of nothing we'd been talking about. The subject was Samhain, where and how we would celebrate this year. "Not to mention their seventh and eighth senses."

"Which are?" asked Deidre. Her cap of golden curls and her impish grin brightened the gloom in the crowded, book-crammed living room of Fiona's fishnet-draped cottage in Plymouth Center. Once she'd lost custody of her darling grandniece, Laura Belle, Fiona had reverted to her former haphazard housekeeping.

"Oh, you know. The sixth is generally a foreboding of accident or death—the impending-doom thing. Next, there's the perception of bodiless spirits, of course—ghosts, you might say—which is the special province of mediums. Eighth is the ability to detect auras and, often, diagnose illness as well. Ninth . . ."

"Ninth!" exclaimed Deidre.

"Ninth is remote viewing," Fiona continued. "The CIA loves that one! But you gals know the drill."

"What about the glamour, your special province?" asked Heather.

"Oh, *that*. Glamour is not extrasensory—it's like hypnotics, a subtle illusion that can make you the center of attraction or, if it suits the situation, practically unnoticed. But, anyway, what I'm saying is, if it weren't for their tendency to panic at extrasensory perceptions, most people would be able to tell when trouble is imminent."

"And do what?" Heather asked.

"Duck, of course. More tea anyone? Another scone?" Fiona's Persian companion Omar Khayyám walked delicately across the coffee table and gave the milk pitcher a quick lick with his pink tongue. Fiona scooped him up with one arm and passed the plate of crumbly morsels with the other. Her tiny cream scones are always delectable, but I make it a point never to look in the kitchen from whence they came.

"That's all very well for Cass with her visions and Phil with her tarot," Heather complained, "but what about me? I never know what's going to hit me until it does."

"But you do, my dear," Fiona disagreed. "That's my whole point. There's a place within yourself from which you can reach out in many more than the ordinary sensory ways. Let your higher self guide you, whatever you call it."

Deidre brightened. "Oh! I call that my angel."

Phillipa looked skeptical. "Catholic holdover?"

"Wiccans have angels, too," Deidre said, pouting.

"I call that little voice in my ear *'conscience.'* I suppose that might be Torah-based," Phillipa said.

"Ghost of my grandma," I said.

"Oh, *that* voice!" Heather said. "That's Hecate speaking to me."

Fiona laughed, with her full-bodied, infectious laugh that none of us could resist joining. "Call it whatever, ladies. It's the timeless and eternal spirit of *you*. So . . . what do you say we have Samhain at Cass's while Joe is away—did you say Miami? I always prefer an empty house, in case of psychic fireworks. My place is a bit small. I'll take a turn in spring when we can celebrate in the backyard."

Thus it was arranged, and I was delighted, my imagination already spinning off into decorating an indoor altar with symbols of the season. Samhain is the last harvest, meaning I had to bring in any fresh rosemary, sage, and parsley I needed. After that, any plant still growing belonged to the fairies and pixies. I didn't know if I believed in fairies per se, but it wouldn't do to take chances with my herb garden. Anyone who's a serious gardener appreciates the quirkiness of nature.

"I have something special I want us to work at Samhain," Heather was saying. "The Nature Conservancy wants to buy some sixty acres of land near Bonds Pond. This would include an important feeding and nesting place for the red-bellied turtle, which is, as you know, an endangered species. Also we'd be getting a pristine pond shore for the Plymouth gentian, which is globally rare. And a nice pitch-pine forest for our declining songbirds and some exceptional insects."

"Nature lover though I am," Phillipa said, "if there's one species that does not evoke my concern, it's creepy, crawly insects, other than to keep them off my body and out of my flour bin."

"No bugs, no songbirds, Phil," Deidre said. "So what's the problem, Heather? Doesn't the Conservancy have the money?"

"Oh, sure—gifts and donations, you know, from individuals who care and companies who want to be seen as community-minded and environmentally sensitive, never mind that they produce beer or handguns. Anyway, the problem is there's a central part of that acreage that used to be working cranberry bogs, owned now by a dyed-in-the-wool Yankee who refuses to sell."

"Well, we'll have to soften him up with a few well-chosen words. Name?" Fiona rubbed her hands together briskly, as if for a psychic warmup. The silver bangles she always wore tinkled madly.

"Clarence Finch." Heather sighed. In small towns, the mention of one name can carry a great deal of anecdotal baggage.

"Uh oh," I said. "Words of dynamite might be more like it.

Isn't he Iggy Pryde's father-in-law-to-be?" We'd already had a run-in with Iggy over the illegal dumping of hazardous waste at his pig farm, and the arguments over who would be made to pay for the cleanup, Pryde or the companies involved, were still going on in the courts. As for the Finch connection, Wanda Finch, Iggy's fiancée, a formidable, frizzy-haired redhead, had once threatened Heather and me with a rifle for trespassing. Clarence Finch, her father, owned a produce farm near Carver and several acres of cranberry bogs scattered around Plymouth.

"I'd venture a guess that Clarence Finch doesn't give a damn about the red-bellied turtle," Phillipa said. "Tight-fisted old sod. Bought all those abandoned cranberry bogs for next to nothing, and now he's probably holding out for big bucks from some developer. The Bonds Pond Estates."

"Never underestimate our powers of persuasion," Fiona said. "But we'll get to that later, at Samhain, when we are working between the worlds, such a lovely place to be. Perhaps we'll invoke some spectral help."

At Samhain, when the veil between life and death is so thin that a soul might traverse from one state to another, we would light candles for those we loved who had gone before us to Summerland. I could count on Heather for bunches of quirky handmade candles. I'd dedicate a special one to Grandma—how I wished she could fly in for a moment and bless my presence in the home she'd left to me, and the gardens, and all the herbal recipes and remedies written in her own spidery script.

Samhain is also the best night of the year for divination. Pagan time is not linear but circular, and on this one evening, when another cycle is poised to begin, the bonds of time are loosened and dissolved into the cosmic chaos. For a few hours, the world exists outside of time, and it's possible to see in all directions, including ahead to the future. So this year Phillipa would read the tarot, and I—perhaps I would have another vision, one that would reveal the face of the poisoner.

*   *   *

"You're on your way to *where?*" I wailed into the phone.

"To Greece, sweetheart. Now, let me explain it again. Picture this. We applied to the port of Miami for one week's berth to re-supply the ship, change crew members—that sort of thing. Well, I was specifically recruited to help conduct a few onboard tours, too, since the *Esperanza* is a retrofitted Soviet Navy icebreaker."

"Sure," I said. "Probably because you're so smart and sexy."

"There's that," he said with a chuckle. "Then a new engineer would come aboard, and I'd fly home."

"The real engineer. A wizened old salt."

"I'm not just smart and sexy, sweetheart—I'm a real engineer, too. But the port's director refused to allow us to dock. Said we'd be too much of a security risk, requiring extra personnel, and cit-ing the ongoing criminal case, although at worst, it's only a mis-demeanor. We couldn't get any nearer than two miles. Helicopters buzzed us, Coast Guard vessels circled us, bullhorns warned us to move along. We faxed protests to everybody—the Coast Guard, the port of Miami, the county manager, the *Miami Herald*. No go. With all the uncertainty, my replacement was instructed to re-main in Amsterdam. So the *Esperanza* is continuing its voyage to Greece for repairs, and I'm going with it. No one is more sur-prised than I."

"Yeah, yeah. Like these detours never happen in Greenpeace. But when will you be home?" I really hated to hear that whining note in my voice.

"I'll be flying back in a couple of weeks or so."

"I guess it's a good chance to visit your mom and brothers, right?"

"Hmmm. Well, my mother *is* getting on in years. I should fly to Athens. But trust me, I'll absolutely be home *long* before Thanksgiving. So what are you doing right now?"

"Getting ready to celebrate Samhain. We're having it here at my house . . . our house."

"Admit it—I would only have been in the way."

"Not at all. We might need a male sacrifice for some weird sexual rite."

"If only you'd mentioned this earlier, I'd have been glad to sacrifice myself. What exactly is it you gals do at Halloween?"

"Oh, never mind. We'll just have to find some other good-looking, lusty Greek guy."

We carried that theme about as far as it would go, and the call ended in a pleasantly sexy mood. Still, when we hung up, I was looking at three or more weeks alone just as I had become used to sharing bed and board with a handsome husband, as well as never having to worry about changing fuses or flat tires. Damn!

Don't feel sad, Toots. You've still got me to cuddle with. Scruffy always understands when I'm feeling a bit melancholy and might need some companionable nudges with a cold nose.

Samhain began just as the sun was setting. Later, there would be a tipped golden bowl of moon and a brilliant Jupiter blazing in the southeast sky. It was a clear, crisp evening, too cool for an outdoor ceremony, although I did light the walk to the back door with solar torches. I follow the New England Yankee tradition of reserving the front door for visiting dignitaries or departing coffins.

I'd decorated the living room window seat as an altar in black, orange, silver, and gold, with bouquets of dried mint, sage, and catnip (fortunately, no felines lived here to roll in the arrangements!), gourds, apples, and nuts, and a statue of Hecate, a loan from Heather, who favored that dark goddess.

Ugh, prickly stuff! And hard old nuts—what do you think I am, a squirrel? If I can't leap up on my watching place, how can I be expected to guard us? Scruffy paced back and forth, with many canine scowls and mutterings, in front of the new altar, where he normally took his ease on throw pillows and kept an eye on the street.

"It's just for one night. If you don't behave yourself like a gentledog, it's into the bedroom you go for the evening."

Hey, Toots—you're always shutting me into or out of that room of yours. How come I never get to sleep on the big bed anymore since we got that furry-faced guy?

"Long story, mutt. Count your blessings, and don't steal anything off the dining room table."

A Sabbat at my house meant I would be the priestess, since it was our custom to take turns conducting the ceremony. For this I'd been saving a long, gauzy green dress studded with silver moons and pentagrams that I'd ordered in a mad moment from a metaphysical catalog—not the kind of outfit a gal could wear just anywhere, especially anywhere in Plymouth.

Twilight was deepening, only a trace of pink over the trees, when we gathered in a flurry of hugs and "merry meet" greetings.

"You look amazing, Cass. A post-midlife Titania." Deidre pulled off a peaked wool cap and shook her short blond curls free. An aura of lily cologne surrounded her. "Will's at the firehouse on Halloween watch. So my mother-in-law, Mary Margaret, insisted on taking the children trick-or-treating. I can't say I like the idea of their collecting a bunch of suspicious sweets. I did impress on M&Ms—so the kids call her—that nothing is to be eaten until I've examined the loot."

"Toss 'em out directly" was Phillipa's glib advice—she who'd never had to reason with thwarted children. Tonight she looked the most traditional of us all, dressed entirely in black. Her straight black hair had the sheen and smoothness of a raven's wing. Attached to her belt, a single note of color, was the scarlet silk bag in which she carried her tarot.

"Be sure your darling poodles don't get into the chocolate," Heather warned Deidre. "Chocolate is poison to dogs." In her pumpkin-colored tunic and dark brown tights, a leather-sheathed ceremonial knife at her waist, she looked ready for a run in Sherwood Forest.

"That's where dowsing comes in so handy," Fiona said for the umpteenth time. "I never eat any strange food without testing it with my pendulum."

"I can attest to that, having been out to lunch with Fiona," I said. "And I find that having your companion swing a pendulum over her crabmeat roll and fries while muttering a spell does tend to attract some unwanted attention at The Walrus and the Carpenter. The place was crowded that day, so we were eating at the bar, and soon were the center of attention."

"Oh, for Goddess's sake," Fiona said. "For all anyone knew, I was saying grace. And what's more important, anyway—other people's opinions or safe food? I'd say, with a madwoman running around town poisoning the church brownies and Phillipa's beautiful breads, it's no time to take chances."

"She has a point there," Deidre agreed.

"We can argue later," I said. "It's the Sabbat, and I'm ready to celebrate."

A general murmur of assent, and we gathered in the living room. Scruffy had already found his sulking spot, stretched out on the hooked rug in front of the fireplace where a small pine-scented fire was ablaze. Between his paws was a Granny Smith apple, stolen from the altar and indifferently gnawed. I gave him my strongest "don't give me any trouble" look, thereafter ignoring his sighs.

With my athame, I consecrated a nine-foot circle, a place for us to work "between the worlds." The mantle was aglow with as many candles as would fit between the animal stone carvings I collected, mostly Inuit and Zuni.

I invoked the four elements, the six directions, the female and male incarnations of the Creator. We proceeded to the work, a simple banishing of the poisons in our midst, a purification ritual to cleanse their evil influence, then various visualizations for healing and other good things. Heather and Fiona each said a few pungent words that the purchase of acreage around Bonds Pond would somehow, for the good of all, and harming none, be smoothly executed by the Conservancy. Then we reached for the invisible force of spirit and pressed each other's hands to pass that energy among us faster and faster until we could contain it no longer, and at a signal from me, we threw our arms upward to let the power of our wishes zoom into the universe—a transcendent moment.

There was a collective sigh, a laugh, a relaxation to our shoulders. It was definitely time to adjourn to the dining room for mulled wine and cakes, pumpkin and apple (lavishly provided by Phillipa). And teasing and fun. We always laughed more deeply after the Sabbat ceremony, the rich, deep laughter of friends who were as close as family. At the brink of winter darkness, we were warmed and cheered by each other.

"You know I've never actually seen a red-bellied turtle," I said. "If the Conservancy manages to pry those old cranberry bogs out of Clarence Finch's grasping fingers, I'd like to see what they look like."

"When," said Fiona.

"When what?"

"*When*, not *if*, Finch gives up that land," Fiona corrected me. "You must believe for good things to happen."

"Sounds like something out of a Disney movie," Phillipa said.

"Say what you will, *believing is seeing*," Fiona declared. She didn't spare us the promised lecture on healing, either, pulling out quotes and pamphlets helter-skelter from the bulbous green reticule from which she is never parted. Sometimes in the past it has been reassuring to know that down in the bottom of that satchel is a pistol, a gift from her late husband.

"As I mentioned at the hospital, a disharmony of the spirit brings about dis-ease." She fished out a leather pouch from the pocket of her coat sweater of many colors. It was decorated with geometric symbols. Taking a pinch of a powdery substance from the pouch, she sprinkled it around the room. "Pollen from Arizona," she answered our unspoken question. Phillipa nudged me and winked. Fiona caught the wink but continued unperturbed: "It's the work of the healer to restore that harmony, however that may be accomplished. Music and dance are often used among the Native Americans. I credit my trip to the Navahos and all I learned there with helping to cure my arthritis."

"And Mick Finn's attentions seem to have loosened you up a bit, too," Deidre said. The Plymouth fire chief had been smitten with Fiona's widow's charms and was a frequent caller. Naturally, all the firemen, including Deidre's husband, Will, teased Finn about Fiona to the limit of his patience.

"I shall remember to dance down the hall the next time I have to visit one of you in the hospital." Phillipa took her tarot pack from her red silk bag, in which she kept a piece of sodalite to enhance psychic awareness. "I was trained in ballet as a girl, you know. Tap, too. Perhaps I'll wear a Navaho headband."

At my dining room table, where jack-o'-lanterns variously leered or grinned, Phillipa read the tarot for each of us, cards arranged in the Celtic-cross manner. Notable among the warnings was the three of swords for Deidre. Ominous-looking thing—a pierced heart. And for Fiona, a fish leaping from the page's cup predicted a surprise. I got the two of swords, of course—stalemate! With my bridegroom steaming away to Greece, what else?

I had the sense that everyone was waiting for my eyeballs to roll back in my head while I swooned into a clairvoyant vision. *It'll never happen*, I thought, and then, miraculously, while my gaze was fixed on a gleaming, candle-lit pumpkin, I slid out of myself. In an instant I was watching a wooden spoon stirring batter in a blue-striped bowl. A box on the table. A chocolate batter, dark as sin. I caught a strong scent of vanilla followed by that fetid hemlock odor. And that was all.

Heather was shaking me. "What, Cass, what?"

"Sweet Isis, more brownies. Chocolate batter being mixed with wooden spoon. But there was a box on the table, you know, like Pillsbury or something. Who are those brownies for? And why is this happening?"

Phillipa spread her deck across the table. "What? From a box?

It isn't awful enough that she's poisoning people left and right, she's using a mix as well? And, really, brownies are so easy to make from scratch. I bet she's adding extra vanilla to kill the taste. Maybe even *artificial* vanilla flavoring, ugh! I wouldn't put it past her. Pick a card while you're hot, Cass," she said. I did as I was told. The nine of cups, reversed.

"Forget culinary niceties, Phil. What does it matter how the brownies are made if they're going to kill you?"

"There are standards, dear. But look at this—greed!" she declared. "No matter how random these events may seem, we'll find greed is the motive at the bottom of all these poisonings."

Chapter Five

You'd think that after all the publicity the poisonings at the church received, national as well as local coverage, no one in Plymouth would ever dare to eat a brownie again. Not so! The batch I'd "seen" being made in my Samhain vision materialized on the following day. This time, brownies appeared at a Halloween get-together for the Silver Lake Senior center. Senior center parties were never held at night. This one took place the day after Halloween, which was actually All Saints' Day. As an advisor to the center's board of directors, the Reverend Peacedale was there with Patty. The Plymouth chapter of the Sweet Adelines, a harmonizing singing group, were entertaining with a medley of songs popular in the Gay Nineties. Also among the guests was our own Heather Devlin with her registered therapy dog, a golden retriever named Honeycomb.

As Patty breathlessly told me later, the minute she'd spotted the brownies at one end of the table, between the Casper the Ghost marshmallows and the vampire-bat cookies, she'd dashed over, slapped at hands reaching for the treats, and rushed them away before Wyn, who's very fond of brownies, or anyone else could be poisoned. I'd mentioned the fetid smell of hemlock to her, and how it might have been overwhelmed by vanilla. So she gave the brownies a knowledgeable sniff. They did indeed smell funny to her. Having no completely safe place to stash the suspect treats, she simply emptied the serving dish into her knitting bag and clapped it shut.

Patty's quick action earned her some strange looks from the volunteers who were hostessing the party. But she was too late for one of them. Vera Lindstrom, who had sampled the brownies while she helped to lay the table, was soon after overcome with weakness, nausea, and difficulty breathing. Heather was already calling 911 when poor Vera began to lapse into unconsciousness.

Patty tried to revive Vera with her ever present bottle of smelling salts. A few minutes later the paramedic team arrived and took over. By then the poisoned woman was barely breathing. Meanwhile, while Heather was reassuring the other seniors, resourceful Honeycomb, following that favorite dog adage, "In confusion, there is profit," seized the opportunity to munch up a few slices of spiderweb cake and was nosing Patty's knitting bag with interest when Heather collared her, literally.

As had happened at the Gethsemane Ladies' League, no one knew exactly when or how the brownies had arrived in the senior center's kitchen among the other donated goodies. Before being grabbed and dumped by Patty, they'd been arranged on a plastic Halloween platter decorated with gravestones. All the fingerprints later retrieved from the platter belonged to the women who had set the table, one of whom was the victim. A chocoholic like Lydia Craig, Vera Lindstrom had consumed a generous amount of the poison and was in critical condition for several hours.

No surprise to me, the poison was again found to be hemlock. The poisoner had to be a woman, I theorized, a herbalist as knowledgeable as myself. Both poison hemlock and privet berries were easily obtained locally and incorporated into foods for someone familiar with both poisonous plants and cooking.

The media loved the ghoulish possibilities. Scary headlines variously reported "Homicidal Botanist Runs Amok on South

Shore," "Mysterious Serial Poisonings Terrorize Plymouth," "Poison Peril in Plymouth, the Halloween Connection," "Are Satanists Poisoning Plymouth? Local Clergy Comments." And the ever popular "Death by Chocolate—Plymouth Police Baffled." Restaurants stopped serving chocolate desserts; no one would order them. But interest in Phillipa's cooking show mushroomed, the public hoping perhaps to see a guest double up after sampling her *Gateau Cocolat*. Plymouth crime news made CNN again, and this time Joe caught the report.

"*Jesu Christos*, sweetheart!" was his informal greeting on the phone.

"Oh, hi, Joe. Where are you, honey? Not jail, I hope."

"I'm calling from the Ulysses ancestral home, where I happened to bring up the CNN Web site on my brother's computer. The poisonings are still going on there! You haven't got yourself involved, have you?"

I wanted to say, "Is your patriarch Greek?" but I restrained myself. "Don't you worry, darling. I was never in danger. The second incident involved Phillipa's show, privet berries in the pumpkin bread. And this last one, a senior citizens' party—well, the Peacedales and Heather just happened to be guests."

"Hey, Sherlock. Have you considered there's a mighty big coincidence here?"

"I have indeed, Dear Watson."

"So my question is, what's next? Or rather, who's next?"

A chilling thought. Fiona. Deidre. The children.

"I don't think it's the circle being targeted." My tone sounded uncertain to my own ears. "And Phil's tarot cards said greed is the motive. So it's not a hate crime, right?"

"Hey, I'm reassured—aren't you?"

"No, I guess not. When are you coming home?"

"As soon as I can get a booking. I'm going to call the airport right after we hang up. I don't trust you to stay out of trouble."

"Little I care, as long as you're coming home. Fly carefully."

"I always do, sweetheart."

But as luck would have it, there was a terrorist incident targeting an Israeli airliner in the Athens airport. Flights were canceled
through the weekend, and all the bookings got jammed up. It
was Wednesday before Joe got to Logan and, as usual, picked up
a Rent-a-Wreck to drive to Plymouth.

"You're still alone?" Heather asked when she called on Monday.
"Come for lunch, then, and we'll brainstorm these poisonings.
Dick's taken the day off and gone to Manomet to help with the
bird banding at the Center for Conservation Sciences. His new
associate, Maury, is taking over for the day."

"Bird banding? I'm surprised you're in favor of that."

"I'm not especially, but at least it's capture and release. Dick
thinks it's important to monitor populations as indicators of dis-
ease and longevity, as well as to follow migratory routes. Did you
know that the Arctic tern has a route of approximately twenty-
five thousand miles? That's the longest. But apparently excitement is running high in Manomet over the hairy woodpecker and
indigo bunting they've captured and banded, and, most thrilling
of all, the seven sharp-shinned hawks. And they get to wear those
nifty T-shirts, 'Manomet Banders Are for the Birds.'"

"You're kidding."

"No. One of the banders had them made up for a lark. So are
you coming? We'll drink, we'll talk—it will be like the old days."

"Nothing's like the old days. We're both married ladies now
with new responsibilities. I'm getting on in years and can't drink
at lunch the way we used to. Not to mention, you don't have a
cook anymore—you have a handyman." It was understood that
Heather herself did not cook if it could be avoided. When
pressed, she ordered take-out, she opened packages, she re-
heated, she tossed the occasional salad-in-a-bag, and she allowed
her husband Dick to grill. None of us expected more.

"No one will ever replace Ashbery, it's true." Heather's long-
time housekeeper and friend had been blown up by a package
bomb during an earlier Plymouth crime wave in which we'd

been involved. After Heather's brief stint with Sicilian house-keepers who ended up in the witness-protection program, the circle had sent out a "call" for a someone new to help with the Devlin menage, and the answer had been a battered old sea-man—demonstrating once more that the Universe of Infinite Possibilities has a sense of humor. "But you know very well Captain Jack is as handy in a kitchen as he is outdoors. And one little bottle of champagne will merely energize you. It's one of nature's great restoratives for women, right up there with Midol and Raspberry Leaf Tea. Furthermore, you're only as old as you feel, my dear. I'm not ready to be called a crone yet, and neither are you. Wisewomen, yes—crones, no. Especially since we're both practically newlyweds. By the way, you can bring Scruffy. Honeycomb will be tickled to see him."

So who could refuse? It had been a while.

"But what about Ishmael?"

"Not to worry. I'll ask Captain Jack to stow his parrot for the occasion. See you at noon?"

Plymouth was a resilient place—has been ever since the first Pilgrim stepped foot on that rock. No one had been poisoned in a week, and the town had resumed its peaceful demeanor. One death did not cause the spiritual descendants of Pilgrims and Indians to run scared. But there was a little buzz in local meeting places, like the dump and the post office. When I stopped to mail some orders on my way to Heather's, the postal clerk, a cheerful, very pregnant gal, asked me if "you ladies are on the case?" The circle's reputation for solving crimes was fast becoming part of the local folklore.

"I'll drink to that," Heather declared, when I related the incident to her. With glasses of '96 Veuve Clicquot in hand, we were lounging in the conservatory of her Federalist mansion, which was strewn with a motley assortment of well-chewed dog toys. Hardly ever were there fewer than a half dozen dogs in residence at the Devlins', an overflow from the no-kill shelter, Animal

Lovers, that Heather supported with her lavish trust income. At the moment, however, most of the Devlin pack was relegated to the fenced yard, while Scruffy enjoyed a tête-à-tête with his favorite blonde, Honeycomb.

"Play nice, kids," I said as they scooted around the potted palms with a rope tug-of-war toy. "You did have Honeycomb fixed, didn't you?" I asked Heather.

"It's okay. She's not in season right now. You know what a champion of neutering and spaying, I am, but Dick insists that Honeycomb, who's a superior therapy dog and has an impressive pedigree as well, should be bred at least once before she's spayed. You ought to have Scruffy neutered, though. A mutt like that can't be allowed to knock up some willing bitch—there are enough unwanted pups in the world already."

"Shhhh," I said. "If he gets the notion that we're planning a little fixing operation, I will never be able to get him into Dick's office for routine shots again."

"Oh, come on, now, Cass. It isn't as if he understands what I'm saying. Neutering will make Scruffy much more docile and also prevent a number of ailments that may occur as he gets older."

Abruptly, Scruffy raised his head from the stuffed squeaky toy he was subduing to impress Honeycomb and gave me a long, accusatory look. *Hey, if that dog lady's cooking up a plot to cut off my nuts, Toots, I'm hitching a ride on the next freight car out of town.*

"Don't get nervous. It'll never happen," I reassured the dog, who was already heading toward the door.

"Really, Cass. Let's not pretend that Scruffy will never age," Heather reasoned with me. "If he were capable of communicating, he'd thank you for having him neutered."

Hasta la vista, baby. Lemme out of here! Scruffy began scratching the door frame. I caught him by the collar and whispered, "No snip-snip, I promise you. Now behave yourself, or you'll spend the rest of the afternoon in the cold car."

By the time I had Scruffy settled down again, Captain Jack had appeared with his superb Three-Cod Chowder informally served in the cooking pot, which he deposited in the middle of the table. Captain Jack, a small gray-haired fellow with merry blue eyes, brought with him a faint whiff of rum. He wore salt-faded jeans, a striped canvas apron over a black T-shirt, and a captain's hat set at a rakish angle.

"Hi, Ms. Shipton. Don't worry about Ish. I got him stowed under his blankey so's he won't hurt that dog of yours. Be back in a jiff with the biscuits."

That flying freak comes near me again, there'll be nothing left of him but a mess of green feathers. Scruffy hadn't encountered the captain's parrot very often, but the memory of his tormenter remained vivid.

"Belay that," I muttered. Captain Jack looked at me sharply but continued to serve lunch. Heather, who was as prodigal with wine as she was klutzy in the kitchen, skillfully opened a bottle of Pouilly-Fuissé to go with the chowder.

Over steaming bowls of seaside heaven, golden crumbly biscuits, and a surprising endive and pear salad, Heather and I talked of poisons and poisoners. "My thoughts keep returning to Lydia Craig," I said. "The thing is, she's the only one who died."

"So far," Heather said darkly. "I hear she's left a fortune to Reverend Peacedale."

"Surely she left her bequest to the church, not to the pastor. That's what Wyn said. She told him about it at Christmas."

"No, dearie. I have it straight from the horse's mouth that the bequest was for the reverend himself to do with as he sees fit. Endow a soup kitchen, yacht around the Mediterranean, or open a bar in Tahiti—it's entirely up to Peacedale. Although Patty may have some input there."

"And I thought lawyers were a discreet lot."

"The late, lamented Mrs. Craig employed the law firm of Borer, Buckley, and Bangs. As it happens, our family has been one of their oldest and best customers ever since my great-great-grandfather sailed out to the Orient and made the family fortune."

"Great Goddess, I hope this bequest doesn't mean Wyn or Patty are suspects."

"Never trust a woman who knits, I say." Heather topped up her glass and mine. "From Madame DeFarge on down the line, they've always been a secretive lot."

"Not Patty. I know Patty, and she doesn't have a sneaky bone in her body. What you see is what you get."

"You're just saying that because she rhapsodizes over your clairvoyant spells."

"No, I'm saying that because Patty is as clear as spring water to my six or seven senses—and besides, she knows nothing whatsoever about herbs. She wouldn't know what to do with a sprig of parsley if it sat up in her refrigerator and cried 'bite me.'"

"Don't get testy, dear. What about Wyn, then? Shouldn't everybody be a suspect, especially those who stand to gain a bundle?"

I didn't answer because Captain Jack had appeared in the doorway with an apple pie, a flaky marvel with an aroma that suggested rum-soaked raisins had been liberally tucked in with the fruit slices. In his other hand, he carried a steaming blue enamel pot of boiled coffee. No namby-pamby latte for the captain!

The strong coffee was amazingly good. I was glad he left the pot when he departed to the "galley," as he called it. Actually, since the back of Heather's house had been rebuilt after the bombing, the new kitchen looked like an ad from *Architectural Digest,* all Mexican tiles and mahogany and restaurant appliances. Even Phillipa, no slouch in the pricey appliance department, was a wee bit jealous of the so-called galley and complained that it was totally wasted on the Devlins and their decrepit houseman. But she had to admit that his cooking skills were surprising.

"So, exactly how much of a bundle is Wyn inheriting?" I asked. "Did you wheedle that information out of Borer, Buckley, and Bangs as well?"

"Bangs is my guy. Youngest of the partners, only sixty-six, and still susceptible to feminine persuasion. The entire estate is worth over five million dollars, if you count the very marketable beachfront property she owned in Chatham. Two nephews and a niece are getting twenty-five thousand each, and the rest . . . ta da!"

"Lydia Craig!" I exclaimed. "She wore the same cloth coat and hand-knit hat for as long as I've known her. She lived in that overgrown mausoleum with the sagging porch and drove a ten-year-old Chevy. Once, when we bumped into each other at Angelo's meat counter, she pointed out to me that the shoulder cuts were a much better buy than the baby lamb chops I was putting into my cart. And I noticed that her cart was filled with markdowns. You know, those dented cans, overripe tomatoes, and past-date baked goods they have on a rack near the back room."

"I bet there were some chocolate goodies, past-date or no. It was her greatest passion."

"Well-known passion?"

"My guess is it was known by the person who laced the church brownies with hemlock," Heather said. "As to her being a millionaire, I think you'll find there's many an old Yankee in Plymouth with a fat bank account and a thin old coat. It's the way we were brought up. 'Use it up, wear it out, make it do.'"

"That Yankee economy didn't rub off on you much."

"Oh, I don't know. I save money buying Veuve Clicquot by the case."

"What do you think about Wyn Peacedale inheriting several mil from the old lady who got poisoned at my Halloween talk?" I asked Joe. It was nine o'clock Thursday morning, and we were still lying in bed, savoring his return home. I'd crawled out from under the quilt just long enough to push Scruffy onto the porch, where he could avail himself of the pet door Joe had installed. Then I brought two steaming mugs of coffee back into the bedroom. We'd declared the day a personal holiday for fooling around and catching up on ourselves.

"What's to think? Have you considered that Reverend Peacedale may not even have known about the bequest until the will was read?"

"He did. He's known since last Christmas. But he may not have understood that the millions would be his personally, as Heather said. She has a useful contact at the Craig law firm—Borer, Buckley, and Bangs. But to my mind, money isn't that important to Wyn and Patty."

"Oh? In my experience, money is important to everyone—although some people are loathe to admit it. But do I think the Peacedales would hasten the end of their benefactor? Probably not. So . . . can I get your mind off murder for a while?" Joe put down his coffee mug on the night table and took me into his arms, kissing my neck and shoulder. A melting sensation ran straight from his mouth to my second chakra. "Are you as hungry as I am?" he murmured, moving his mouth lower.

"For breakfast?"

"That, too—but later. . . ."

Chapter Six

Deidre was in the upstairs sewing room of her brick-fronted garrison Colonial, making costumes for Jenny and Willie to wear at the school Thanksgiving pageant. Bobby was pedaling a red car up and down the hall. The toy poodles, Salty and Peppy, skidded along after him, yapping, while Baby Anne revved up her own little motor from the playpen nearby. The scene brought me back to when my own three, also close in age, had been a full-time concern. I sighed a grateful sigh. Getting older has its compensations.

"So I wondered if you might go with me to the pageant," Deidre said. "I'd like to take these two to see their brother and sister on stage, but Will's on duty and M&Ms is off to Atlantic City with her gambling pals."

"Sure. There's nothing I like better than a six-hour elementary school Thanksgiving pageant. It's the thing I've missed most since my children grew up."

Deidre stitched a fake-leather fringe onto a little brown cotton shirt. "Remember when you needed me and the kids to be your cover while you scouted around that serial murderer's homestead in Carver? And his two crazed Dobermans attacked my station wagon?"

"Okay, okay. I owe, and I'll go. I'd love to. Same old plot, is it? The Pilgrims invite the Indians to share a meal and sign over North America?"

"Yep, same lousy deal. Jenny's a Pilgrim lass, and Willie's an Indian brave. I'm making an Indian costume for Bobby, too. Even though he's not in the pageant, he doesn't want to feel left out."

"And Anne?"

"Papoose. You wouldn't mind carrying her on your back, would you? I'd like to be able to move around freely with the video camcorder, in case anything unexpectedly delightful occurs."

"Sure. Good for the posture, I bet. How do you find time for all this?"

"No problem. Time stretches to fit the things you have to do, I always say."

Deidre had the knack all right. Watching her busy hands, I marveled at the way the costumes seemed to appear out of nowhere and were remarkably well-made. When I used to whip up costumes, my stock-in-trade for fast effects had been safety pins and Scotch tape. "I think you must have those little brownies out of Grimm's fairy tales coming in at night to help you. Made them tiny shoes and shirts, did you?"

"Funny you should say that, Cass." Deidre reached into a copious workbag hanging on the back of her chair and fished out a stuffed elf wearing a cobbler's apron with a tiny awl sticking out of its pocket. "It's a new product I'm introducing into Deidre's Faeryland. This one is Bobbikins the Brownie Shoemaker. Wait a minute . . . yes, here's his wife, Bettikins."

Bettikins wore a kerchief and an apron; she was holding a little sewing basket.. "Adorable. You'll sell a million of 'em. And seeing it's you, I believe those million orders will be filled on time. Who needs sleep?"

"I have *you* to thank, Cass, for getting me started selling on the Internet. I do sometimes miss the stimulation of running that vitamin place at Massasoit Mall, but when Baby Anne arrived, it was just too much." She propped the two dolls on the windowsill and went back to her sewing machine. I couldn't resist opening Bettikins's miniature sewing basket. Tiny spools of thread, a strawberry pincushion, some postage stamp–sized scraps of cloth. While I was playing, Deidre continued dispensing folklore. "Those legends of the brownies may have been inspired by the history of the ancient Picts, you know—small, dark pixie people who had a way of disappearing into earthen tunnels when the Romans began to hunt and kill them for sport. Only came out at night to collect the food left for them by kindhearted Celts."

"I've heard something about that from Fiona."

"Yeah, I guess I did, too. She's like a walking *Golden Bough*. The unabridged edition, of course."

"Speaking of Fiona and pixie food handouts, did you dowse the kids' Halloween candy?"

"Huh! I did better than that. I dumped it out in the trash and substituted good stuff. I don't think they ever knew the difference. This poison thing has me freaked."

"You can't be too careful," I agreed. "You've heard about the Peacedale windfall? What's your take on it?"

"It could be that old Mrs. Craig was a target, but, then, the poisonings just keep right on happening. That woman at the senior center had a close call."

"Patty's the one who saved the seniors. Took one look at those brownies and smelled a rat."

"Bizarre coincidence, isn't it. Here I am making brownie dolls and someone else in town is making poisoned brownies."

"But not necessarily someone who *lives* in town. When did you begin this new project?"

"Just before Halloween. I got to thinking about trick-or-treating, which reminded me of the Picts, or brownies, in their nightly foraging expeditions. Hey, do you think that was a clairvoyant thing?"

"Very likely. Because your particular magic is so often expressed by handicrafts. So, my dear, if you get any new inspirations, we ought to give them serious attention."

Deidre looked at her hands and smiled. "Well, what do you know. Clairvoyant fingers—there ought to be a special name for that."

"If there isn't, we'll make one up. Maybe it's a form of psychometry, though. That's, like, when you put your hand on an old brooch and suddenly 'see' the history of the person who wore it."

"I'll stay out of the antique business, then. Might be overwhelming."

"Oh, yes, the Picts," Fiona said. Intrigued for reasons I couldn't quite fathom, I'd stopped in the Black Hill Branch Library to inquire after books referencing the Picts. "Supposedly they went to earth, literally, when the Romans invaded, hiding in burrows like prairie dogs. Not only were they smaller in stature, with darker skins, than the Celts, they probably emerged covered with dirt—hence the name 'brownies.' Some scholars insist that the Picts and Celts were one and the same, but I favor the theory that the Picts predated the Celts in Briton and were a truly aboriginal people. There's some evidence that they spoke a different language. It was said that the Irish saint Columba needed an interpreter when he spoke to the king of the Picts on the banks of Loch Ness."

"Loch Ness?" I was getting confused.

"The Picts were the original inhabitants of Scotland—I've always thought my tiny Aunt Gwenny MacDonald must have been a Pict throwback. Sharp little bird eyes, never missed a trick. Stood no higher than my shoulder. A true pixie. Taught me just about everything I know."

"Which is just about everything there *is* to know," I commented, still looking through the disappointing history section. Branch libraries are pretty poor pickings. I'd have done better at Fiona's cottage, which was crammed with esoteric references that rivaled the collection at the New England Center for Physical Research.

While I grumbled over the shelves, Fiona busied herself making tea for the two of us. This was her kingdom, a minimalist library housed on the first floor of a cozy twenties' bungalow. It was owned by the Plymouth Women's Cooperative for Folk Arts, who still had a quilting room in the cellar. Furnished with warm, aged oak, it would have seemed like a step back in time except for the computer buzzing and gurgling on Fiona's desk.

"Strange coincidences," I said, giving up on the Black Hill reference books. "Someone is poisoning people with homemade brownies. I make an offhand comment about brownies sneaking in at night to help Deidre finish her dolls, and I find out she's creating prototypes for a line of brownie dolls to sell on the Internet. What do *you* make of all these 'brownies' popping up?"

Fiona poured fragrant ginger tea into two thistle-decorated mugs, handed one to me, and opened a tin of shortbread. Immediately, Omar Khayyám wafted in from mouse patrol in the stacks and jumped gracefully onto her desk. "Never be surprised that synchronicity is woven into our lives. Everything is interconnected in spirit, my dear. The ultimate oneness of the universe is the basis of all magic. And healing." She gave Omar a shortbread crumb and passed me the tin. "So when you perceive the pattern underlying these ideas and events that seem weird coincidences to you now, you'll solve the mysterious poisonings." She turned to the computer, punched a few keys, and clicked on a search item. After starting the printer, she turned back to her tea.

"I expected to do that with a vision. You mean I'm going to have to puzzle this out?" I wondered what she was printing.

"A little of one, a little of the other is my guess. I'm printing out a little essay on the Picts and the pixie-brownie connection for you to take home with you. That's what you were looking for, wasn't it? I have some things at home, too, that I'll set aside for you to read. Maybe something there will strike a spark in your psyche. That's all it will take, my dear. But I wonder, don't you, who the next target will be?"

Chapter Seven

A note on the table informed me that my bridegroom had gone shopping at Home Warehouse again. What worrisome home improvement was he planning now? My little house didn't offer all that much scope for remodeling. I felt guilty that Joe hadn't had the Wagoneer for transport, but relieved that I'd missed having to go with him to that big, drafty, barnlike place filled with the scent of raw pine, bins of dull, utilitarian tools, and toilets lined up like theater seats.

Scruffy had seized the opportunity for a nap on my white chenille bedspread. "Off, off, *off!*" I commanded. He sprang down instantly and trotted into the kitchen for a long drink of water, as dogs do when they're embarrassed. *What's the fuss? No one else was using the big bed*.

After booting the dog outdoors, I booted up my computer and was pleased to see a note from Freddie, my former protégée who now worked for a computer firm in Atlanta—an entry-level job at Iconomics, Inc. that she'd wheedled out of my son, who was a resident whiz at that firm.

From: witch freddie freddie13@hotmail.com
To: witch cass shiptonherbs@earthlink.net
Subject: what's up?

hi, cass. it's me, don't have to email from the library
thanx to adam generously donating his old computer when
he upgraded.

job's going great. haven't screwed up the works yet, so i
got another mini-raise and a shot at fem management training (so iconomics gets to keep their government contracts.)

things are not so great, tho, at my apartment building.
first it was the frizzling of the laundry room, for which i got
blamed (hey, i do my best to keep control, but every time i
was a wee bit late getting my stuff out of the dryer, someone dumped my undies all over the floor. third time it happened, i was major p.o.'d and the dryers blew up. *quelle
surprise!* as the french say.) then there's this thing with all
the buzzers ringing every time i come in or go out. well,
you get the picture. i am renter non grata, sez her royal
majesty queen of the tenants' org. doesn't know i got a cat,
tho. yes, am trying not to think bad thoughts about her,
harm none and all. but you know that zen saying, enlightenment will come when you stop thinking of the white
horse. . . . sure, baby.

i'm guessing married life with the greek dude is groovy,
since i haven't heard from you for awhile. maybe i'll give it
a try myself one of these days if i can dazzle some hot hunk
like your boy, ha ha. ☺

what's this i've been reading about some alice b. toklas
brownies poisoning you guys in plymouth? like i bet you're
up to your eyebrows in this one, am i right? need advice
from yr favorite pixie, i'm available. i could, like, catch a
ride up there with adam at thanksgiving.

send full details—inquiring minds need to know!

stay healthy
hugs to all the witches. tummy scratches to Scruffy.
> freddie.

P.S. i'm thinking i might, like, take some college
courses, maybe catch a degree one of these days. what do
you think?

The word "pixie" rather leaped out at me, but I decided I was really being silly now. It seemed that Freddie still had her eye on my son, Adam, who was much too old for her. Apparently he'd resisted her wiles so far, and since he'd been transferred to upper management offices in a different building, it would be more difficult for her to practice her spells on him. Hence her offer to drive up with Adam at Thanksgiving. A long ride, usually a sleepover. Oh well, I could hardly say no. Being with Freddie was like opening a window to a fresh breeze from the west, cleaning the cobwebs right out of my brain. Of course, there was that little problem of her amazing talent for psychokinesis. I'd tried to teach her to master her mind-over-matter ability, but from time to time it jumped out in maverick poltergeist activity. Still, it would be great to see her.

From: Cass shiptonherbs@earthlink.net
To: Freddie freddie13@hotmail.com
Subject: Yes!!!

Love to have you here for Thanksgiving! Didn't know
Adam was planning the trip. A word of warning: *do not* stop
at Atlantic City this time. If you hit that dollar machine big
time *again*, someone may get nosy about you. A low profile
is the Wiccan way.
    About your apartment—if you don't want to have to
keep moving, behave yourself with the tenants. You know
it's within your control, even the buzzers. Remember the

threefold law—those frizzles could boomerang right back to you!

Someone is indeed poisoning people in Plymouth. Seems to be indiscriminate. First a church social, then a TV cooking show (Phil's), and then the senior center. But we think there may be a method in this madness.

The "Greek dude" (isn't it time you called him Joe?) and I are still officially on our honeymoon until our first anniversary at Yule.

See you at turkey time. We'll have a talk about college, great goal! Meanwhile, keep in touch and I'll keep you posted, too.

Love,
Cass

Once I got started writing e-mails, I kept on, sending a short note to each of my three children, who were much more liable to answer this impersonal form of communication than some tedious message on their answering machines in their mother's well-remembered nagging tone.

In order of age, the oldest first, I began with my Becky, who worked for a firm that specialized in family law. She'd recently separated from her husband, Ron Lowell. I had to tread carefully around this one—she might make up again with that philandering jerk.

From: Mom shiptonherbs@earthlink.net
To: Becky rlowell@katzandkinder.org
Subject: How are you?

Hi, Honey.

Been thinking about you and wondering how things are going. Still loving your job?

Thanks again for the sweet get-well card and your call.

Only one night in the hospital, and no lingering effects. And don't worry, I'm barely involved—I just happened to be speaking at the church when the incident happened. I don't have to tell you that the world is full of crazies. You must meet them every day at K & K.

Have you made any plans for Thanksgiving? Would love to have you here, with or without Ron, up to you! Freddie writes me that she and Adam are driving up, so it will be a real family get-together. Well, it's a tad early—no rush letting me know.

Love,
Mom

Adam's metamorphosis from computer nerd to confident, upwardly mobile, highly paid professional had been a matter of joyous amazement to me. Our warm and easy relationship never veered into those muddy waters I sometimes found myself in with my daughters, but he did maintain a certain distance, not entirely due to the mileage. So I was somewhat surprised and pleased that he was planning on a Thanksgiving visit, if that wasn't a figment of Freddie's fertile imagination. I decided to proceed on faith.

From: Your Ma shiptonherbs@earthlink.net
To: Adam adamshipton@iconomics.org
Subject: Thanksgiving

Hi, Adam.

Delighted to learn from Freddie that you're planning to spend Thanksgiving with Joe and me, and that she's going to hitch a ride with you.

Hope the job is going great, and you're well!

As Joe explained when you called, I'm not really

involved in the poison problem in Plymouth. It was only by a bizarre coincidence that I happened to be giving a talk at the church when the first incident occurred. Not to worry!

Do send a note to confirm about Thanksgiving!

Love,
Ma

My youngest, a hopeful actress, lived with her partner, Irene, in California. We'd wallowed in some emotional quicksand while she was in therapy, but I felt we'd pulled out of it finally. Recently, the girls had moved from San Francisco to Los Angeles in pursuit of film work.

From: Mother shiptonherbs@earthlink.net
To: Cathy ireneandcathy@aol.com
Subject: How are things?

Hi, Cathy!

Thinking of you and wondering how things are going in your new place. I'm saying a prayer that you and Irene will each find some great career breaks in L.A. I remember that you planned to change agents, too—hope you found someone who appreciates your talent and works hard for you.

Also wanted to tell you that Adam and maybe Becky will be in Plymouth for Thanksgiving—just in case you and Irene are coming East around that time. Wouldn't it be nice if we could all get together!

I hope you're keeping healthy and haven't lost any more weight. I know Irene worries, and so do I. Take care of yourself!

Love,
Mother.

All these plaintive e-mails left me feeling rather melancholy, so I welcomed the sound of Joe crashing through the kitchen door with supplies from Home Warehouse. "Want some help, honey?" I called from my snug little office, which in an earlier time had been the borning room, right beside the kitchen.

"Just open the cellar door for me. I thought I'd rough together a better worktable for you. There's not enough room on that thing you've got in your old storage room, which appears to be on its last gateleg anyway."

"I know, but it belonged to Grandma. It's got a certain sentimental value for me."

"Sure, I get that. My idea is to move Grandma's table to stand against the unshelved wall, and then to build you a new, bigger one under the light. Speaking of which, I got some track lighting, too. What you've got down there now is much too feeble for a workroom."

"It has a sort of atmosphere," I ventured. "Spooky and inspiring."

"I don't know how you can even see the labels when you're putting together your herb mixtures. You ought to think of your workroom as a kind of laboratory, not some alchemist's cave."

Joe's face shone with do-it-yourselfer enthusiasm. His eyes hoped for praise. What's a gal to do?

"You're wonderful, honey! I'm so excited!" I opened the cellar door and snapped on the light, noticing for the first time that it *was* a bit gloomy down there. Even the stairs were in shadow. "This is such a thoughtful idea. Will you have time to finish it, do you think, before Greenpeace sends you off to tilt at windmills?"

What's the big furry-faced guy doing now? I ought to go first down the stairs. It's a canine tradition, in case there are dangers down there.

But I held Scruffy out of the way while Joe trotted past me with an armful of boards. I heard them hit the cellar floor with a thud. Then he was back upstairs, barely winded. "Got about five more trips," he said cheerfully, stopping for a quick kiss from his admiring wife.

"I'll help you." I had to let Scruffy go, which meant the dog danced around and in front of us with every trip from the over-loaded rental car to the cellar.

By the time we got through, my workroom was a sea of boards, tools, and lighting equipment. How in the world would I be able to fill my orders while all this home improvement was going on? Oh well, it could have been worse. He could have got an urge to remodel the kitchen. Opening the refrigerator, I took out a slab of salmon from its bed of ice.

Instantly, Scruffy was under my elbow, inhaling deeply. *Hot-diggity-dog! Is that fish? I love fish. The fishier the better.*

"I know you do. I remember all those times you rolled in dead fish on the beach and I had to give you a vanilla bath. But don't worry. You'll get your share in your supper dish tonight. Now move out the way so that I can get what I need for the sauce."

Fish oil is good for my gleaming coat. We French briards don't need baths. Baths are for retrievers, those saps. Hey, what's with the green weed, Toots?

"Fresh dill. Now, will you stop nagging?"

"I haven't said a word." Joe, who was now washing up in the half-bath with the door open, felt the need to defend himself.

"Not you. *Scruffy.*"

"You really do talk to him, is that it?"

"It's hard to explain."

Hey, get used to it, bearded guy! What do you think I am, some kind of dumb animal? My senses are sharp and my paws are stealthy, so watch yourself, fella.

It was just as well that Joe didn't hear what I heard.

Chapter Eight

During the next few weeks, my third eye, the clairvoyant eye, remained stubbornly closed to whatever dangers were brewing. Perhaps the constant pounding in my cellar workroom kept me distracted. There was definitely no chance of slipping into an alpha brain-wave state while Joe was at work in the house. I did my best to visualize him finishing the project soon—particularly before he was called away. Meanwhile, I was forced to put together my herbal orders in the kitchen, an additional mess, just when I was trying to focus on Thanksgiving, only a week away.

As I suspected, Adam hadn't been thinking about driving up to Plymouth for the holiday but had been maneuvered neatly into it by Freddie. Becky seemed pleased to join us, too, as well as glad to throw cold water on Ron's hopes that she'd spend the day enjoying the Lowells' chilly hospitality and perfectly presented Norman Rockwell bird. "We're in a bit of chaos here now," I warned her, "but no doubt Joe will have everything shipshape by the time the turkey goes into the oven."

"With Grandma's secret Nine-Herb Stuffing? Which you keep promising to write out for me."

"Of course, Grandma's stuffing. I'm a firm believer in tradition." I still relied on Grandma's notebooks of handwritten recipes.

Shipton women had always been famous for their herbal lore: not only for well-seasoned New England food but also for medicinal teas, herbal cosmetics, and useful potions of all kinds.

"Oh sure, Mom . . . you're the quintessential traditionalist."

"Actually, I am. Only my traditions go back a long, *long* way. Anyway, I'm looking forward to a lovely family party. Cathy won't be coming east, but that was really too much to hope for. She and Irene are organizing a vegetarian feast for out-of-work theater friends."

"I bet that will be a rockin' good time." Becky's tone betrayed a trace of envy for her sister's lifestyle.

"If you like tofu-turkey and chili. It's a hand-to-mouth existence, Becky. Not for you or me, but the very insecurity seems to suit them. So far away from home, too—I'm just glad that Cathy has Irene to watch over her."

"Wouldn't you rather she found a *guy* to look after her?"

"I don't even think I was surprised that she chose differently. Besides, I like Irene, and I think she's good for Cathy. I'm just happy to see all you little birds fly off on your own chosen flight paths."

"So you can fly off on yours?"

"You're too canny, my dear."

"Maybe I've inherited some of your sixth sense."

I hoped not, but I didn't say so. So many terrible things I'd seen—and seen twice. Once in my mind's eye, and again when they happened. Remembering some of those occasions while Becky talked on about the merits of following hunches in her family law practice, I let myself gaze too long out my office window at the gold of the late-afternoon sunlight settling on the ocean. I felt myself slipping away. I saw a pair of hands wearing work gloves, carrying a canvas bag. Gardening boots, like Wellingtons. Bright green. The corner of a navy jacket. *Now what was that? And where?*

"Mom? Are you there?"

I gave myself a mental shake and zipped back to the present.

"A sixth sense can be a mixed blessing, dear. Bad things happening to good people, you know."

Thanksgiving was a case in point. But for me personally, it was a truly blessed day that filled me with a rich sense of well-being. I'd put the work gloves and green Wellingtons right out of my mind in favor of concentrating on Grandma's stuffing and my usual tussle with the pastry for pies. I have been known to hurl the whole mess against the wall, just to see if it would stick, but on this magic Thanksgiving, the pastry mixed up perfectly—neither too wet nor too dry. I baked a slew of pies: pumpkin-pecan, mince-pear, and two apples, one French with cream and one regular New England. All thoughts of the murderous herbalist were banished from my spicy, steamy kitchen.

Joe and I *had* got it all together—not only together, but polished and shining. And, as always, it was glorious to have most of my family—with lively Freddie as a bonus—together around the table. Fiona was sharing the holiday with us, adding her own particular zaniness and wisdom, a nice foil for Freddie's kinetic energy.

From the moment Adam and Freddie stepped out of his Lexus, however, I'd had to submerge the nagging little notion that their friendship was becoming a lot less than casual, which, of course, had been Freddie's intent ever since they'd first met here in my house. I remembered how Adam had come downstairs looking for a boot Scruffy had stolen. My tall, fair-haired son was wearing only a towel at the time, and Freddie had been turned to awestruck, worshipful stone, Pygmalion in reverse.

Oh, let those little birds fly free! I reminded myself, trying not to visualize Freddie as a prospective daughter-in-law—*Great Goddess! What a challenge that would be!* I loved the girl dearly, but she was Volatile with a capital V. Still, she'd saved my life once—I owed her one, though not necessarily one of my children.

From sheepskin jacket to Gucci loafers, Adam looked as if he'd just stepped out of *Gentlemans Quarterly.* Even the perfectly faded jeans had an Armani label. Freddie, on the other hand, sported her usual bohemian chic—micro skirt, clingy top, thigh-high boots, and a sporty ankle-length black leather coat. Her pale face emphasized heavy eye makeup, more skillfully applied than it once had been. Her hair was midnight black again, jelled into pixie peaks, and her earrings were plentiful, but never mind—at least she'd given up the nose ring. They were a wildly divergent couple, but maybe that was the attraction.

Since the days she worked at Hamburger Heaven, Freddie had always been a favorite with Scruffy. *It's the girl. The girl is here! Let's keep her this time.* He danced around Freddie, leaping and snapping his teeth together, until she crouched down and allowed herself to be greeted with sloppy kisses.

Becky came in later, breathless from an emergency hearing for an abused wife seeking a restraining order. "She's pregnant, too," she declared angrily. "Holidays seem to bring out the monster in estranged husbands." Still wearing her all-purpose court outfit—suit, stockings, and pumps in monochromatic navy—she was just a shade plumper, but radiant in her own new freedom.

I wondered if Becky and Adam were planning to visit their father, perhaps tomorrow, but I didn't ask. Gary Hauser, my ex, a chemical engineer, unfortunately was employed at the Pilgrim Nuclear Plant and lived in a nearby condo development called Governor Bradford Village. I did my best never to run into him.

And now that I was newly married, it was heartwarming to see how well my children responded to Joe's earthy affection. In the Mediterranean way, he hugged everyone, including Adam.

Fiona, in a striped skirt and quilted top, stood beside me, breathing in, I knew, the essence of everything I was feeling about Becky and Ron, Adam and Freddie, my dear, absent Cathy, even Gary and Joe. "All things will evolve as they are meant to do, in the best of possible ways. Don't you worry, Cass," she murmured in my ear.

"Oh, thanks, Dr. Pangloss," I hissed. But before I could ask her for specifics, Freddie had dragged her away for a conference on "finding the unfindable," which was Fiona's specialty.

"She knows enough right now," I warned Fiona.

"But I always want to learn more, you know that, Cass." Freddie's tone was deferential, but the wink she directed toward me was her own saucy self.

"Freddie's ability to learn complicated material is almost intuitive. She never stops amazing me," Adam said, causing Freddie's pale face almost to blush. "She's on her way to becoming a master troubleshooter at Iconomics."

"She never stops amazing me, either," I said, thinking of an entirely different set of skills that Freddie possessed. Had he seen her ability to addle a delicate machine? Yes indeed, as I soon learned, he had witnessed just such an incident, but he hadn't realized what was going on.

It was a lovely feast, filled with warmth, affection, and laughter. Joe told engaging stories about his Greenpeace missions. Becky described her craziest family cases. Adam related how a "curious but humorous intermittent virus" had infected a competitor's display at the Atlanta Computer Show. At this, Freddie looked away from my raised eyebrows to busy herself cutting meat off a turkey leg, while Scruffy leaned devotedly against her side, sensing that bits of crispy skin were about to fall his way. Fiona refrained from dowsing the food, for which I was personally thankful, both for her trust and for not having to explain what was going on to Becky and Adam.

So I was in a rather mellow mood, still humming "We Gather Together" and putting sheets of foil over leftover pies when Patty called me, gasping and crying. "It's Wyn, Cass. He got dreadfully ill right after dinner—the dinner we give at the church, you know. For the elderly or anyone else who's alone." More sobs. I had to strain to understand her. "Poor, dear man. And Wyn's not the only one. I'm calling from the hospital now. I thought you ought to know. It's probably hemlock again. In the chocolate cake. Oh, Cass . . . Wyn's favorite. He gobbled up two pieces, while complaining that the coconut was 'off.'"

"Oh, Patty, I'm so sorry. Would it help if Joe and I came over there? Has someone notified the police?" All the time I was being reassuring, I was wondering why Wyn and Patty hadn't been more careful about the provenance of every food at the church dinner. And surely Patty had warned Wyn to watch out for chocolate.

"The police know, Cass. Wyn insisted on having an officer present to keep us all safe. Officer Notley personally vetted all the donated foods, attached a label with a name to them all. But the problem was Bevvy Besant's cake. 'I'm white cake,' she said, so Ned Notley okayed the two 'white' cakes. But Bev had only brought one. And what do men know, anyway? Ned thought *coconut frosting* meant *white*."

"Where's Officer Notley now? Do you think I could talk to him?" *The idiot.*

"He's having a gastric lavage, dear. Wyn gave him a big piece of the coconut cake. Sorry for him, you know, getting stuck with Thanksgiving Day duty. But those two nice detectives are here again. So you stay put, dear. You have your family there. Just go ahead and enjoy them. There's nothing you can do. I simply had to talk to someone outside the church, you know. Mrs. Pynchon is acting as if I'm somehow at fault in all this for not keeping a closer eye on the donated food and a tighter rein on Wyn's sweet tooth. I even heard her telling Detective Mann that he ought to investigate me. *Me!* Can you imagine that?"

"Stone Stern and Billy Mann are always running into crackpots like Mrs. P. They'll know enough to ignore her. But tell me, Patty, has anyone been able to track down the chocolate cake. I mean, who brought it?"

"Oh, *I* should have known," Patty wailed. "But I was so busy serving the dinner, and by the time I had a bite myself, then started cutting up the desserts, there was Wyn digging into a chocolate cake. What was I going to do? Grab the fork out of his hands and wrestle the cake away? Of course, I instantly checked the label, and it said Besant, big as life. The pies were donated by Bunn's Bakery, you know, but the cakes were baked by the Ladies' League."

"What about the rest of the food?"

"The cooked turkeys were a gift from Forker's Turkey Farm. Angelo's Market sent over most of the fixings. Oops. There's Dr. Blitz. Have to go now."

"Patty . . . wait . . . I want you to keep me posted. I'll try to stop by later." But I didn't know if she actually heard me.

Joe and Fiona had been hanging over me, listening with concern to my end of the conversation and what they could hear of Patty's squeals. "You'd think the Ladies' League would have been much more careful after what happened the last time," Joe said. "They should have vetted every single food item themselves, never mind the cop, and kept tabs on who actually carried each one into the kitchen."

"Okay, I won't say they should have *dowsed* the dinner," Fiona said. "I know that's not their *thing*. But for Goddess's sake, a modicum of care. Talk about 'Death by Chocolate'!"

Hearing our excited voices, Becky, Adam, and Freddie came in from the living room, where Freddie had been taking all their money in a cut-throat game of Monopoly. I'd warned them that Freddie was a wizard with dice.

"What is it?" Adam demanded.

"Not another poisoning!" Becky cried. "What kind of a pervert would poison people on Thanksgiving?"

"Chocolate cake this time. Might be hemlock again." I found I needed to sit down and take deep breaths for a moment. Joe put a consoling hand on my shoulder. "That was Patty Peacedale. The cake turned up at the Gethsemane Thanksgiving dinner for the lonely and elderly. The pastor is very ill. He's at the hospital now with several of his parishioners."

"Awesome," Freddie declared. "Some nutty dude, no doubt about it. Wish I could stick around to help catch this guy. But you go, girls! Chocolate lovers are getting to be an endangered species around here."

"Yes, this has gone quite far enough!" Fiona was drawing herself up into her most imperious glamour. "We simply must get together posthaste."

"Maybe at Phil's," I agreed. "She's entertaining family, but I believe they'll be leaving sometime tomorrow."

At seven, Becky said good-bye, pleading the merciless caseload she was carrying for Katz and Kinder. Leaving Joe, Adam, and Freddie to deal with the last of the dishes, Fiona and I jumped into her ancient baby blue Lincoln Town Car and headed to Jordan Hospital to see how Wyn and Patty were faring.

"You don't suppose the reverend is being targeted by evil forces, do you?" Fiona asked as she drove at her usual lulling pace of thirty-five miles an hour.

"Nothing so medieval," I said. "If he *is* a target, it's those millions he's just inherited."

"Evil is the root of all money." Another of Fiona's pixilated proverbs.

Chapter Nine

As we entered the Jordan Hospital lobby and headed for the reception desk, Fiona dug in her reticule and took out a small bottle of sage oil. "Here, rub a little of this on your wrists, my dear. There are always lingering negative vibrations when a madwoman is running around town indiscriminately poisoning innocent people." The receptionist looked up from her computer with a startled expression. Fiona paid her no attention, continuing her lecture to me. "You'll want to step outside yourself now, dear, if you've a mind to have a healing influence on the pastor. We're all connected to each other, cells of one body. You remember, I explained how that works when we were in Salem on the Donahue case."

The receptionist, who no longer made any pretense of looking at her computer monitor, was hanging on Fiona's every word.

"My friend will be fine just as soon as she gets her medication," I said. "Could you tell us, please, in what room we can find Selwyn Peacedale?"

"Well, I . . ." Looking hesitant, she punched a few keys. "He's not allowed to . . ."

Fiona drew herself up for battle, but just then I caught sight of

Phillipa's husband striding across the lobby. "Stone . . . Stone . . ." I called to him. "How's Wyn? Is Patty still here?"

"Hello, gals." He smiled down at us, pushing the fine brown hair out of his eyes in a preoccupied manner. "Peacedale will live, which is more than we can say for some of his Thanksgiving guests. He's in Room 202, second floor. Patty Peacedale is up there, too, in the clutches of some women from the church. I think she'd be grateful for a rescue."

"This is so terrible. Was it someone from the church crew who died? Or that young officer?"

"No, the victims were guests. Elderly ladies. Let me get back later to you on the details."

Stone looked so harried and worried, I couldn't bring myself to give him the third degree. So I just said, "Okay, thanks. I'll talk to you later then. Maybe we can help. I mean with the herbalist connection."

"Cass, believe it or not, I'd welcome even a psychic insight to this case."

"I wish I could offer one. I'll keep trying." We said good-bye and rushed away in opposite directions.

As we came out of the elevator, I heard a familiar strident voice. ". . . never had such goings-on as we've had to endure since your husband took over Gethsemane. And now these murders . . . *murders* . . . surely some sort of curse . . . you and your witchy friend."

Fiona may be plump and arthritic, but when the spirit moves her, she can outdistance me with ease, as she did now, racing down the hall into the family waiting room at full sail with cannons blazing. We found Patty in tears, not entirely because of Wyn's narrow escape. Mrs. Pynchon was there with two other League ladies, obviously her acolytes.

"Avast and begone, evil tongues!" Fiona cried, holding both little fingers straight out in the classic banishing mode. "We'll have no more harangues this night. You ladies will want to leave here *this minute* and not be bothering dear Mrs. Peacedale *any longer* with your ill-considered remarks. For your own good, you know. It wouldn't do for any of those mean-spirited thoughts to come home to roost. Not that I'm wishing you ill, although I could, I could. No, it's just the way of the Universe of Infinite Returns . . ."

I didn't think Mrs. Pynchon and her minions heard the last part of Fiona's homily, because they were out the door and running for the elevator before she was half through her speech.

"That was a *bit* over the top, Fiona, but it worked like a charm," I said.

"Oh, I'm so glad to see you," Patty breathed. "Mrs. P. has been working herself up to a fever pitch for the last half hour. I'd be surprised if she wasn't convening another '*Dump Peacedale*' committee."

"Not to worry. Fiona took her down very neatly. How's Wyn?"

"Asleep, poor baby. What a terrible time's he's been having. I pray that this poison person will be caught soon."

"She will," Fiona said grimly. "We're on the case now."

"Oh, goodie," Patty caroled with some of her old ingenuous zest. "Several of my own friends are organizing a prayer circle, and your good thoughts and wishes will be most appreciated. What is it, exactly, that Wiccans do in a case like this?"

Before Fiona could reply, I said, "We'll say some words that are very like prayers for the best possible outcome—healing of the sick, comfort to the bereaved, and harming none, the banishing of the evildoer."

"Putting a stop to this wicked woman's poison spree is first on our agenda, then locking up her ass in jail forever." Fiona's menacing tone was somewhat muffled as she fished around in the bottom of her reticule. "Ah, here it is!"

Good Goddess, I thought, *let her not pull out that pistol*. But no, she had found a crystal pendant, not as large as the one she usually wears around her neck, probably a spare. "Here, dear, if you will take this crystal and hold it over whatever you plan to eat—"

Patty seemed quite enthralled as Fiona described the basic uses of the pendulum and then how it could be employed to dowse food and pronounce on its wholesomeness. But since a pendulum must work through one's unconscious mind, would it perform for someone who might not have that sixth sense for good and evil that Fiona possessed?

"But Fiona . . . that's your own very special crystal," Patty protested. "Now, if I understand you correctly, any pendant could signal its approval or disapproval of a particular food."

"Oh, yes," Fiona agreed. "Even better if it's been worn on your person and absorbed your vibes."

"Well, then, I think I'll just try your most interesting game with *this*." Patty reached under her Peter Pan collar and pulled out a silver cross on a chain.

Fiona gently lifted the pendant in her hand and, leaning close to Patty, examined its curious design. The elegant basket-weave pattern of the square cross was set against a slightly smaller circle. In its center was a green stone, like a rough emerald. "Oh yes, dear, this should be fine. Worn it for a long time, have you?"

"It was a gift from my favorite relative. Aunt Mae. Aunts can be such angels in the lives of young girls."

"What was your aunt's last name, dear?" asked Fiona.

"McDonigal. Mae McDonigal."

"Celtic, of course. For best results, give the cross a wash in mugwort tea."

"Mugwort? What's that? My, my . . . Won't Wyn be fascinated," Patty breathed, wiping away the last traces of tears from her cheeks.

"I always think it's a mistake to burden a husband with too many details that are best handled by a woman," Fiona said, letting go of the cross. "Your Wyn has so many parish matters on his mind, especially now with these malevolent goings-on. It might be a kindness simply to dowse the food and say nothing more about it."

"Perhaps you're right. I'll just say it's a kind of blessing."

"A fine thought." Fiona put her plump arm around Patty's shoulder and hugged her warmly. Silver bangles tinkled softly. "Now about your problems with Mrs. Pynchon . . ."

"Enough, Fiona!" I said hastily. "Let's just duck into Wyn's room and say a few healing words. I think that's what we came for, wasn't it?"

The pastor lay flat in bed, eyes closed, face pale, his hands in a prayerful pose on his chest, like a saint in effigy on his tomb. We sat down quietly in the two plastic chairs, not wanting to disturb him if he was dozing. I tried to remove myself from my own concerns and concentrate on healing thoughts. Fiona reached over to lay her pudgy fingers on the pastor's arm.

"Hell and damnation," said the crabby voice of the reposing saint. "I suppose I'm going to have to follow your advice and give up chocolate." His eyes opened. "Oh dear. I thought that was Patty."

"That might be good advice to follow, Wyn," I said. "At least until we discover the crazy chocolatier with the poisonous herbs. I mean, until *the police* solve the case."

He smiled wanly. "My money's on you ladies in the circle."

"Your money may very well be the motive, Wyn. I've heard it's quite a lot."

He sighed. "Millions. It's like having won some terrible lottery, when I think how I've benefited from Lydia Craig's untimely death. I was hoping the money would be a force for good."

"It will be," Fiona said grimly. "As soon as we banish this wicked person."

"Amen," Wyn said.

I didn't have to call Phillipa. It was she who called me early the next morning. I was slumped against the counter sipping my first cup of coffee, waiting for the caffeine to kick in, when the kitchen phone jangled my nerves like an alarm clock. "We have to do something!" she screamed in my ear. "Did you know two people who dined at the church yesterday died last night?"

"Yes. I met Stone at the hospital."

"It was two of the really frail elderly dears, the Luckey sisters. Did you know them? I guess Peacedale has some kind of cast-iron gut. I can't stand any more of this!"

"Me neither. Stone didn't say who they were. I think Fiona introduced me to the Luckeys one time at the library. The sisters were quilting with the Women's Cooperative in the basement. Fiona will be wild. She's already insisting that we meet, possibly at your house, and conjure up a way to stop this evil character. Is your family leaving for home today?"

"Yep. Noon flight. Will you call Deidre and Heather? I've got to go whip up a farewell breakfast. Oh, and, Cass, it *was* hemlock again."

"But it's November," I said. "The stuff should have died back in the fields by now. I wonder if she put by some chopped hemlock leaves in her freezer. Not much different than freezing parsley or basil. You can do it in little foil packets. Turns black but is perfectly usable in cooked dishes."

"Personally, I always use fresh herbs," Phillipa said.

"This gal really knows how to manage her herbal arsenal."

"Or guy."

"Maybe. But her boots looked to be a woman's size nine."

"You saw *her boots*, Cass?" Phillipa's voice was hitting that shrill note that's so unsettling first thing in the morning.

"Green Wellingtons. You go dazzle your guests, Phil. I'll explain everything tonight. What time do you want us?"

"Oh, come at seven. And come hungry. I have leftovers to die for."

"Unfortunate expression," I commented. "See you later, then."

I telephoned the others. Deidre was happy to take a break from the family scene. Cooking was not her forte, but she waded into any holiday with her usual grit and gusto. To Deidre,

Thanksgiving meant candied yams with marshmallows and green bean casserole with condensed mushroom soup and petrified onions, and, by Goddess, she would produce them.

Fiona said she'd hardly ever been more tempted to invoke a curse—what kind of madwoman would harm two lovely old ladies like the Luckeys? So she was pleased that her concerns were being taken up by us all before she could stray from the white way, so to speak. Nevertheless, she complained, "But, Cass, it's you who always tell us who to look for. What's happened to you?"

"Do you suppose finding true love has taken away my witch's powers, like in the movies?"

"Oh, garbage, Cass. True love sharpens all the senses, five or six or nine—whatever you've got. You know that."

"Yeah. Listen, Fiona, I'll surely zero in on some telling detail. Just give me a little time."

Chapter Ten

"*Cherchez l'argent.* Again!" Phillipa turned over another tarot card, this one the four of pentacles.

"I thought that was supposed to be *cherchez la femme.*" Deidre put down her fork and empty plate with a sigh. "That was the loveliest mince pie, Phil. I suppose you made the mincemeat yourself, right?"

"Maybe it's both," I said. "Seek the woman who's after money. Divine lemon, too, and with a double-crust—superb." I had to admit that Phillipa had a way with flaky pastry that was far beyond my poor culinary powers. Pure magic!

We were lying around Phillipa's living room in various stages of surfeit. I made the zipped-lip sign to our hostess so she wouldn't mention that the mincemeat was made from venison, which would get Heather riled just as we were gearing up for a united effort. That dedicated animal activist had even picketed one of Plymouth's trendiest restaurants, Winston's New England Nuovo, for the offense of serving Provimi milk-fed veal.

A blazing fire in the copper-hooded fireplace highlighted a Moroccan brass table where Phillipa was studying a tarot layout. "And the *six* of pentacles, too," she said, as if that confirmed everything.

"I don't know how someone could cause all this heartache and bellyache out of greed," Heather said. She was sitting cross-legged on the floor near the fire. Her bronze hair glinted with light, looking like part of the décor.

"That's because you already have money, honey," Deidre chided her.

"Ladies, ladies . . . let's just concentrate on who has something to gain in this series of poisonings." Fiona brought us back on track. "Reverend Peacedale, for instance, has become a millionaire, thanks to the Lydia Craig legacy. Perhaps she intended him to set up some kind of trust to do good works, but, as I understand it, he can do anything he wishes with the money." She gently stroked Phillipa's fluffy black cat, Zelda, who had found a comfy napping nest in Fiona's lap. Perhaps Zelda remembered, in the mysterious way of animals, that it was Fiona who'd rescued her from a Dumpster and conned Phillipa into giving the discarded kitten a home.

Heather took out a faux-leather bound notebook and gold pen from her hand-loomed bag with the legend *Moonchild* woven into the pattern. "I'm making a list of suspects connected with the money. Selwyn Peacedale is number one. Has to be, because he got the dough. It is, after all, possible that he might have feigned getting poisoned himself. Second, his lovely wife, Patty, who may very well have had enough of that drafty parsonage and living a life of good works. She knew about the Craig legacy, and could have been impatient to collect. Now, who else? If something happens to Peacedale, for instance, what becomes of his inheritance?"

"Good point," Phillipa said. "And as a matter of fact, I've looked into that. Or, rather, Stone has looked into that, and I've wheedled the information out of him."

"Who?" "Who?" "Who?" we demanded, sounding like a parliament of owls.

Phillipa's dark eyes, often so difficult to read, betrayed a gleam of pride at her clever research. "If Wyn Peacedale were to go to his heavenly reward within a year of receiving the Craig bequest, Patty P. would get *not one red cent.* The money would revert to the estate, to be divided between Lydia Craig's nephews and niece. But, if the pastor lives longer than the specified year, the bequest will be inherited by whomever he chooses, probably his wife."

"Do you suppose that there's a plan afoot to get rid of Peacedale before the year is up?" Heather asked, busily jotting down notes. "And what are these relatives' names, ages, occupations, marital status? It certainly would be in their interest to polish off Peacedale while his bequest is still entailed to the Craig family."

"I know something about them," I said. "Patty has made me her not-of-the-parish confidant. The funeral civility of the Craigs, she's complained, disappeared the moment the will was read, and they've been trashing the Peacedales ever since. But you want names, Heather. As I recall, the oldest nephew is Geoffrey Craig. That's Geoffrey with a 'G-e-o.' He's a CPA, married to an attorney named Heidi Pryde. A distant cousin of the pig-farm Prydes, I might add."

"Plymouth!" Deidre said. "Six degrees of separation docsn't apply here. It's barely two."

"I wouldn't trust a Pryde as far as I could throw her," Phillipa said. "I'll bet she's a personal injury attorney."

"Okay, Geoffrey Craig and Heidi Pryde Craig." Heather continued her note-taking. Was that a Mont Blanc pen, I wondered. It flashed richly in the firelight.

"The Geoffrey Craigs live in a posh part of Marshfield, and Heidi belongs to the very exclusive Gardeners of the Mayflower Society," I continued. "Which makes her a prime suspect in my book. We're looking for someone who knows her herbs."

"It's not easy getting into the G.M.S.," Heather said. "As it happens, the president is related to me by marriage, Violet Pickle Morgan, and a more snobby old harridan you'll never want to meet."

"Don't tell me! To get into G.M.S., your family has to have come over on that overrated, overweighted boat?" Deidre demanded to know.

"No, but it helps to be related to some founding mother who hand-carried English herbs to her New World garden. I wonder how a Pryde made the cut?"

"Blackmail, obviously. Old Violet Pickle must have had a skeleton in her ancestral closet, and Heidi Pryde ferreted it out. Children?" asked Deidre.

"No. Not yet anyway. Lydia confided to her pastor that Geof and Heidi were thinking of adopting a Russian orphan, and she *did not* approve."

"Next?" Heather's blue and gold pen was poised at the ready.

"Bruce Craig, rather the black sheep of the Craig family. Ace mechanic, works at Johnny D.'s garage and lives in an apartment over the Wampanoag Deli in North Plymouth. Married to Sherry Wojcik. They have two children—Bruce Jr. and Shirley, both elementary-school age. On weekends, Sherry works as a cocktail waitress."

"And Lydia Craig does not approve of cocktail waitresses?" Phillipa inquired.

"You got it," I said. "And it also came to Aunt Lydia's attention that the police were called to Bruce's apartment more than once for a 'domestic disturbance.' Then we have the niece, Jean Craig Deluca, married to Arthur Deluca, a painter of the seagulls-over-dunes school of Cape Cod painting. Jean's something of a potter, plus she runs a little gallery in Plymouth Center near Fiona's place, where she sells her husband's work to tourists who want to take home a piece of the Cape. Lydia Craig did not approve of the Delucas' artistic friends. She felt that her niece, Jean, was wallowing in bohemian decadence, possibly getting drunk with a bunch of artists and smoking pot as well."

"Art! I know Art," Fiona said. "And Jean, too. He's a pleasant enough fellow, and so prolific. Her pots are . . . well . . . pretty little things," Fiona said. "They've always seemed like a harmless couple to me. No raucous parties or police raids, at any rate. There's a teenage son, too, I believe."

"Yes, Leonardo," I said. "Goes to Assumption. But Lydia Craig felt that a Catholic high school was a waste of money and would turn the boy popish like his father, when a plain old public school education that her taxes paid for was available for free."

"Lydia Craig is clearly depicted here holding on to her four pentacles for dear life." Phillipa tapped a card in her layout. "She would not have approved of any wild expenditure such as education fees."

"Patty said that Miss Craig told Wyn about the bequest last Christmas. She said she wanted him to create a foundation to help the 'deserving poor,'" I continued. "And she instructed him to commission an engraved bronze plaque with an embossed portrait of herself and the Craig coat of arms to be erected over her pew. Oh, and the family motto, 'Live that you may live forever.' The plaque, of course, would barely put a dent in the Craig millions."

"I'm surprised she didn't hold out for a stained-glass window," Deidre said. "So poor Peacedale was supposed to let the *undeserving* starve on the church doorstep? I know that type of do-gooder. But poor, miserly Miss Craig died in an untimely and horrid way, and I mean to find out who did it."

"So do we all," Fiona declared. "She must have wanted that foundation to ensure her immortality, without her having to go to the expense of hiring a foundation financial manager recommended by Borer, Buckley, and Bangs. We all know what a tightwad Lydia was. On the other hand, simply leaving everything to her own family would have yielded no everlasting profit in heaven. She probably counted on having plenty of time to work out the parameters of the foundation with Peacedale, never suspecting that a yen for brownies would cut short her plans."

"Brownies!" I said. "I can't get over the notion that brownies—the elfin kind—are connected in some way."

"Well, Craig is a Pictish name." Fiona polished off the last of her lemon pie with a flourish of her fork. "Craig means 'rock,' by the way, and the original Craig tartan was soberly designed in various rock colors—black, gray, tan, white, and a thread of orange. Sometime later, the Craigs added crimson and a rather raucous blue. The MacDonald tartan, I'm happy to say, is sober green with a dignified red accent. . . ."

"Picts are connected to brownies, and Craigs are connected to Picts," Deidre interrupted. "Hey, Cass . . . synchronicity rules!"

"Okay, here's the list." Heather tore the page out of her notebook. "The Peacedales, Selwyn and Patricia. The nephews, Geoffrey and Bruce, and their wives, Heidi and Sherry. The niece, Jean, and her husband Arthur Deluca. So, what's the next step, Cass?"

"Why is everyone looking at me?"

"Past history, based on who sent us off into danger before," Phillipa said. "Anyone for more pie?"

A chorus of groans. Then Deidre said, "Have we got any kind of sorting spells in *Hazel's Book*?"

"Aha! I thought you'd never ask." Fiona reached into her remarkable reticule and pulled out that useful volume, a treasure she'd unearthed at a yard sale. Faint purple letters etched into the black cover read *Hazel's Book of Household Recipes*. Along with stews, soaps, sachets, cough syrups, and other nineteenth-century staples, the book included recipes with magical ingredients and purposes. "Hmmm. Sorting, sorting . . ."

Fiona licked her finger and paged through, her silver bangles chiming. I wondered what ancient viral infection might lurk on those back pages. *I'm definitely getting paranoid*, I thought.

"Now, here's the very thing!" Fiona pulled forward the raveled, faded pink ribbon marker to hold the page. " 'Sorting for Rot or Any Evil Influence.' Ah yes. No surprises there." She mumbled to herself, reading the ingredients through the gold-rimmed half-tracks perched on her nose.

"Aloud, aloud!" Heather insisted.

Fiona read in a low, strong voice, taking on Hazel's persona. "Line up in a row your fruits or livestock or whatever you question as to its wholesomeness, and sprinkle them with a strong tea of sweet wormwood, chervil, and *Herba benedicta*. Light a yellow candle whilst chanting, 'Mother of wisdom, dispel all doubt, evil at the bone will out.' If you are close put upon by curious neighbors, a verse of 'Rock of Ages' can be sung instead and will also work. The rot will be sorted from the wholesome, making itself known by ooze."

"Do you suppose that applies to names on a piece of paper?" asked Deidre. "Shouldn't we have photos or something like that? And what's *Herba benedicta*?"

"Avens," I said. "The Blessed Herb. *Geum urbanum*. Also called bennet. A long medicinal history, and also used to ward off demons. Where she writes 'whatever you question,' I believe she may have used slips of paper. You know Hazel, with her cautious wording and red herrings."

"Yeah, like, I can see her piously humming 'Rock of Ages,'" Deidre said.

"On the other hand, one doesn't expect slips of paper to 'ooze.'" I continued.

"Never know till you try it," Fiona said. "Magic is in the eye of the beholder, I always say."

"Well, yes, I can put together the herbs," I said, "and, Heather, you do the yellow candle, but don't get carried away. A plain yellow candle will be quite good enough. Let's get together at my place, say, on Friday night. Give me a chance to show off my newly refurbished workroom."

"What do you mean, 'carried away'?" Heather demanded. "What you need here is the piercing ray of the Goddess, yellow grain, Ceres Incarnate sorting the wheat from the chaff."

"Okay, okay," I said. "Whatever."

"I'll write the names on parchment," Deidre said. "Maybe

parchment has some latent ooze properties. I've been practicing calligraphy in my spare time."

"How does a mother of four youngsters get any spare time?" Phillipa asked.

"As you know, Deidre has a special relationship with time," I said. "Friday at eight, then?"

As soon as Patty got Wyn home from the hospital and settled into bed, she called me, her regular sounding board, to bemoan the fact that he was insisting on officiating at the Luckey sisters' funeral.

"Can you get someone to help him?" I wondered.

"Alas, our parish is too small to support an assistant, as Mrs. P. has always drummed into Gethsemane's board of directors. I thank God she's only the treasurer and not the president," said Patty, in what sounded like a fervent prayer of thanks.

"When's the funeral?" I thought maybe I'd better be there to see if I got any guilty vibes from any of the mourners.

"Visiting hours today and tomorrow. Funeral on Saturday morning at ten. Are you coming? I suggest you walk over early. I think it will be well-attended."

"It will be *mobbed*, Patty. Every time a victim of murder is laid to rest, the sympathetic, the curious, and the just plain morbid come out in flocks."

"Yes, I suppose you're right." Patty sighed. "And that will make it so difficult for me to count the house. I do like to keep track, you know. Wyn's head is always in some heavenly cloud. But he does like me to check attendance. So then if Mrs. Pynchon complains that people are put off by his ecumenical view, I can point out that his sermon on Saint Francis and blessing of the pets was standing room only."

"Right, Patty. Wyn's lucky to have you watching his back, so to speak. Yes, I will be there—and early. I like to keep an eye on the crowd myself."

Chapter Eleven

"Let's *all* go to the wake," Deidre said. She was helping me to set up the old wooden folding chairs in my cellar workroom. "I love a good wake, don't you?"

"That's your Irish genes doing a jig, Dee," Phillipa said. "In my family, the dear departed were buried with all haste, but then we sat shivah for seven days, which is like a wake sans the body."

"We ought to say a few words among ourselves for those poor Luckey sisters as they journey to Summerland," Fiona said. "And catch the wake, too."

"Outstanding idea!" I agreed. "Wouldn't it be grand if some of the Craigs showed up! I'd see them up close, get Patty to introduce me, and maybe even shake hands. The touch of a stranger's hand often gives me a quick psychic flash, although I must say I'm getting discouraged."

We'd gathered for our foray into Hazel's "Sorting for Rot" spell. I'd turned off the marvelous track lighting that Joe had installed in favor of my ancient green hanging lamp and a few scented candles—lavender, rosemary, and myrrh. Our shadows danced against jars of dried herbs on the old wooden shelves. It was all marvelously evocative.

Out of her *Moonchild* bag, Heather took the yellow candle

she'd made and set it up in the center of my brand-new pine worktable. Possibly it was as plain as Heather ever gets, just tiny sprays of wheat and a few honeybees embedded in the golden wax. "I found these bees dead in my Widow's Walk," Heather said. "I wouldn't want you to think I'd kill harmless insects just for my art."

"One girl's harmless insect is another girl's menacing sting," Phillipa said. "That's Dyer's Funeral Home, isn't it, Dee? I haven't been to a whole lot of wakes, but I suppose you can clue me in to how to behave."

"Just murmur something like 'terrible tragedy, untimely loss,'" Deidre suggested.

"Tragic maybe, but hardly untimely," Phillipa said. "Weren't the Luckeys close to ninety?"

"Doesn't matter," Deidre said. "If it wasn't in the Goddess's good time, it *was* untimely."

"Hush, you two!" Fiona clapped her hands together. "Let's concentrate on what Hazel has to tell us."

Heather lit the candle. The aroma of warmed honey joined the other fragrances in the room. "This is so lovely, Heather," I said, as I hastily put an old plant saucer under the candle lest it drip hot wax on my bridegroom's handiwork.

Deidre laid out the slips of parchment on which she'd lettered the names of Lydia's relatives as well as the Peacedales in beautifully decorative calligraphy. I sprinkled them lightly with the infusion of sweet wormwood, chervil, and *Herba benedicta*. Fiona began to sing in a soft low monotone, "Mother of wisdom, dispel all doubt, evil at the bone will out," and we joined in, repeating the hypnotic words with more and more fervor in every round. Soon the whole cellar rang with our chanting, the green light swung back and forth like Fiona's pendulum, and the glass jars rattled.

Suddenly Deidre screamed, "Oh, look!" breaking the rhythm. Everyone's gaze zoomed to where she was pointing. A tiny bit of sticky stuff had oozed out of the wood under one slip of parchment.

"Holy shit!" exclaimed Heather reverently.

"Jean Craig Deluca," Fiona read aloud in a somber tone.

"Good old Hazel," Phillipa said. "I'm not saying Jean's the one, but just in case, I think we ought to investigate her thoroughly. For instance, does she garden? Does she know her herbs like Cass? Did she have access to the places where poisoned foods were introduced? I wonder if I should mention this to Stone."

"Well, he did say to Fiona and me that he'd welcome even a psychic insight on this case," I said. "If I were you, I would whisper the name in his ear, let him look into it for you." I peered more closely at the little ooze near Jean's name. Would it still, count, I wondered, if that were some glue of Joe's or natural sap from the pine? But I didn't want to throw a bucket of cold water on the circle's enthusiasm.

"And I'll see what I can find," said Fiona, whose expertise with library and Internet resources and her own dowsing skills always served us so well. "Murder will out, and murderers, too."

"What was that racket you had going on downstairs?" Joe asked after everyone had left. "I haven't heard anything quite like it since I was in Zimbabwe. Scruffy went upstairs and put a pillow over his ears."

"I think you're exaggerating, dear. We were only chanting. It's just something we do." I picked up our cups and saucers and stashed them in the dishwasher.

"I don't mean to complain, sweetheart, but your chanting seems to have done something weird to our phones. Listen to this—"

He punched number one on his cell's speed dial, and my kitchen wall phone rang. I picked up the receiver. "Shipton's love potions and exotic massage oils," I sang into the phone. It sang back. Or rather, it squealed, grunted, and moaned. *Very weird indeed!* I thought guiltily of all the times I'd been tempted to hex Joe's cell phone so that Greenpeace couldn't get through to him with yet another assignment halfway around the world.

And now, without my even trying, the damn phone was having a nervous breakdown.

"Is this static on your phone, too?"

He handed me the cell. The same, but worse, with a kind of electrical pop and crackle followed by subterranean groans.

"Sounds as if the Rice Krispies elves are having an orgy."

"Can you fix it? Unchant it, maybe?" His expression was faintly accusatory.

"Gosh, I don't know. This has never happened to me before." I went to the refrigerator and opened the door, looking for the excellent merlot we hadn't finished at dinner. Something to steady my brain while Joe busied himself taking the kitchen phone apart and peering suspiciously at its interior works.

At the sound of the refrigerator door opening, Scruffy trotted downstairs, ears perked. *Hey, Toots, even though I come from a long line of brave French briards, that caterwauling you had going on was too much for my sensitive auditory equipment. I really need something to get my teeth into, to restore my natural canine confidence. Any pork chops left?*

"Sorry about that, Scruff. No chops left over, but how about a nice raw carrot?"

I beg your pardon. Have I suddenly sprouted rabbit ears?

"Let's not get hoity-toity. You're only *half* briard, you know. The other half is pure mutt, some fly-by-night terrier, I imagine, judging by your manners."

It's probably thanks to my daredevil sire that I'm super-savvy, Toots, instead of being a victim of overbreeding like some stupid, sissy show dog.

"Okay, superdog, how about a supersize, special-occasion, liver-flavored gourmet dog biscuit?"

Now you're talking dogspeak!

"Are you having a conversation with Scruffy right now?" Joe asked wonderingly. Satisfied that there were no interior gremlins, he put the phone back together.

"Hmmm. I guess you could say that. Say, who called you on the phone anyway—? Don't tell me!"

"Yep. My boss did call me with an assignment, but before I could find out what it's about, the phone went into its gobbledygook phase."

I laughed. "Well, I'll try to undo the spell, but my heart won't be in it."

"Can you? Undo the spell, that is?"

"I haven't a clue. Let me call in reinforcements." I picked up my kitchen phone and hit the speed dial for Fiona.

"Cass? What in Hades . . ." Fiona's voice sounded garbled and far away.

"The Hazel chant zapped my phones," I shouted over the din.

"What? Cracked your bones?"

"ZAPPED MY PHONES," I yelled even louder.

"OKAY . . . GOT IT. TRY SAYING THE CHANT BACKWARDS. IN FACT, SAY IT TWO TIMES, AND CALL ME IN THE MORNING." I distinctly heard my friend cackle merrily before she hung up.

"What did she say?" Joe demanded. "Let's do it, whatever it is."

"Even if it's a weird sex thing?"

"Is it? Good old Fiona." The man was positively smirking.

"Just kidding. She said to say the chant backwards . . . twice." I scribbled the words down on the notepad by the phone. *Mother of wisdom, dispel all doubt, evil at the bone will out.* Then I reversed them. *Out will bone the at evil doubt all dispel wisdom of Mother.* "Will you read this with me twice?"

"Okay. Then can we do the weird sex thing?"

"There is no weird sex thing. I made it up."

"So? Even better . . ."

"Are you going to say this with me or what?"

Joe stood beside me, arm around my shoulders, hip against hip, reading over the words. Sensing a party, Scruffy trotted over and leaned against my other side. I scratched behind his ears.

Then Joe and I recited the charm twice, and Scruffy added a couple of woofs. I had my doubts whether Fiona's hasty charm would work, but magic is always worth a shot.

"Now give it a chance to perk for a minute." I poured the merlot into two glasses and gave Scruffy the promised supersize biscuit. He grabbed it and trotted into the living room to enjoy his treat on a proper rug.

We drank and waited. At the last sip of wine, Joe's cell phone rang. He glanced at me shamefaced as he answered, "Ulysses here. Yes . . . Yes . . . I understand. What's your transport? Sure, I can do that. Right. Right." Then after a few moments of silent listening, "Yes, I'll leave as soon as I can."

"Oh, Good Goddess," I wailed. "I should have left bad enough alone."

Joe took me into his arms, laid his cheek against mine, and patted my back, as if comforting a child. "I'll be saving the Tongass, but I'll be thinking of you."

"Yeah?" I wouldn't have admitted it, but I never could be angry with Joe when he was holding me against his deliciously brawny body. "So what's the Tongass, and from where exactly will you be thinking of me?"

"I'm surprised at you, Cass. The Tongass is our largest national forest. Part of the Roadless Area Conservation Rule in Alaska." He murmured a description of its untamed beauty into my ear, which actually made the place sound sexy. "The U.S. Forestry Service is planning to exempt Tongass from the roadless rule. In other words, to clear the way for chopping it up."

"So what are you going to do? Sail to Alaska in an icebreaker in protest?"

"Well, not exactly, sweetheart. I'm meeting activists from Alaska in D.C. We're going to bring our protest to the Forestry Service offices in the USDA building. Delivering a letter asking them to quit logging in protected places."

"Not sailing? Just delivering a letter? So why do they need you?" I pulled away, the better to see his face. Yes, something more definitely was going on. It could be read clearly in the corners of his mouth and his eyes glancing away from my direct gaze.

"I guess someone's decided that I can be useful in other ways."

"I can imagine. Like what, exactly?"

"Like engineering how to move a heap of sod." Joe took his duffel bag out of the coat closet and headed into the bedroom to pack.

"Sod? What's sod got to do with it? You're not leaving *now*, are you?" I followed after him, whining.

"No, sweetheart, but I've got to catch tomorrow's first shuttle to D.C., so I do have to leave at four."

"In the morning?"

"Yep. That's the next four we've got." He began throwing shirts and jeans into the duffel. How long was he planning to be away?

"Washington's not far. But it's almost December. You'll be home for our anniversary at Yule, right?"

"Absolutely." He zipped up his duffle and gave me a lingering kiss. "No way would I miss that." His hands slid down my arms and around my back, pulling me close, pushing me gently toward the bed. "Meanwhile," he murmured into my ear, "what was that you were saying earlier about a magical sex rite?"

"They're all magical, lover."

Much later, when we were lazily contemplating a late supper, I said, "So, you never answered me about the sod."

"The sod is a surprise for the Forestry Service, and I think I'll let it be a surprise for you, too. Check the six o'clock evening news the day after tomorrow."

So I did. And it *was* a surprise. Because there was Joe, getting arrested again, this time for helping to dump twelve tons of sod in front of the USDA building. His companions in crime were a bunch of guys from Alaska and the executive director of Greenpeace. All of them were wearing inappropriate smiles and looking mighty pleased with themselves.

Chapter Twelve

At Deidre's urging, we attended the wake en masse, where we found that mourners in the Luckey room had overflowed into the halls of Dyer's Funeral Home. Frail friends from the church and the Women's Cooperative, struggling to view the twin caskets, were nearly being trampled by a crowd of townspeople morbidly attracted to the cachet of a local murder. But none of them, I was disappointed to discover, were the Craigs.

The circle, of course, wasn't guilty of any such lowbred curiosity. We were engaged in the high-minded activity of sleuthing. Or so Deidre kept reminding us as we read our way through gift tags on the enormous bank of flowery tributes. "Ah, the *Pilgrim Times*," she murmured, shaking her blond curls in disapproval. "I'll bet *their* circulation is getting a nice little boost from another poisoning. Attractive arrangement of mums, though. And look at this, 'The Geoffrey Craigs.' Elegant basket. White and yellow carnations. At least their *flowers* made it to the wake. Here in spirit if not in flesh. I wonder how they knew the Luckeys."

"In Plymouth everyone knows everyone at least by nodding acquaintance," Phillipa muttered. "Can we, for mercy's sake, get out of here now? Miss Etiquette's book, *Etiquette for Dummies*, declares that twenty minutes is quite long enough to pay one's respects. And this crush of people and flowers, plus a trace of eau d'embalming fluid in the air are oppressive. I'm feeling quite nauseous."

"Now, wait just a minute," Fiona grabbed Phillipa's arm as if to prevent her from bolting out the door. Although Phillipa's signature black outfit was perfectly appropriate, Fiona, conceding nothing to mourning custom, was wearing a striped jacket, patchwork skirt, and her usual armful of silver bracelets, which jangled fearfully among the discreet whispers. "Maybe I should have been dowsing these floral tributes?"

"No, you should not!" I declared firmly. "And Phil's right, it's high time we made our way out of here."

"Ah, but Fiona hasn't swung her crystal over the Luckeys yet!" Deidre's blue eyes sparkled mischievously.

I was about to caution Deidre not to give Fiona any ideas when Patty Peacedale tapped me on the shoulder. "Don't the sisters look wonderful!" she enthused in a refined murmur. "Gloria's Crowning Glory did their hair and makeup—very tasteful. And isn't this a grand turnout for the poor dears?"

"Oh, hi, Patty. Bodes well for the funeral, does it?"

A corner of Patty's mouth twitched into a half smile, perhaps all she would allow herself at a wake. "So, what are you girls up to today? Checking the vibes? I've read that in the Middle Ages, a corpse often identified its murderer by bleeding when he approached the bier. The guilty party could be tried and hanged on that evidence alone."

"That must have made for some exciting wakes," Phillipa said.

Heather, who had been viewing the Luckeys and saying a few Wiccan words of farewell, joined our circle. "Probably the same savants who tossed their suspect in a fast-moving river and called her a witch if she floated. Of course, if she drowned, she was found innocent. An early Catch Twenty-two."

"Can we *please* go now?" Phillipa whined.

"I'm ready to go when you all are," Heather agreed instantly.

"Everyone's expressed sympathy to the cousins, right? So, frankly, Cass, your house is closest, and I'll be looking for a good, stiff brandy after this. By the way, Patty, what happened to that fiesty feline companion that belonged to the Luckeys? I assume the cousins are offering him a home. Prize Maine Coon cat, wasn't it? Brown tabby. Buster, if memory serves. Not a great traveler. The Luckeys used to have a wicked time trying to bring that character into Dick's office."

Patty looked bemused. "Cat? Did the Luckeys have a cat? Oh, yes, I believe they tried to carry it into church for the blessing of the animals. Nearly scratched his way out of Emma Luckey's arms and gave Wyn a good slash, too. Maybe you could ask that gentleman over there, Heather. I believe he's the Luckeys' executor, and he's probably been through the house to check whatever an executor checks in cases of sudden death. Oh dear. I do hope the poor thing is all right. How many days has it been now?"

"Oh Great Isis!" Heather cried. "You mean no one's been looking after Buster? We're going to have to get into the Luckey house immediately. Patty, I want you to go right over to that executor and demand the key. Poor deserted cat may be wasting away in that big old place."

"Well . . . I . . ." Patty's expression was desperately uncertain. She looked around, possibly for her husband. No help in sight.

Not one to delay when an animal's welfare was concerned, Heather put her arm through Patty's and simply marched her over to the small man with the brush mustache, who listened and nodded and smiled encouragingly.

"The house is open this evening for out-of-town relatives, and refreshments have been laid out in the dining room," Patty said when they rejoined our huddle. "Mr. Shortsleeves says to go on over there and search for ourselves, it's perfectly okay with him. He says no one has seen the cat since the Luckeys were taken ill. He's been in the house himself, of course, and those cousins, the heirs, and a woman who was hired to clean the place and set up for the reception after the funeral tomorrow. He thinks maybe the little bugger ran away."

"I don't believe it. We'll find him," Heather said grimly. "And a Maine Coon cat is hardly a 'little bugger.'"

"Maybe you'll want to give the kitty a good home, Patty," Phillipa suggested, with a sly wink in my direction. "You have lots of room in that big parsonage, and a cat can be such a comforting companion. As foster mother to an abandoned waif myself, I should know."

"Great idea!" Heather beamed approvingly.

"Oh dear, no. My goodness, Wyn would be hacking and coughing, I'm sure. His bronchial tubes are so very delicate. And that's the very cat that scratched Wyn when he was blessing the critter. No, no, I couldn't do that," Patty said.

"Yes, better not," I agreed. "Mrs. Pynchon would be quite upset if you started to take homeless animals into the parsonage. And there would be nothing she could do about it, either. With Wyn working on his book about Saint Francis and needing a bit of inspiration, Mrs. P. wouldn't dare interfere. After all, Wyn already has a publisher—didn't you tell me that Beacon Press is interested? Having Wyn as pastor could turn out to be quite a feather in the church's cap. Yes, if you took in the Luckeys' sweet cat, Mrs. P would be flummoxed for sure."

"Flummoxed? Mrs. P.? And nothing she could do about it?" Patty seemed to be turning this notion over in her mind.

"Nothing," I declared, "no matter how high her blood pressure rose with the frustration of holding her tongue."

"Well. I suppose Wyn could give it a try. See how his allergies react and all. And if Buster would refrain from spitting and scratching. But I've never had a pet to take care of. I'm not sure I'd know what to do."

"Oh, a cat's no trouble at all." Phillipa smiled brilliantly at Patty. "That's what these friends of mine assured me when they thrust Zelda into my care."

"Let's move it, ladies. I'd like to search the Luckeys' before the family gets back to the house." Heather walked briskly toward the door, her chestnut braid swinging, and all of us followed like sheep. We hadn't meant to barge in on the Luckeys' relatives' domain, but now that we'd been summoned to a rescue operation, what else could we do?

The Luckey sisters' house was a three-story Victorian of the haunted-mansion architectural style. It had twin turrets, several odd chimneys, and long double-windows that looked like sad eyes. This would not be an easy search.

The hired helper had already set up coffee and tea for the cousins, and when we arrived, she was in the midst of laying out glasses around a decanter of sherry. Heather helped herself to two glassfuls in quick succession before directing us to separate for the search. Deidre paused to explain matters to the surprised woman, whose name was Mrs. Pigeon. She shook her head—no, she hadn't seen the poor kitty anywhere.

We reconnoitered in the front hall beside a looming oak coat-tree with beveled-glass mirrors that warped every image. Surely it was bad luck even to glance in them. My face looked spectral, and it was clear that I needed to do something about my hair, which was hanging in my eyes like Scruffy's.

Phillipa looked over my shoulder. "Mirror, mirror, on the wall . . . Who's the spookiest of all? Do you think it's about time for a visit to my hair salon, Cass?"

"My very thought. As long as it's not Gloria's Crowning Glory."

"You girls go on." Deidre pushed us aside and ran her fingers expertly through her curls, leaving a few attractive pixie wisps on her forehead. "I'll stay to give Mrs. Pigeon a hand laying out refreshments." Then, in a stage whisper, she added, "Someone ought to check for brownies, don't you think?"

"Absolutely," I agreed. "Or anything chocolate. Or suspect in any way. What a catastrophe that would be!"

"I don't know where to look," Patty whined. "And I don't feel right about poking around in the Luckeys' house without their permission."

"They're *dead*, Patty," I reminded her. "But I know what you mean. It does seem so intrusive."

"Yeah, yeah," said Heather. "Will you gals stop admiring yourselves in those weird mirrors and get cracking? Think about that poor, bereaved cat dying somewhere in this mausoleum because no one cares. Patty, you check in the bedrooms and bathroom— and I *charge* you to open every drawer, cabinet, and closet. Phil and Fiona, you search the parlor and the library, particularly behind any heavy pieces of furniture. In case the relatives return from the wake, you two have the kind of presence that no one will question. In fact, they may not even *see* Fiona if she gets herself into that invisibility glamour. I'm going up to the third floor. Cats can get in anywhere, but sometimes they can't get out again. And this place is cubbyhole-heaven."

"What about me?" I was beginning to feel left out.

"I'm saving the best for last. I want you to check around in the cellar. Ask Mrs. Pigeon if she's seen a flashlight anywhere that you can use. I have one in my bag, but I'll need it if I have to go on up to the attic. All right, everyone check her watch. It's seven forty-five on the nose. Try to meet back here at eight-thirty."

Mrs. Pigeon didn't have the faintest idea where the household flashlight might be, but after I assured her again that we were here at Mr. Shortsleeves's behest, she didn't seem to mind my looking in the kitchen drawers. I found a rusted flashlight in the junk drawer that every large old kitchen seems to have—along with small-appliance parts, rubber bands, metal rings of dubious origin, and assorted small tools. The battery was a bit weakened, but, after all, the cellar had a light. I might not even need the flashlight.

But I did. The cellar light dangling on a cord was a 40-watt bulb trying to do a 125-watt job in that cavernous old cellar, whose strange turns, odd partitions, and variety of wall surfaces suggested something out of Edgar Allan Poe. I stumbled around from one cobwebby corner to another, and, not being a fan of spiders, turned up the collar of my jacket, wishing I had a scarf to cover my hair.

That poor cat! I finally found Buster in what must have been the old coal room. I'd had to swing the door open. Perhaps he'd accidentally imprisoned himself, or he'd sensed his companions' tragedy and hidden from possibly perfidious strangers. Not much light, but the faint flashlight beam caught those two gleaming, baleful eyes behind an overturned galvanized-tin pail.

"Here, kitty, kitty, kitty," I called soothingly. The cat's eyes slitted with suspicion.

"Okay, Buster, let's get a move out of here," I ordered firmly. The cat statue peered at me unblinkingly in the dark.

"How long since you've had a square meal and a lick of water, hey? I bet Mrs. Pigeon can find you a nice can of kitty salmon," I coaxed.

Buster hissed. It was a mean hiss with real claws behind it. And he was a big, burly cat, a tabby with a long sweeping tail curled around his paws in a most dramatic and regal pose. His hair-tufted ears kept moving as if collecting sounds from all directions. His stare was calculated to intimidate; nevertheless, I moved in closer. Why hadn't I thought to bring the gloves I keep in my Jeep? I stretched out a tentative hand toward the cat. Buster gave a cat scream and executed a warning slash through the air, like a fencer testing his rapier. I snatched my hand back out of harm's way.

I really didn't want to have to call Heather down here for help. Besides, Buster might disappear into another hiding place while I was gone. I thought about how well I communicated with Scruffy. But I'd never really talked to a cat before. Or more to the point, listened to what a cat had to say. Well, I would give it a try.

Closing my eyes, I attempted to empty my mind and move my consciousness into Buster's brain. When animals communicate with humans, they speak in pictures that can be read as words. With Scruffy, of course, when he takes on that alpha-dog look, his stance jaunty and his ears perked, it's more of a real conversation.

(I won't go into the discussion of whether animals think or not. Every Wiccan knows the answer to that one, and we don't have to implant electrodes in some chimp's brain to test the theory.)

So there I was crouched in the old coal room with only the rapidly fading beam of a weak flashlight, trying to move myself into the mind of a strange cat. Softly, I murmured, "Why don't you tell me what you'd like to do, and I'll try to help."

My caretakers have gone away. Maybe they're not coming back. Wooooe, wooooeeee, it's so hard to find good caretakers.

"Yes, they have gone. And I'm sorry to tell you, they've journeyed to Summerland forever. But I've found another caretaker who will make you comfy in a home of many rooms with all the scratching places and hidey-holes you could wish for. Her name is Patty, and I know she'll minister to your needs quite adequately."

Patty? Ow, ow. Silly little name. Will the new caretaker cater to my wishes and whims? I also require a soothing belly rub from time to time.

"You can call her Patricia. With patience and persistence, Patricia can be well trained, I'm sure. I'll tell her everything that you require."

I want to bathe myself now. I wouldn't want Patricia to see me like this.

"In a crisis, it's sometimes necessary to forgo one's toilette. Right now what you need is a proper dinner to keep up your strength."

Ha! A great nocturnal hunter need never go hungry. I am adequately fed on mice and beetles I myself have captured in this dark place. But as a change of pace, I would enjoy a dish of poached salmon with egg sauce or a broiled chicken liver with bacon.

"Wouldn't we all, Puss. I'll see what the kitchen has to offer. Can I give you a lift up the stairs?"

Buster crept forward, and in a sudden burst of confidence, leaped into my arms. At my age, it's not that easy to rise from a crouch with a twenty-pound cat hanging on you.

Ugh! What is that disgusting smell?

"Dog, probably."

Why don't you get rid of him, and then you can be my caretaker. I will call you Tabitha—a decent human name.

"Actually, my name is Cass, and you're Buster."

If a cat can be said to snort in derision, Buster snorted. *Listen, Tabitha, my name is Loki of Valhalla. And I want you to make it clear to Caretaker Patricia that I will no longer answer to Buster.*

"Yes, of course, your lordship." I freed one hand to stuff the flashlight in my pocket and trudged upstairs with the cat.

Mrs. Pigeon screamed when she saw us. Fiona and Phillipa came running from the living room. Naturally, this spooked the poor deserted cat, who hissed, jumped out of my arms, and darted away into the parlor.

"Oh the dear wee, timid little thing," cooed Mrs. Pigeon. "What's its name?"

"Loki of Valhalla."

Hearing the ruckus, Heather loped down the stairs with Patty following breathlessly. "I heard a cat down here. You got Buster?"

"Almost. He's dashed into the parlor somewhere."

"Look behind the piano," Fiona suggested. She was right, of course. When it's a matter of finding, you can't do better than Fiona. Phillipa, Heather, and I edged the heavy old upright away from the wall. I wondered how Buster had managed to wedge his plump self into that narrow space.

"Come now, Loki of Valhalla," I said. "It's time for your new caretaker Patricia to pledge you her loyalty."

Patricia? Wooooe, dear me, I look such a fright. I haven't even had time to groom my ears.

"Patricia will understand about your ears. She's a bit disheveled herself, after looking for you in all the bedrooms."

"Oh, Great Goddess," Phillipa said. "I believe Cass is *now* conversing with that mangy Buster."

"Shhhhh, will you, Phil!" I warned. "And it's not Buster any more. It's Loki of Valhalla. Come on now, dear Loki, we are all waiting eagerly to greet you."

Loki backed out with infinite slowness and no lack of grace.

"Your lordship, Loki of Valhalla, allow me to present Patricia, your new caretaker. Patricia, this is Loki, who's agreed to accept your hospitality on trial. Do you happen to have any chicken livers in the fridge?"

"Chicken livers?" Patty shook her head in a bemused fashion, an oily lock of brown hair falling over her broad white forehead. "Right now, I don't think there's much of anything in the refrigerator. Do you think that Dick Devlin might declaw Buster . . . eh, Loki . . . before I bring him home? I have all that parsonage furniture to worry about—they notice every little scratch. And where will the cat be relieving himself? Outdoors, I trust."

Heather sighed deeply. "Patty, I know you speak out of ignorance, so I won't hold it against you that you would imagine that my husband allows any cat in his care to be declawed, thus leaving him with no defenses. And you must *never* allow Buster to roam outdoors, where he will surely become lost, injured, or diseased. Cats must be nurtured within the house always. And Goddess knows, you have acres of rooms. Come on now, I'll drive you and Buster home, and on the way we'll stop at our place for a litter box and various other supplies you'll need. Just like having a baby left on your doorstep, isn't it? All kinds of things to learn. I think Dick has some pamphlets you should read."

"Maybe I should call Wyn. It's not like me to bring home a guest without consulting his wishes." Patty looked uncertain, but Heather put a strong arm around her shoulders for reassurance.

"Most men love surprises, my dear," Fiona said. "Gives them a chance to roll with the punches, so to speak. Have you ever thought of becoming a redhead? They say redheads really put fire into a marriage."

"I'll bring Loki," I hastened to volunteer before Patty got any more agitated. "You'll recall that he isn't a great traveler? I think he and I can communicate well enough to get him over to the parsonage. Maybe."

"If the herb business ever fails, Cass, you could probably

make your living as a pet psychic." Phillipa hummed a few bars of "Talk to the Animals."

Loki hissed and circled around my leg. *Ow, ow . . . I am not going to go anywhere in that horrid belching box, Tabitha.*

"Oh, yes, you are." I scooped up the cat firmly in my arms. With hasty good-byes all around, I headed out for the Jeep and plunked Loki in the back. Then I opened the folding divider that screens the back of the Jeep from the seats, a kind of doggie gate I never use for Scruffy, and took off without further conversation. Suffice it to say, I learned some interesting feline oaths on the way over to the parsonage, along with having to endure much spitting, screaming, and loose fur flying inside the car. Fortunately, it wasn't a long trip.

When I arrived, though, I had to wait for Heather and Patty, who had stopped off at the Morgan place for supplies. Except for the porch light, the parsonage was dimly lit, the only bright lamp being upstairs in Wyn's study. I smiled, listening to the swearing cat, thinking of what a Saint-Francis sort of challenge the pastor had in store.

Chapter Thirteen

The next morning, I was truly tempted to let the answering machine deal with Patty when she called before my coffee was ready, but somehow I couldn't bring myself to desert a novice pet parent.

"I don't know how I let myself get talked into taking in this insufferable creature," she began at once. "Cass, you have to help me get rid of the beast. It started in at four this morning pacing back and forth, hollering and nipping my toes. I gave it a tin of that nice cat food Heather Devlin gave me, and it turned up its nose in a most insulting way. It has ignored its litter box and done the most disgusting mess in Wyn's study. I have never smelled the like in my whole life."

"Calm down, Patty. You're just going through a minor period of adjustment. You're going to grow to love Loki, you'll see. Where did you put the litter box?"

"*Never!* It's never going to work out. Wyn had to go over to the church to finish up his sermon. He's beside himself. He says I should certainly have consulted him, it's not like me to go ahead and make a major decision like this without our praying together over it. I put the litter box in the third-floor bathroom."

"Yes, dear, I understand. Try to remain calm. Would you check and make certain that the third-floor bathroom door is open and that Loki knows it's there for his convenience?"

After quite a bit more in that vein, Patty cried into the phone for about twenty minutes. *Foisting Buster on Patty was Phillipa's idea,* I thought, *and I am going to get her for this.* Then I had a brainstorm. When I finally got Patty to hang up, by promising to stop by with some savory tidbits for the new king of the parsonage, I called Deidre.

"Hey, Dee . . . do I remember correctly that you are on a school committee with Mrs. Chester Pynchon?"

"That old dragon! Yes, and what do you want with her?"

"I want you to call her up and complain that the Gethsemane parsonage is infested with cats."

"This will help?"

"It's drastic, but worth a try. The reverend is giving Patty a bit of grief over the new cat. Loki, a.k.a. Buster, is liable to end up at Animal Lovers unless Patty has an irresistible impulse to hang on. Such as a chance to turn up her nose at Mrs. Pynchon."

"I hope you know what you're doing," Deidre said.

"That's not the way I operate."

"Hi, sweetheart." The deep, sexy voice of my beloved always surged through my nerves and descended like a hot rum toddy to my midsection. Wasn't it time for me to cool down? After all, we'd been married for almost a year.

"You're out of jail, I hope?" I said.

"Oh, sure. Rather a publicity stunt on both sides. What have you been up to?"

"Not much. We went to the Luckeys' wake and funeral. You know Plymouth, they were standing six deep in back. And we rescued the Luckey cat. A lovely Maine Coon cat. Everyone had forgotten about the poor thing's existence, I guess. Found it in the old coal cellar. We talked Patty Peacedale into adopting the critter. Just good works, honey."

"Me too. But I'm taking the shuttle home the day after tomorrow. Keep my dinner warm."

"And everything else."

Splashing cool water on my flushed face in the downstairs lav, I caught sight of my hair, wild as usual. One good thing about sandy hair, I'd always told myself, it doesn't show gray, but that was no longer quite true. I vowed then and there to get a stylish cut and a reviving rinse at Phillipa's hair salon before Joe got back from Washington. Those Greenpeace gals were always blond, tanned, and looking as if they were on spring break from Bryn Mawr. Maybe I'd get Scruffy groomed, too.

"Phillipa!" I said without preamble. "Could you get me a really early, really urgent appointment tomorrow at your salon. What's it called? I'd like to get my hair out of my eyes before Joe gets home. *And* colored." I'd carried a cup of tea into the living room and was perched on the window seat with Scruffy, already watching the road as if Joe's Rent-a-Wreck might be zooming in the driveway at any moment.

"Out of jail again, is he? I'll see what I can do. It's called Sophia's Serene Salon. Not your usual clip joint—very classy. Mozart, Vivaldi, no big hair. Yes, you could use a color rinse, too. Although I wouldn't go so far as to suggest you become a flaming redhead, as Fiona recommended to Patty."

We chuckled, but I said, "Never underestimate Fiona. Maybe a merry shake-up is just what the parsonage needs."

"One shake-up at a time. Right now they have Buster to deal with."

"True. And from what I heard from Patty this morning, it hasn't been going well. Say, how about I come over to your place after I get clipped, and we'll go snooping—I mean, shopping—at that Deluca art gallery, and have a look at Jean Craig and her garden."

"Oh dear. I'm supposed to be getting a start on writing a column for the *Pilgrim Times*. Restaurant reviews. I'm going to call it

'Whine and Dine in Plymouth.' *Whine* with an *H*. What do you think?"

"Catchy. But crime-fighting is more exciting. That's probably why Stone does it. Men keep all the fun stuff for themselves."

"Okay, you talked me into it. Your car, right? Are you bringing that horsey dog?"

"Yes, but I'm going to drop him off at the groomer's."

At this, Scruffy instantly sprang up off the window-seat cushions, ears at full alert. *Hey, Toots. What do you think I am, some wimpy, water-loving retriever? We briards don't need baths. It's against nature to dunk us in water. I won't go, and you can't make me.*

"You'll go if I have to drag you in by the scruff of your neck."

"No need to get nasty," Phillipa said.

"Will you stop gazing at yourself and keep your eyes on the road!" Phillipa demanded.

I moved the rearview mirror back to its rightful place and eased into a parking place near Deluca's Sea Garden Gallery and Gift Shoppe. "I love what Sophia did to my hair, Phil. It's lighter, but not that ubiquitous old-lady color, and this ethereal fringe—it's just like Crystal whatshername's. And my skin—my skin is all aglow from that Inner Light facial."

"You know, girlfriend, you could actually treat yourself to a salon more often. Say, twice a year instead of once. Especially if you want to keep that attractive color. Well, well—isn't this nauseatingly charming."

We studied the cute *shoppe* housed in a white Cape Cod cottage with Wedgewood green shutters and window boxes, the latter overflowing with fake ivy and dried flowers in autumn colors. A small side building appeared to be an art studio. The curtained upstairs windows, with various objects on the sills, looked as if the family lived there. Past the cottage, one could see an assortment of fishing boats in the harbor. The deceptively bright sunlight of early winter made their colors seem sharper than at other times of the year, when a hazy vista prevailed. The white picket fence enclosed remnants of a patterned garden with crushed seashell walks. Two picture windows offered glimpses of gray-framed seascapes of the kind that can be seen in every gallery on the South Shore.

"It's perfect, like Disney World." A sudden gust of cold air off the Atlantic was making me shiver. "Let's go inside and meet the proprietors. I'm interested to see that a true gardener has been at work here, albeit a little too cute in her tastes."

As we entered, a musical bell announced our presence. The shop didn't seem much warmer than the outdoors. Perhaps I simply hadn't shaken off the chill of winter by the sea. But a moment later, I decided the coldness was emanating from the shop itself. Just then a small brown-haired woman appeared through mossy curtains from a doorway in back. She had dark eyes, golden skin, and the kind of permanent smile that gets frozen in place over the years—how many years it would be difficult to guess for one so petite. Her leafy green smock was clean and crisp, and she was carrying a tray of painted cups or pitchers that at first glance looked like Toby jugs.

"Great Goddess of Avebury, those little critters are pixies!" I exclaimed. There's nothing quite so gratifying to a clairvoyant as having many bits and pieces of intuitive knowledge finally click into place, like completing a giant jigsaw puzzle. "Getting the picture" in its truest sense. So this was the pixie person! Even her short, casual haircut echoed the theme.

"Good morning, ladies. May I help you?" Her voice was high and girlish, but pleasing.

"Our friend Fiona Ritchie lives just a few doors down the street, and we must have passed your gallery dozens of times," Phillipa said. "We thought it was high time we said hello and had a look around. Such as charming place!"

It's always a shock to discover how well one's friends can dissemble. "I was particularly attracted to your garden," I said. "Those lovely shell paths. I'd love to see what comes up in the spring,"

"Fiona Ritchie. Ah, yes. Has those merry parties in her back-yard." Jean Deluca was still working on Phillipa's first remark.

"Herbs, perhaps?" I pursued.

"A variety of lavenders, heathers, sages, and other small shrubs. I don't have a lot of time, so I rely on hardy perennials. Do you garden yourself?"

"Oh yes. Cassandra Shipton." I fished a business card out of my pocket and laid it on the counter. "And this is my friend, Phillipa Stern. You may have seen her cooking show on PBS?"

"I'm Jean Deluca. I rarely watch television, but your names certainly sound familiar. But that's Plymouth, isn't it? Welcome to our shop, ladies. Is there anything special I can show you?"

Hoping Jean wouldn't connect our names with certain lurid crime stories of the past few years, I plowed ahead. "Adorable little jugs. Brownies, or pixies, are they?"

"Oh yes," she said vaguely. "Elfin creatures, to be sure. We Scots are always attracted to the fey."

"Lovely paintings!" my duplicitous friend enthused, gazing at the sand dunes, seagulls, beach roses, and picturesque boats that sailed across the walls in weathered gray frames. "So original."

Jean's smile deepened, lifting the upturned corners of her mouth a bit more and exposing tiny white, even teeth. "Yes, aren't they marvelous! And so reasonable, too. I'm always telling my husband, 'Arthur, work like yours of museum quality should command a price to match,' but he assures me he's much more interested in sharing his work with ordinary people of modest means."

Phillipa pinched me on the arm and flashed her brilliant smile at Jean Deluca. "How generous of him!"

This insincere exchange might have continued to the point of nausea if a young figure hadn't darted through from the back room. "Mom! Mom, you *promised* me. I need those keys *now*. They're *not* on your dresser like you said." The teenage boy's eyes flashed with exasperation.

"Lee, calm down, honey. We have customers, dear." His mother fished out the desired keys from the pocket of her leafy smock and dangled them in the air. "Allow me to introduce my son, Leonardo. As you can see, he's in a flaming hurry." No one would have doubted that this was Jean's son, the same dark eyes and diminutive stature, although beautifully muscled. His hair was darker, a cascade of Italianate curls. His mouth, upturned at the corners like his mother's, resisted suggesting a perpetual smile.

"Hi. *Nice* to meet you." Lee's voice lowered to an agreeable range, and he gave us a charming smile before snatching the keys out of his mother's hand, carelessly hitting the tray on the counter as he did so. The elfin jugs careened into one another. "The *audition's* today. Don't you *remember*, Mom? I *told* you at breakfast."

"Of course you did, dear. Would I forget that?" But Jean was talking to the closing front door, with its musical tinkle somehow turned into a jangle. "Boys!" she exclaimed. Her smile never wavered as a green Volkswagen revved up outside and peeled out of the shop's driveway. "It's the Assumption Drama Club, you know. They're auditioning for *A Midsummer Night's Dream*."

"*A Midsummer Night's Dream!* At Assumption?" Phillipa exclaimed. I kicked her ankle bone lightly.

"Yes, the kids have persuaded the drama coach. I'm not so sure the principal will find *Midsummer* an acceptable choice, the old fart. The thing is, Lee wants that part. Puck, you know—it's made for him. And I can tell you, I'm going to be pretty pissed if our youngsters get guided toward something safe and banal that happens to have the Church's imprimatur. The kids want *Midsummer*, and they should be allowed to have it. I simply won't stand for my boy to be passed over." Jean's smile never faded during this whole tirade, but her voice got a little shrill. "Are you taking that?"

Without thinking, I'd picked up a fat little jug from the tray—a cute brown-garbed figure with green shoes and pointed ears. Not my usual sort of objet d'art. I was much more at home with a Zuni fetish. Still, I was moved to buy the thing. "How much?"

Jean tapped a few keys on the Mac computer next to her cash register. "Twenty-nine, ninety-nine," she said. "I call that one

Syllabub." I took out my wallet and handed over two twenties, studiously avoiding Phillipa's incredulous expression. Jean gave me change, and carefully wrapped Syllabub in pale green tissue paper and a plastic bag bearing the legend *Deluca's Sea Garden* and decorated with several seaweed fronds.

"Well, good-bye, then. Love your shop!" I stuck out my hand hoping I'd get to shake Jean's, but instead she handed me the package.

As soon as we were safely in the Jeep, "What crap!" Phillipa exclaimed. "Well, what do you think? Any vibes?"

"There's a chill in the shop, and Jean Deluca herself is a bit of a creepy character—that pasted-on smile—but still, I have to say I'm not sure," I confessed. "I was hoping she'd shake my hand, but no luck there. It's my feeling, Hazel's spell or not, we should check out the other Craigs as well."

"I noticed the chill myself, but I just figured they were saving on fuel. Can't be too many customers this time of year, judging from the way she leaped on you, dearie. Syllabub, indeed! I guess she knows her medieval treats, eh? But in the interest of fairness, if nothing else, I agree with visiting all the Craigs. Unfortunately, today I really need to get right back to my computer and bang out something for my new column. Already I'm racing the deadline."

"I wonder if Jean Deluca knows her medieval herbs as well? So, then, who are you skewering—I mean, reviewing—for openers?"

"Why, Winston's New England Nuovo, of course. I love the place, but at times he gets too, too desperately fusion. I mean, really—enough with the Tabasco-marinated cherries and maple aioli on an otherwise decent chop."

"That's okay. You're off the hook after inspiring my amazing makeover. Scruffy won't know me." I touched my chic hair with awe.

"Will you, for Goddess's sake, keep your eyes on the road,

Cass!" Phillipa insisted. "Scruffy will know you, essence of jasmine and lavender. It's Joe you've got to worry about."

"Fiona says that men love surprises."

"Speaking of change, get Heather to go with you," Phillipa advised. "She's our lady of leisure. And it will do her good to get away from the doggies for an afternoon."

"Good idea. Although it may be Deidre who really needs to escape. Did you perceive a continuing theme at Deluca's?"

"Kitsch, you mean?"

"There's that. But I was thinking more of the leafy green motif. Jean's smock, the curtains, the tissue wrap. Even the Volks was green, did you notice that?"

"So?"

"That's what I'm working on . . . what does that motif indicate? Poisonous Herbs-R-Us? You know, Phil, I was hoping you'd get her chatting on the subject of cooking."

"Ho ho. Like, inquire if she'd been baking any lethal brownies lately?"

"Exactly. But maybe Fiona. They're neighbors and both Scots, after all. Yes, that's it. Fiona will have to invite Jean Deluca for tea and scones. Bring up the subject of baking. Or maybe indigenous poisonous plants."

"That's a tea party I won't mind missing. What if Deluca brings an edible gift, say, brownies?"

"Not to worry. Fiona will check out any food gifts with her pendulum."

"Does that work, do you suppose?"

"Each of us has her own magic, that works for her, if not for anyone else. That's one of Fiona's, and I have boundless faith in Fiona."

"Okay, but warn her off anyway. What did you say hemlock smells like?"

"The bottom of a mouse cage."

"Well, then. A good nose is as useful as a pendulum any day."

Chapter Fourteen

"Joe's still away, and I have a new gorgeous haircut 'n color, practically a makeover. So how about you and I go out for drinks?"

"This *afternoon*? Sure. But I can't believe I'm hearing this from Cautious Cass," Heather said. "Where? What are you up to?"

"Oh, ye of little faith. What's the name of that little bar where Bruce Craig's wife, Sherry, works?"

"Why her? I thought it was Jean Deluca we're after. It's called the Wander Inn. Affectionately known as the Wander-Inn-and-Stagger-Out. Not the place to order a fine wine, but I hear they make a very decent Margarita."

"I've never actually had a Margarita," I confessed. "Phillipa and I checked out Jean Deluca this morning, after I emerged from Sophia's Serene Salon as a new woman. I came away from Deluca's shop with a handmade elfin jug called Syllabub and no firm conclusions. I'd like to have a look at Bruce Craig, too, but I can't think of a good excuse."

"That's easy. We'll take Ashbery's Dodge over to Johnny D's garage for a tune-up and whatever else it needs. Captain Jack's been after me to get that old car up and running again. He craves wheels. Do you know the upholstery still smells of cinnamon and cloves?"

"Ashbery was a wonderful cook. Remember those sticky pecan rolls?"

We reminisced for a few minutes over Heather's former house-keeper until we were both teary, then agreed to meet later that afternoon for a run on Johnny D's before rattling over to the Wander Inn to knock back a few Margaritas.

"Sounds like a plan. I'll follow you, then, in the Jeep." I wondered what condition I'd be in when Joe finally got home. With Heather, somehow the simplest occasion often got out of hand.

Bruce Craig didn't look much like his cousin Jean. True, he had the same dark hair and eyes, but his skin was as white as if he never got out in sunlight—except for the heavy shadow of one-day's beard, the fashionable stubble look. Of medium height, he walked with a thin-hipped swagger. Quite good-looking in a *Saturday Night Fever* way.

"No way he gardens," I whispered to Heather while Bruce was having a look at the Dodge. "Or whips up batches of brownies."

"Maybe his wife. They could be working together. Bonnie and Clyde sort of deal."

"They robbed banks, my dear."

"Because that's where the money was," Heather explained. "But in the case of the Craig relatives, the money is in Reverend Peacedale's pocket."

"Later," I whispered. Bruce was through with the exploratory examination and ready to deliver the bad news with a suitably grave expression. I wondered if he knew that Heather was mistress of the Morgan mansion. Probably, I decided. Most Plymouth tradesmen had an internal *Who's Who* of the town's "old money."

Bruce outlined the work that would have to be done to bring the Dodge up to code. As I'd expected, it would be cheaper to

buy Captain Jack a "new" used car, but the Dodge had its sentimental value, after all. Heather signed some kind of agreement,
and we took off in the Jeep.

"So what did you think?" she asked.

"I wouldn't want to be Sherry. Bruce Craig is the lean-and-
mean type. But I don't think he's a murderer."

"Let's go check out the wife, then." Heather was still hopeful
of an investigatory hit.

Soon we were nestled in a dark booth with a red tablecloth at
the Wander Inn. The walls, too, were red, the ceiling was black,
and the windows of the former L-shaped farmhouse were ob-
scured by heavy red drapes. A laquered black bar stretched across
the back wall. Several men and one woman were watching a
NASCAR race playing on a color TV above the bar, the sound
turned down to a dull roar almost entirely drowned out by the
jukebox wailing "Everybody's somebody's fool . . ." with the characteristic nasal twang of country music. I thought there were couples in some of the other booths, but I couldn't quite see them,
the bleak winter sunshine replaced by the light from tiny lamps
with red shades.

Heather was studying a laminated snack list by this faint light
when a tall, slender girl with pink cheeks and mahogany hair cut
short as a boy's appeared out of the gloom. I was encouraged to
see *Sherry* embroidered on the black bolero she wore over a low-
cut white blouse that almost laced up the front. "Ladies?" she inquired dully. As far as I could see, she was the only waitress
serving the booths. No one was seated at the small round tables
in the center of the room. One concluded this was a hideaway sort
of place. Rumor around town suggested that although Wander Inn
was an inn in name only, there might be a few rooms that could
be rented by short-term guests.

"Sherry, dear," Heather read from her waitress's chest. "May
we have a basket of Riki Tiki Shrimp and a pitcher of frozen
Margaritas?"

"Ma'am, it's only beer in pitchers. But I could bring you two

Big Ritas. The Big Rita comes in a frosted twenty-ounce glass with extra lime and salt on the side." Sherry seemed to brighten up, perhaps sensing such a thirsty couple might leave a bigger tip.

"Right. We'll have those, then. Big Ritas." Heather fished out a handful of quarters and dropped them into the pocket of the ruffled red apron Sherry wore over her black miniskirt. "And for Goddess's sake, would you see if there's any music on that box and play it for us? Jimmy Buffett would be my first choice. And you, Cass?"

"Oh, I don't know. Vivaldi. Or Albanoni." I spoke absently, my attention wandering to a picture that was forming in my mind's eye. There was an overpowering urge to reach out and touch the girl, to receive the rest of the picture.

"Never mind her," Heather was saying. "Buffett, or the Beach Boys. Or even the Rolling Stones."

Sherry smiled wanly and turned to leave. I put my hand out and took hers, framing an instant excuse. "Oh, wait just a minute, Sherry. Those Riki Tiki Shrimp—could we have some ketchup to go with them?" She turned back, and I quickly removed my detaining hand.

"Ketchup's right there on the table, miss. And there's sweet 'n sour sauce that comes with the shrimp."

"Okay. Sorry. I didn't notice." The vibes from Sherry's limp white hand enveloped me like a dense, warm mist. What I needed to clear my head, I decided, was that frosty twenty-ounce Big Rita.

"So . . ." Heather whispered in a stagy voice as soon as Sherry had left to give our order, "what did you feel? Is she the one?"

"Just give me a moment to process my impressions." I really couldn't communicate my visions until they'd sorted themselves out into words.

"Oh, what a prima donna!" Heather complained but let me sink into silence for a few moments. Soon, however, Sherry was back at our table with the Big Ritas.

My companion took a sip. "Sweet Isis, it's perfect. Cuervo tequila, triple sec, actual real lime, and, yes, a splash of curaçao! It's Margarita paradise."

"It's just a drink, Heather. But a colossal one, I'll give you that. It'll take me all afternoon to drink this," I said, hoping to forestall the notion of ordering seconds. "Okay, what I feel is that Sherry is involved in some scheme concerning money, but there's *no* suggestion of poison or murder. Of course, I don't get more than a fleeting sense of the person from such a brief contact."

"Hush!" Heather warned as Sherry appeared again and plunked down the crispy shrimp in a plastic basket. Some familiar Beach Boys' hit began to surf through the Inn. *Fun, fun, fun . . .* "Thanks for the tune, Sherry."

"No problem. Enjoy!" She trailed off tiredly in the little outfit that was meant to flounce with every step.

"A money scheme," Heather whispered. She picked up a crusty shrimp by its tail and dipped it into the sauce with a thoughtful expression "I knew you'd come up with something."

"Yeah, but not necessarily the right thing."

Later, when we staggered out into the sunshine, drunk with sudden light as well as tequila—I'd successfully resisted another Big Rita, but Heather hadn't—Heather suggested we continue our investigations with the Geoffrey Craigs. "Maybe I can get Violet to introduce us. Violet Pickle Morgan, my cousin by marriage, runs the G.M.S with an iron trowel."

"If you can arrange something, that would be great."

"You can count on me, Cass. Old pickle-puss will be putty in my hands." Heather closed her eyes and fell to humming the *fun fun fun* song while I eased around the curves of Route 3A with unusual care, not wanting to be stopped while breathing out the fumes of Big Rita.

After I'd poured Heather out of the Jeep at the Morgan mansion, I crept along home with the windows cracked open for a sobering blast of cool air.

And, oh, joy! There was Joe's rental, a blue Honda, parked in the driveway. I found him in the kitchen, opening a bottle of Australian merlot. *Just what I need*, I thought, *more booze*. Then I was enveloped in my lover's passionate hug and spicy aura. This went on for some time until Scruffy began to nose between us in an alarmed fashion.

Say, Toots, what am I, chopped liver?

We broke apart a little. While Joe poured wine with his other hand, I patted Scruffy consolingly and wondered when this guy of mine was going to notice my great new hair. "So, how was jail, honey?"

"American jails are okay, but there was that one little jail in Belgium I liked better. The usual overcrowding, of course, but great hot chocolate." He took a deep swallow of merlot. "Ah, that's good. I've brought a couple of steaks, too—got 'em at Angelo's. Thought we could grill them."

"In case you haven't noticed, honey, we don't own a grill. But I do have a broiler. Same thing, only no carcinogenic carbon." I sipped cautiously, eyeing the large package on the counter. Scruffy pranced around the kitchen, pointing toward it with his nose from time to time. *Hey, Toots. Make mine really rare.*

"You'll get it the way I cook it," I said.

"Of course, sweetheart," Joe said. "Whatever you cook up will always be fine with me."

In that case, it might be a good moment to tell him about our recent forays into detecting. While I made a baby-spinach salad and scrubbed baking potatoes, I described the Deluca gallery, Jean Deluca, Bruce Craig, and Sherry at the Wander Inn.

"I noticed that you got an early start on the happy hour," he commented. "And you've done something different to your hair—shorter, is it?"

"Lighter, too. Sophie mixed this color especially to reflect the real me. She calls it Sahara Spring. And the bangs are just like Crystal whatshername's. And I had a mini-facial called Inner Light by Zensations. I thought you'd never notice."

"I notice everything." Joe's voice got that low, husky tone. "Like that trace of salt on your lip . . . Margaritas?"

"Very good, Watson. Very good, indeed. Wouldn't you like another taste? Actually it was called a Big Rita. That Heather. She's *such* a bad influence."

Joe spent some time looking for more traces of salt on my lips while Scruffy thumped around in a disgusted manner on the faux-sheepskin bed I keep for him in the kitchen.

Finally I nuked the potatoes and broiled the steaks. The rich, fatty taste was deliciously decadent. The dog sighed with satisfaction over his share, and licked his chops plaintively when it was gone.

Later Joe made a fire in the living room fireplace, and we lounged around on the big sofa watching Joe's favorite, the Discovery channel. I heard all about the intricacies of sneaking twelve tons of sod onto the steps of the USDA building.

"When I saw you standing there grinning with the Greenpeace director," I murmured into his shoulder, "I wondered if you're getting so popular with headquarters that they might want to offer you a permanent management position. Do they have an office in Boston? Wouldn't that be ideal?"

"Washington's the closest, and there's an office in San Francisco, too, sweetheart. Either of those suit you?"

No! I thought instantly. *I love my home, I love this town, I have roots here . . . friends . . . an agenda. What will I do if Joe should want to move? Maybe I should never have married.*

"Wow! All your muscles just tensed up. Not to worry, sweetheart. I'm just one of those guys who's not meant to hold down an office job, no matter how tempting. I'm an old sea dog, and, to tell you the truth, I enjoy the challenges and the company of like-minded idealists. And I believe you're much the same. Aren't you hell-bent to solve these poisonings with your own team?"

"Not such an *old* sea dog." I sidestepped admitting the truth of that insightful remark by falling instead into a long, tender clinch that soon had us heading for the bedroom, peeling off clothes as we dove into the timeworn softness of Grandma's quilts.

"She's coming to tea? Really? Outstanding, Fiona!" I crowed into the phone. Now Fiona would have her chance to divine the truth about this woman that Hazel's sorting spell had fingered.

"Three o'clock, dearie. Be here."

"Me? You want me there, too?" *Tea with the Plymouth poisoner? Oh, why not!*

"I don't know what to think," Fiona confessed. "Jean has always been a pleasant neighbor, not like some I could mention, with their snide remarks about our circle gatherings. The notion that we might feel free to dance in the moonlight does tend to get on people's nerves around here. So you'll come?"

"Backyards are a trifle close in your neck of the town," I said. "Sure. Good to have another go at the gal."

"Jean said she's bringing a treat from her own kitchen."

Hecate protect me! "You don't suppose Jean's onto us, do you?"

"Oh, do you think so? How fascinating. And a wonderful chance for you to see how dowsing for poison works, Cass."

"I can hardly wait."

Chapter Fifteen

"I'm off to Fiona's for tea." I leaned my head into the bedroom, where Joe was occupied with measuring floor and walls with an eye to enlarging the closet. Perhaps he was getting tired of having to keep most of his clothes upstairs in the guest room. "If anything happens to me, you will take good care of Scruffy, won't you? And remember that I loved you and the children."

Joe shot to his feet, dropped the tape measure, and put two strong hands on my shoulders, pulling me into the room. "What are you talking about? Are you in some kind of danger you're not telling me about? But you're saying 'tea with Fiona'?"

"Oh, it's nothing, honey. Don't you worry. It's just that a person never knows what may happen on the road. And I don't even have a will."

"Okay, that's it. I don't know what you're up to, but you're not going to do it."

"I am too. Good Goddess, what a fuss you're making. I'll be home by five." I ducked away from his restraining hands, grabbed my bag, and was out the kitchen door faster than Joe could take hold of me again or Scruffy could leap up off his sheepskin to demand a ride. "I'll be just fine," I hollered back in the door before closing it quickly and scuttling down the porch stairs.

Better not turn on the cell phone, I thought as I sped away. A light drizzle was falling. ICE POSSIBLE, the dashboard informed me. The outside temperature was exactly thirty-two degrees. It was true, what I'd told Joe. Driving can be dangerous. Even air travel, they say, is safer than automobiles. I slowed down and turned the radio up, WCRB, my old standby. I only wished the music programmer weren't so fond of double-trumpet concerti.

Warm amber lights were shining in the windows of Fiona's fishnet-draped cottage, and Jean Deluca's green Volkswagen was parked out front. I noticed the little car had actual seaweed fronds painted on its sides. Very leafy and suspicious. "Hello . . . it's me," I called as I stepped in the door. It looked as if our hostess had made some effort to clean up; at least there weren't the usual piles of magazines in the entry. The fragrance of Fiona's freshly baked cream scones wafted past my nose.

"Oh, Cass. How lovely!" Fiona crooned. "You know my neighbor Jean, of course. You're just in time for tea. It's Lapsang Souchong." She filled thistle-decorated mugs with the steaming, smoky brew. On the table were plates of scones, shortbread, salmon and cucumber triangles, and, *yikes!* brownies. The brownies were arranged on a plastic plate, not Fiona's thistle pottery.

Wearing a prim green twin set and a tweed skirt, Jean sat stiffly on the sofa, where Omar Khayyám, was parading back and forth behind her head, hissing. That permanent smile affixed to Jean's face never wavered. Perhaps Omar would lick up a crumb of brownie and we'd all learn something. *No! No! Banish that thought*. I wouldn't want any animal to be harmed just to save my own hide.

"Jean! So nice to see you again. I was in your shop recently . . . bought that adorable Syllabub jug, if you remember."

"Yes, of course. Cass Shipton, the herb lady. You were there with your friend, the lady in black. She put me in mind of the stepmother in Snow White."

"Oh, that must have been Phil," Fiona said with a chuckle. "Amazing gal. Reads the tarot for us all. Writes poetry and cookbooks. She even has her own cooking show." She got up and bustled to the window, taking down the crystal that hung there catching the afternoon light. Then she turned back to me. "Jean made those delicious-looking brownies, Cass."

"Oh, I'm afraid the credit for those belongs to Baker Boy." Jean's smile beamed modestly. "My little specialty is simply to add extra vanilla and a drop of Godiva liqueur."

What about the poison hemlock? I wondered. *That adds a unique touch to a mix.*

"How very original, dear. There's a secret ingredient in my scones, too, but I have to admit I rarely reveal it. Have you ever played with a pendulum, Jean?" Fiona was swinging the crystal over the coffee table in a seemingly absentminded fashion.

"Is that an old Scots thing?" Jean watched with fascination as Fiona zeroed in on the brownies. "I think I recall someone's grandma . . ."

The pendulum swung in sedate circles. Fiona smiled in a satisfied way and handed the crystal to Jean. "Not exactly Scots," Fiona said. "Pict, maybe."

"They say that the Craigs—I was a Craig before I married— are descendents from the Picts," Jean said.

The kitchen phone rang jarringly, and Fiona went to answer it while I brooded on what subterfuge I could use to take hold of Jean's hand. Absent a genuine vision, I had to use my secondary talent for receiving impressions from physical contact.

"It's Joe, for you," Fiona said.

I ducked into the kitchen to answer, averting my gaze from the bowls and dishes piled haphazardly in the sink. "Hi. What's up?" I said. Picking up a piece of toweling hanging on the sink, I began to scrub bits of drying pastry off the countertop.

"You got me worried with that touching farewell speech, sweetheart. I just wanted to be certain you made it to Fiona's in one piece," Joe said.

"Yeah. Route 3A isn't too bad at this hour. I *told* you not to worry."

He laughed. "Okay. Something's going on that has you alarmed, and you'll tell me what it is in your own good time?"

"Hmmmm. Sure I will. My tea's getting cold. Talk to you later, honey."

"Drive carefully."

"Always." It was *eating* carefully that concerned me at the moment.

But when I went back to the living room, Fiona was already halfway through a brownie. If worse came to worse, I'd call Rescue and have her pumped out immediately.

"Extra vanilla—very tasty." Fiona offered me the platter. What could I do? I might claim I was allergic to chocolate, but I really wanted to do my own kind of dowsing. So I accepted a brownie, placed it on a napkin and brought it up into sniffing distance. No telltale mousy odor, but that might have been masked with so much vanilla. Artificial, I deduced, not the natural flavoring. Wretched stuff but strong.

I put the napkin down on the coffee table and sipped my tea, determining to chat serenely while I watched over Fiona for any trace of faintness, numbness, or shortness of breath. "So . . . how did Lee do at the play reading?" I asked. A question about someone's youngster generally elicited several minutes of discourse from the doting type of parent, which I suspected Jean was.

I wasn't disappointed. Although her smile remained in place, her face flushed angrily as she complained that *A Midsummer Night's Dream*, with its pagan and sexual content, had been bumped by Assumption's principal in favor of a stage adaptation of Franz Werfel's *Song of Bernadette*. "In *Midsummer*, Lee would have been Puck, of course. He really wanted that role, too."

"Well, he can't very well play Bernadette, but how about one of the Doubting-Thomas priests?" I suggested.

"There's really nothing in *Bernadette* that's equal to Lee's special talents. Oh, if I could, I'd transfer him to Phillips Exeter

Andover right after the Christmas break. I wouldn't even wait for the school year to end. Andover has a wonderful theater department and state-of-the-art facilities. Well, I mustn't burden you with my frustrations. This tea is so deliciously bracing, Fiona!"

"You must believe in your dream if you want a dream to come true," Fiona said as she refilled Jean's mug.

"Is that a song from *South Pacific?*" Jean looked bemused.

"I've never been to the islands. Tuition out of sight, is it?" Fiona asked.

"Might be *South Pacific*. But Fiona is referring to the philosophy, or rather, the article of faith," I said. "Positive thinking."

"Positive *magic*. For the highly evolved," Fiona added, continuing to muddy the waters.

"It's this way, Jean. If you focus on your heart's desire, really visualize it as you wish it to be, sometimes the Universe of Infinite Solutions will bring your vision into reality." *What was I saying?* This woman's heart's desire might very well be to reclaim the Craig millions by poisoning the Peacedales so that she could send her son to a pricey private high school.

"Yes, yes, Cass has it exactly right. We're working on an interesting problem along that line right now. An environmental matter. It's one of our specialties, when we aren't . . . well, when we aren't working on bigger things." And Fiona went on to blab details of the Samhain spell we'd set into motion over the sale of land around Bonds Pond to the Nature Conservancy. She threw in the plight of the red-bellied turtle, and even mentioned that Clarence Finch, with his overgrown cranberry bogs, was the holdout we were targeting. No shortness of breath in evidence there! Jean's brownies must be harmless, after all. Or at least this batch was safe to eat. Now I would have to listen to Fiona crowing about the efficacy of dowsing.

Still, someone had to keep a clear head and check things out in a scientific way. While Fiona had Jean's attention, I scooped up the brownie-in-napkin in front of me and dropped it into my bag, the deep, soft leather one that Joe had brought me from Italy, which was almost as copious as Fiona's reticule.

Jean seemed a little surprised when I wanted to shake her hand as we parted. It's not usual among women, who generally favor the airy wave or the just-missed kiss, but she did put forth her small hand for a limp salute. With a quick hug for Fiona, I left immediately, wanting to sort impressions quietly as I drove home. That kind of psychic exercise is not conducive to safe driving, so I forced myself to take extra care on roads that were beginning to be icy.

On the way home, I called Phil on my cell. "I've been to tea at Fiona's," I said. "Jean Deluca brought a platter of brownies."

"Sweet Isis! You gals didn't eat any, did you?"

"It's okay. Fiona dowsed them, and I gave them the smell test. Well, to tell the truth, I didn't eat mine. I have it wrapped in a napkin, and I thought I'd drop it off at your place for Stone. Maybe he'd like to analyze the thing, see if it's the same mix as the one that polished off Lydia Craig."

"What a good idea! But is Fiona okay?"

"Fiona is fine. Jean said that she uses a Baker Boy mix and adds vanilla and Godiva liqueur. Smelled like artificial vanilla and a cheaper chocolate liqueur to me."

"Ugh. Even when you're poisoning someone, there's no excuse for resorting to *that*. Shame on her."

Shortly afterwards I turned into Phillipa's driveway and dropped off the purloined brownie. Then I wasted no time in hurrying home before Joe could get anxious again. Men can be such worrywarts.

What with one thing and another, I figured Joe would be pleased that I survived tea at Fiona's.

And he was. Greeting me with a big, warm embrace as soon as I got in the door, he murmured in my ear, "Sweetheart, I need some plywood and things. Mind if I borrow the wagon for a quick run to Home Warehouse?"

A ride? Oh joy! Take me, take me, take me! Scruffy was bouncing around Joe's legs, tail waving at top speed.

"The Jeep is going to be loaded with bulky supplies," I pointed out.

Joe stepped back and looked at me oddly. "Well, of course it is."

"I was talking to Scruffy. He's asking you to take him along."

"Oh, *Scruffy*. He can go. I'll manage. Hey, you won't mind a little chaos in the bedroom for a few days, will you? I think I can construct an addition to the closet using the space I've detected behind that inside wall."

"Wow. You're my hero. We can sleep upstairs in the guest room." *In twin beds, what fun is that?*

After they left, Joe huddled deeply into his pea jacket, the Greek fishing hat jammed on his head, and Scruffy dancing his way to the Jeep, I found myself imagining the peace and quiet that would reign when Joe got his next assignment.

I shook my hands briskly to shake off that negative thought.

"Hey, I'm feeling left out," Deidre complained the next afternoon. We were in her yellow kitchen drinking whiskey-laced tea and looking out at the cheerless backyard while I caught her up on our recent investigations. "So you got a chance to shake hands with Jean. Any impressions?"

"Nothing definitive, unfortunately. Only a great deal of unfocused anger. Maybe because her son just had his theatrical hopes dashed at Assumption. I'll have to wait for the analysis of that brownie."

"I used to know Jean's husband, Arthur Deluca. We both went to Assumption, only he was *years* ahead of me, but I'd see him at church things when he was on break from Boston College. Took himself and his painting very seriously. That's easy to do when you're growing up in the boondocks without much competition.

Wanted to escape the stifling commercialism of America and take in the art scene in Paris, but rumor had it, he got Jean knocked up and that was that. The usual story. So he settled for seagulls."

"I gather that the seagull business isn't exactly booming."

"They're getting by, like the rest of us. You know how it is, working for yourself. One feels freer, but it doesn't usually support a lavish lifestyle."

"And Jean wants to send son Leonardo to Phillips Exeter. Harvard to follow, I don't doubt."

"Some women will stop at nothing when their kids are involved. That Texas-cheerleader mom, for instance. But what about Bruce Craig's wife, Sherry? You said she's involved in some kind of suspicious money scheme."

"Yes, but don't ask me the details. Well, actually, I think it has something to do with the Wander Inn, not the Craig fortune. I sure hope Sherry's not actually stealing. It's impossible not to feel sorry for that poor girl. A manikin with punkish mahogany hair. Looks as if she's badly in need of some fresh air and vitamins. Listen, Heather's going to set something up with Geoffrey Craig's wife, she of the garden club. Why don't you come along with us on that one?"

"Oh, goodie. Will's working nights this month, so he can look out for the kids for a few hours. And I'd just love an excuse to get out on my own."

From the sounds of the roughhousing going on in the living room, it seemed as if the Ryan brood would be perfectly happy with Dad. "But what about Annie?"

"I'll see how Will feels. If he's too tired for Annie, I may bring her with me. But don't be concerned. She's such a good little girl, you'll hardly know she's there."

I remembered being conned into carrying the Ryan baby in a papoose rig while Deidre videotaped her two oldest in their school's Thanksgiving pageant. I had to admit I hadn't heard a peep out of Annie the whole time. For all I knew, since she was on my back and out of my view, she might have slept right through that endless theatrical event crammed with wildly applauding parents. Lucky Annie.

"If Heidi Pryde Craig has made it into that snooty Gardeners of the Mayflower Society, they can't be as much in need of the Craig fortune as the other Craigs. He's a CPA, she's a lawyer. And by the way, personal injury *is* her specialty. I caught her act in a TV ad for her firm, Fisch, Barter, and Dodge. She was talking about the comfort of having a woman lawyer to confide in concerning personal female matters. A convincing, sympathetic manner. A wee drop more?" Deidre lifted the teapot in one hand and the bottle of Irish whiskey in the other.

I waved away the offer. Joe might begin to wonder about me if I started coming home every afternoon reeking of alcohol. "Professional couples with two good salaries can get themselves into financial difficulties, too. Or simply may want to move up the food chain to a richer lifestyle."

"Yeah, you're right. Who wouldn't want to be a millionaire?"

"That's what sells lottery tickets."

"And every Craig in the immediate family must feel gypped by this huge bequest to Pastor Peacedale when all they're getting is a few measly thousand. What's he going to do with all that money, anyway?" Deidre picked up her workbag and began to stitch a Bettikins dress.

"I think he's still too much in shock to have made any decisions on that."

"Sure. But Patty's got to be making plans for him. Real women always know how to spend money. Probably wants to start by taking out a contract on that Pynchon dame Fiona was telling me about. Imagine going into that tirade while poor Peacedale was still in the hospital recovering from poison!"

"Fiona sent Pynchon and her cronies flying in short order."

"Good thing we have Fiona on our team, isn't it?" Deidre took out a doll and fitted the dress to her. Bettikins, I noticed, was wearing a tiny silver pentagram under her bodice.

Salty and Peppy came skittering across the tile floor following a soft spongy ball. Bobby, now a robust kindergartner, came giggling after, then his older sister and brother, Jenny and Willie. Deidre's husband Will followed, holding Annie in his arms. Suddenly the kitchen was overflowing with grinning Ryans seeking sustenance. Willie and Annie had Deidre's blond mop of curls. Bobby was a carrot-top like his dad once had been, but Jenny's hair was straight and brown, a reflection of her quiet demeanor. Like many older children, she looked somewhat burdened with the responsibility of younger siblings.

Crackers and various jars were brought out. Zwieback for Annie, who gummed it happily, gagging from time to time. The poodles were vigilant in their task of cleaning up crumbs, and there were lots of those.

"Awesome," I said as we dawdled over the last of our tea and the Ryan kids snacked at the counter. "I don't know how you do it. I raised three, and I don't know how *I* did it, either."

"Sure you do. The trick is, just don't think about the big picture. Do the next thing, whatever it is. Put out small fires promptly. Jenny's nine now already, and a genuine help to her mom. And, Annie is the positive *last*."

"I don't know about that. You're just a prolific gal. It's a good thing you're not a gardener. We'd all be swimming in vegetables."

"Yeah, well from now on, I'm turning my prolific nature to doll-making."

"So you say. Hey, I'm glad you're getting out to the Mayflower thing, whatever it is. Your family is beautiful, but possibly you could use a break."

There was a crash, a scream, and a few sharp barks, as the tin of crackers hit the floor.

"You think?" Deidre said. "Good thing I love them to pieces."

Chapter Sixteen

"This is simply too good to be true." In honor of our afternoon of social aspirations, Heather was chauffeuring us in her newly washed, beautifully waxed Mercedes. The car's back windows, usually sticky with an excess of dog drool, bore only one nose print. Heather had transported Honeycomb to my house, leaving her in Joe's care so that the golden retriever could romp with Scruffy. The two dogs appeared to have formed an attachment, and Heather was inclined to be indulgent with Honeycomb, her genuine therapy dog. "It's the Bonds Pond thing—you remember we worked on that at Samhain? There's been a break in the negotiations with Clarence Finch."

"What? What? What?" Deidre and I chorused.

"The ringed boghaunter, an endangered dragonfly, has found the Finch bog to its liking and moved there in droves. Ergo, the habitat of this rare insect *cannot* be sold to anyone *but* the Nature Conservancy. In fact, it was strongly hinted to Finch that he ought to donate the property, but he threatened to set fire to the place first. An ugly encounter, according to Dick. As a bird-banding member of the Center for Conservation Sciences, he was present at the Conservancy meeting."

"Boghunter?" Deidre's tone was full of wonder.

"No, *haunter*. Boghaunter. And that's just what the dragonfly is doing, haunting Finch's bogs. Reach in my handbag, Cass, and take out the snapshot. Dick loaned it to me for your edification. Some Campfire Girl took that photo on a spring field trip. She swears they were crossing Finch's bogs at the time. But it didn't come to light until last fall, believe it or not, right after Samhain. By and by, it got into the hands of a member of the Dragonfly Society of America. An official odonatist from the DSA was dispatched to Bonds Pond to investigate, and the rest, as they say, is history."

I removed the photo from Heather's bag and studied it. "It's a miraculous endangered living thing, but it's a repulsive one."

"And I thought you were an animal lover!" Deidre took the photo out of my hand. "Gracious! What a revolting creature. Actually it looks more like two creatures. The day that insects take over the world, I'm leaving."

"It *is* two creatures," Phillipa said. "What you're looking at is the mating of a ringed boghaunter dragonfly with a willing damselfly. He's grabbed her by the back of the neck and she's curving up to collect the sperm on his abdomen. The thing is, that means there are dragonfly nymphs in the waters of the bog who may spend two years in that aquatic stage until they emerge and take wing. Isn't nature fantastic?"

"And isn't it interesting how things work out?" Deidre said. "Now this is a solution we never would have dreamed of, and yet it's perfect. Of course, we really don't *know* if we had a psychic hand in this, but it *is* rather a coincidence."

"I love it," I said. "And I'm perfectly willing to take the credit. Just among us five, of course. But what is an odonatist?"

"Specialist in dragonflies, which are of the order Odonata. Once they start looking closely, I'll bet the odonatists and other interested environmentalists will find additional endangered creatures in Finch's bogs." Heather was steering sedately into the large circular driveway in front of a handsome old mansion, yellow with a white trim, surrounded by large, well-tended trees: beech and oak, with a backdrop woodland of evergreens. "I almost, but not quite, feel sorry for Finch. Okay, get ready, gals, to meet my cousin by marriage, Violet Pickle Morgan. We'll be sharing a coffee hour with the Gardeners of the Mayflower and hearing a talk on seaside gardens by a Japanese fellow. Violet is going to introduce us to Heidi Craig. I've told Cousin Violet that I have a friend who might need the name of a good personal injury lawyer, but we'd like to meet the Craig woman informally before consulting her officially."

"Not bad," Deidre said. "Who's the friend?"

"You, dear. A malpractice incident with your last pregnancy. Try to look a little sad and wistful."

"Geez, Phil. Why me? Why didn't you use Cass?"

"Cass is here as a well-known seaside herbalist who would naturally be interested in the gardening problems thereof. You're here as a victim. That's the way I worked it out, so sue me. Or rather, sue your obstetrician for interfering with your fertile cycles."

"Don't I wish," Deidre said. "With me, even the pill can't be trusted."

If a Boston terrier could be reborn in human form, the result would have been someone much like Heather's cousin Violet, a small, frisky woman whose dark hair was striped with white. She had button-bright eyes and an aggressive pug nose.

"Heather!" she barked from across the room, scampering to meet us at mid-aisle in the lecture room, "It's about time you got yourself to one of our meetings, my dear."

"Cousin Vi," Heather murmured. "How lovely to see you! You're looking very fit and trim." They kissed the air over each other's shoulder.

"You know I'd be delighted to put you up for membership anytime, my dear. With a little inspiration from us and a decent gardener, your house and grounds could be a showplace." Violet's little round eyes shone with recruiting zeal. "Of course, you'd have to get rid of that wolf pack."

"I would, I would . . . if only I could find loving homes for those rogues. Say, Vi, could I interest you in a sweet little Lab who's recently come to live with me?"

I couldn't help but chuckle imagining the Lab, whose name was Luke Skywalker, zooming down the road with little Violet Morgan at the other end of the leash.

Violet jumped back as if from a contagion and shook her head emphatically. "Heavens to Betsy! No dirty dogs for me, my dear. Messes on the lawn, holes in the flower beds, tulips and peonies behcaded at the height of their glory. No serious gardener would tolerate those destructive creatures."

"I have to admit that I prefer my 'wolf pack' to a perennial border any day. But let me present my friends," Heather continued smoothly. Deidre and I were duly introduced, sniffed at, and dismissed as being of negligible social value. Violet remembered, however, that she'd promised to put us together with Heidi Craig. Once that had been accomplished, she trotted away to engage the afternoon's speaker, Professor Ishimoto, on the subject of beach roses.

Despite her calm expression and deceptively bovine aura, there was something formidable about Heidi Craig that made her someone I wouldn't want to encounter as an adversary in a courtroom. Her hair was brushed smoothly away from her face, a long, straight fall of pale brown, her limpid eyes a darker brown. The charcoal suit she wore was cut like an Armani, emphasizing shoulders and slimming hips, its severity broken by a glimpse of aqua silk shell and a rope of pearls.

When we were introduced, she immediately shook hands. Hers was dry, cool, and firm. My immediate impression was unequivocal. This was one upwardly mobile lady, a social and professional climber. Obviously, she'd zeroed in on the right garden club. All around us, the Mayflower wives were circling in their Talbots classic plaid skirts, cashmere twin sets, and Ferragamo flats, exchanging gardening tips and gossip in cultivated low tones. Every one of them probably employed a professional gardener.

With one quick, sharp glance at Deidre, Heidi said, "Vi tells me that you might be interested in my professional help in a personal matter. Call me if you'd like to talk it over. Any friend of Vi's—"

Subduing her usual perkiness, Deidre assumed a wan demeanor and nodded sadly, her eyes downcast in order to hide their irrepressible mischievous glint.

"We knew your dear aunt Lydia," I said, figuring I'd get Deidre out of the limelight. "We're all so sorry about that sad affair."

A cloud passed across Heidi's smile. It would be difficult to tell if that sudden shadow was brought forth by the thought of her aunt's death or of the disposition of the Craig fortune. I was betting on the latter.

"An untimely tragedy. She'll be missed," Heidi said. "But life must go on."

"Still, you must be so distressed," Deidre said. "At least if the police had made an arrest, you'd feel a sense of closure."

Heidi smiled. "Closure," she echoed, looking directly at Deidre. "Closure is what you get when the culprit pays . . . and pays big. Otherwise, you just go on waiting for justice to be served. But I don't have a great deal of faith in law enforcement, I'm afraid. A brutal and primitive effort at best."

"How true." Heather sighed. "It must be very satisfying, though. Winning a civil suit in a worthy cause."

"My satisfaction comes from seeing my clients get the justice they deserve and have been denied by callous corporations and careless professionals." The way Heidi said it was like a prayer.

"Amen," Deidre responded.

"Call me." Heidi gave just a little squeeze to Deidre's arm. "There's no obligation, no charge at all. We'll see if there's anything—"

"Oh, I think your cousin Violet is about to introduce Professor

Ishimoto." I broke into that tender moment, wanting to get to the subject of Heidi's garden and what might be lurking in it. "Do you have a special interest in seaside gardening, Heidi?"

"Oh yes. Our property is just across the road from a lovely private stretch of beach. Windemere Road. Perhaps you know the area."

Indeed I did. The priciest property in Marshfield. "Yes, some lovely old houses on that road. Herbs are my major interest, of course. Are you fond of herbs yourself?" I asked as we moved to take seats among the rows of folding chairs.

"I have a number of lavenders," Heidi whispered. "Sages, rosemary, various thymes. All ornamental. I'm far too busy to harvest and preserve anything, alas." She sighed as if cherishing a secret longing for domesticity.

What an actress! I thought. *Could the Geoffrey Craigs' upscale lifestyle also be an act? This dame must rake in the contingency fees, but what if there are extraordinary expenses we know nothing about? Gambling. Blackmail. Addictions.*

I made a note to ask if Stone had checked into everyone's finances, although who could hide debts better than a CPA?

By the time we got out of there, I'd about had it with slides of massed blue hydrangeas, Russian olives, and *Rosa rugosa*. On the way home, we raked over Heidi and her perennial herbs without being able to reach a conclusion on whether she was still a suspect. Heather dropped off Deidre, then me, and came in to pick up her dog. We found Honeycomb drooping over Scruffy's sheepskin, looking exhausted. Scruffy, who usually greets me as if I've been gone for months, was nowhere to be seen. Joe was at the kitchen table, hunched over his drawing of the extended closet.

"No thanks, no tea," Heather declined my offer. "This pup looks pooped. I wonder if she's coming into season?"

"Ask Dick," I suggested. "Where will you keep her safe, if that's the case?"

"Dick wants to breed her once before she's spayed, considering her outstanding pedigree, so he'll probably whisk her away to the kennel he's selected. When the time comes."

After Heather left, I leaned over Joe's shoulder to admire the sketch. "That looks grand, honey." He turned for a sweet welcoming kiss, but when I nuzzled his neck, I sensed clearly there was something wrong. So I put on the kettle for a calming cup of kava. "Where's Scruff?"

"I had to close the little bugger into the guest room. Is that sassy little gal by any chance *already* in season?"

"Uh oh," I said. "Tell me they didn't."

"Unfortunately, when I let them out for a run around the yard, they took off together into that stand of pines, and I think they may have done the deed. Or partially, before I got to them."

"Honeycomb's about to get shipped off to be put together with a champion golden."

"You might want to tell Devlin to save the breeding fee. Or not. Up to you, sweetheart! I'll go upstairs and let the bugger out of detention, then. Quite the opportunist, isn't he?"

"He's an unneutered male acting the way nature programmed him. But I sure wish he hadn't."

After trotting into the kitchen at Joe's heels, Scruffy raced around the downstairs searching for Honeycomb. Having satisfied himself that she was indeed gone from the premises, he sank onto his sheepskin sniffing her scent with a gloomy expression.

"So . . . what do you have to say for yourself, fella?" I asked.

Hey, I had everything going just great with that sweet little blonde until your furry-faced pain-in-the-butt pulled me away.

"Uh oh. I think you may have got us all into trouble, you mutt."

What do you want from me, Toots? I'm in love.

"I may have got them in time," Joe said. "We could just forget about this incident. Let Devlin proceed with his plans, and nature will take its course."

That's exactly what I wanted to do, but lies of omission are still lies. I drank two cups of kava and gave Heather a call.

"Didn't I *tell* you to have that scamp neutered *for his own good?*" she screamed, "But would you listen? No way." Then, surprisingly, Heather began to giggle. I could hear the reassuring sound of ice clinking and a drink being poured. "Well, so much for Dick's plans to produce a superior therapy breed."

"I'm really so sorry. And we don't even know if Scruffy caught her or not. Will Dick be very cross?"

"Never. He's a real teddy bear, you know that. The nicest guy I ever married. We'll quarantine the little hussy, and Dick will give her a pregnancy test as soon as he can. Meanwhile, I think we'd better call off Honeycomb's other rendezvous. Maybe next year, as the Red Sox used to say. But if Honeycomb *is* preggers, what will I do with a litter of mixed-breeds? I suppose I could ask Dick to—"

"No, don't do that!" The words I heard myself saying seemed to be bypassing my brain. "They'll be champs in their own special way. And I promise to take one myself and help you to find homes for the rest."

"You bet you will. I'll drink to that," Heather said.

"I can't believe what I just heard," Joe muttered after I'd hung up. "Another Scruffy! The patter of little paws. Do you suppose this one will converse with you, too?"

I was rubbing my forehead as if to get my thinking processes back into gear. "It may not even happen. You probably separated them in time. You do think you did, don't you?"

Joe just smiled and raised one eyebrow. "*Que sera, sera.*"

Chapter Seventeen

It was soon determined, alas, that Honeycomb was in a family way, but Heather nobly forgave this canine indiscretion. She admitted to having been partly responsible, arranging a "play date" for the two dogs when there was even a suspicion Honeycomb might be coming into season sometime that month. There should have been warning signs, of course, but there were always a few females who kept everyone guessing.

In a spirit of clemency, Heather even insisted on hosting an anniversary party for Joe and me. After all, it has been in her Victorian red living room just one year ago in December that we'd been married by the Reverend Peacedale and handfasted by Fiona.

Heather's hospitality tended to be on a grand scale. She planned to hire the same troop of medieval players, The Greensleeves Strollers, to provide music. A decorator was being brought in to garland the rooms in holly, mistletoe, pine, and fir, but Heather herself was designing the tree—seashells and real candles. (A slight worry, but I knew Dick would insist on keeping a fire extinguisher nearby.) Captain Jack would lay out one of his spectacular fish feasts, with its lavish centerpiece of bright red lobsters on a bed of green seaweed. And, naturally, there would be a case of Veuve Clicquot.

Who could resist such a lavish festival so lovingly planned? Joe and I agreed to it gratefully and began to rough out a guest list.

It would be Yule, the Winter Solstice, the Wiccan season of the sun's rebirth as the Child of Promise—the promise of life's renewal. We would burn the Yule log using a bit of the old year's log and dry sprigs of holly to ignite it. There would be peace and hope for earth's return to spring in our hearts.

But as Yule approached and the sun reached its weakest days, there was at least one heart in which not peace but murder reigned. The scene I had envisioned last fall came to pass, a stealthy intruder into the Peacedale kitchen, the addition of lacy greens to a plastic bag of prepared salad.

That Monday evening, pastor's day off, Patty had set up two tray tables in front of the TV and popped into the VCR a favorite Christmas movie, *The Bishop's Wife*. She'd carved up a barbecued chicken from Angelo's, nuked two baking potatoes, and doused two bowls of salad with garlicky blue-cheese dressing, strong enough to kill the mousy flavor of hemlock snipped into the baby greens. (Actually, Patty thought her taste buds were encountering a particularly pungent arugula.) But before the angel, Cary Grant, could skate away with the neglected wife, Loretta Young, Patty had doubled up in pain and nausea, while Wyn Peacedale was seeing heavenly visions and gasping for breath.

Somehow Patty managed to call 911. The rescue wagon arrived in a matter of minutes to whisk the couple to Jordan Hospital, where the ER nurses and doctors were becoming all too familiar with the symptoms of hemlock poisoning. Treatment was swift and sure.

Loki of Valhalla, a.k.a Buster, yowled plaintively from the third-floor bedroom, where an insensitive animal-control officer had incarcerated him with dry food, water, and his litter box. Loki's feline brain had been fixed upon the remnants of that barbecued bird now being swept into plastic bags, along with the rest of the Peacedales' last supper. Well, not really their *last* supper, since both of them managed to survive the ordeal, although it was touch-and-go with Wyn.

Deidre alerted us to this new crisis. She and Will had been in the emergency waiting room with Willie, who'd crashed his sled—and head—into a tree and needed to be checked for concussion, when two ambulances screeched up to the entrance. The scanner on Will's belt told the rest. Deidre rushed into the ER in time to see the Peacedales, pale as beeswax and barely breathing, being given oxygen as they were rushed away to be detoxed. By the time everyone had been called, Phillipa had the news, too, from Stone.

Heather made it her mission to rescue Loki from the parsonage. After a fearful tussle getting the obstinate cat into a carrier, she tucked him up at the Animal Lovers cat wing for safekeeping until the Peacedales recovered and were released.

So that Deidre could keep watch over Willie while we discussed this latest attack, we met in Deidre's living room for a council of war. We gathered around the truncated oak dining table that served as her coffee table, surrounded by Deidre's prolific handiwork, from gleaming refinished pine pieces to needlework samplers and her family of poppets. Heather had brought what she called "a divining candle," a thick purplish stub with orange streaks. Imbedded in the wax were runic symbols: the messenger, Ansuz, and the breakthrough, Dagaz. When Deidre lit the wick, familiar odors wafted around us. "Mugwort and peppermint for prophecy," Heather said.

"Goddess help us," Fiona said. "We have to stop this woman."

"I've become so fond of the Peacedales," I said. "And I'm upset with myself for not having divined the murderer's identity before this latest attack."

"Maybe you're trying too hard," Fiona suggested. "Psychic knowledge comes in its own good time. Sometimes you just have to *'let go and let Goddess.'"*

"One thing we do know for sure—it's the Peacedales who are being targeted," Heather said. "No matter who else got poisoned along the way."

"Okay, say that one of the Craig heirs wants to eliminate Peacedale before the year is up and the pastor's permitted to will away the fortune elsewhere," Phillipa said. "Why bother to poison the breads on my cooking show?"

"Have you forgotten that Patty was there, chaperoning the Sizzling Seniors, who were part of your audience that day? Maybe the poisoner thought Wyn—" I paused, letting impressions of the audience form in my mind's eye. There was some elusive knowledge hovering on the edge of my consciousness, but what? "You usually do pass around samples of whatever you've been cooking as soon as the taping is finished."

"I thought we'd tagged Jean Craig as the likeliest suspect," Heather said. As usual, Salty and Peppy had established themselves in her lap, and she continued to scratch them in the sensitive chest area as she developed her theory. "Cass and I had a look at Bruce and Sherry Craig, and, really, they simply don't *fit* one's psychic profile for poisoners. Isn't that true, Cass?"

My attention was caught up in the light of the candle. I felt too tired and heavy to reply.

"Dee, you were with us at the G.M.S. meeting. Did you think Geoffrey Craig's wife, Heidi, was a possible? I mean, in your bones?" Heather asked.

"My bones are dumb as posts." Deidre refilled our teacups and passed a plate of arrowroot cookies, her nursery staple. "But my common sense suggests that a personal injury lawyer as sharp and hungry as Heidi wouldn't be fussing about in the kitchen whipping up poison brownies when she could probably hire some lowlife of her acquaintance to plant a bomb in the Peacedales' Buick."

"On the other hand, I went with Cass to have a look at Jean Craig," Phillipa said. "And I agree with the Hazel sorting spell that Jean might be the genuine article. There's something desperately determined about that woman, in spite of the outward pleasantness she projects to customers. Also, she impressed me as the type that would go a long way to help her son achieve his dreams. The boy has his heart set on being in the theater, and Assumption doesn't give him much scope in its drama department."

"That description fits most parents," Deidre said.

"True," Phillipa agreed, "But now we have the evidence of the lab report. Stone says the brownies Jean brought to Fiona's tested the same—minus the hemlock, thank Goddess—as the ones that polished off Lydia Craig. Baker Boy, with a jolt of extra artificial vanilla and chocolate liqueur. Must have been sickening. However, that's beside the point. Cass, you share the view that it's got to be Jean, don't you? But where do you suppose she got her hands on fresh killer greens at this time of year? Cass? *Cass!*"

At that point, as I was told later, it appeared that I had fallen into a trance. But to myself, I had left Deidre's living room and was standing outside a small, decrepit greenhouse, trying to peer in the small-paned windows. It was difficult to see through the filth of years and the steam of some interior heater. But I could detect someone moving within. I rubbed one pane and pressed closer. A small person, spraying and watering the plants. Too slender to be Heidi, too short to be Sherry. And the plants . . . There were several varieties. I recognized some of the leaf shapes.

"Leave her alone," Fiona was saying when I came back. "Let her follow the sighting as far as she can."

Nausea and weakness overcame me, but after a while I said, "Hemlock growing in pots. And some other plants. I think I recognized tobacco leaves—nicotine can be deadly. In an abandoned greenhouse. And you're right, from the general outline of the figure tending them, it must be Jean. But I didn't see her closely enough to make a positive identification."

Fiona patted my hand, the silver bangles on her arm tinkling their soft music. "You've brought us even closer to our good goal, dear. We know who we're going after. All we need to do is to find that greenhouse. That might be a job for me and my pendulum."

By the time we'd finished our conference, it was too late to visit the Peacedales. All we could do was hold hands, summon energy in our usual way, and send our best healing vibrations to the recovering couple. Before we parted, Fiona promised to use her particular talents to find the greenhouse where deadly plants were growing in December.

When I got home, Joe had the kettle on and was spooning chamomile mint tea into the pot. As his muscular arms held me closely, the doom and gloom of my visions melted away. "The Peacedales will be okay, sweetheart," he murmured into my hair. "While you were out, I called the hospital again. They're both out of intensive care, although Wyn is still a pretty sick puppy."

"Good news so far. Thanks." I sighed, enjoying the reassurance I always found in his embrace.

"And speaking of sick pups, this dog of yours has been moping around all evening. I think he misses his lady love."

He's got that right. After the most perfunctory of greetings, Scruffy had slumped down on his faux sheepskin again. Now he gave me a baleful glance.

"I suppose, since the damage is done, I may as well take him over to Heather's for a visit. If he's not *canine non grata*."

"Otherwise, who knows what he might get into his head to do," Joe said. "Some spin-off from *The Incredible Journey*, perhaps?"

Don't knock it, dude. We superior tracking canines can follow a scent trail to the far places. Scruffy perked up suddenly and began to pace around the kitchen. *Love and danger bring out our amazing skills and perseverance.*

"For the time being, I think all walks had better be on L-E-A-S-H," I spelled.

"Right," Joe agreed, letting me go so that he could pour the tea. "And I managed to connect with Stone, too—he was in Patty's room to ask her about that infamous salad. Patty said she's been so busy with parish work, she's had the groceries delivered from Angelo's. Also, she explained to Stone that as an affirmation of Christian principles, they never lock the parsonage. Also, she says it drives Mrs. Pynchon crazy."

"Laudable goals, but a risky policy. Gosh, I'm bushed."

"Take your tea and go straight to bed, sweetheart. I'll take Scruff out for his last walkabout. And, yes, on L-E-A-S-H."

A leash! Moi? What does he think—that I'm some kind of pin-headed greyhound? It would serve Furry Face right if I dragged him into a ditch. Scruffy stalked to the door and scratched the patch of bare wood on the frame in a disgusted fashion.

"You'll do no such thing!"

"You're talking to the dog right now, not me, correct?" Joe said.

"Yes, of course. You watch your footing out there, honey, in case you-know-who makes a dash for you-know-what. And by the way, don't bother to spell L-E-A-S-H anymore. He's got that one."

"Yeah? Well, maybe he'll get this one, too. I'm the A-L-P-H-A male here, and we'll have no mutiny on my watch." Joe looked Scruffy right in the eyes as he snapped on the leash, and I could swear that Scruffy blinked first.

The next day, I visited the Peacedales as soon as I thought I'd be allowed to sneak in, just after lunch. Patty was much recovered. She was wearing a pink velour jacket over her hospital gown, part of the pants suit she'd had on when she arrived. I found her sitting beside Wyn, holding his hand while he slept, his cherubic cheeks looking slack and gray. Patty held her finger to her lips, and we tiptoed out of the room and down the hall to a rather pleasant alcove with a window. A light, nonthreatening snow was falling, melting as soon as it encountered trees and roofs. The real winter in New England arrives in January.

"What *do* you make of this, Cass? Detective Stern has as much as told me that it's no coincidence the poisoner got us twice—someone is trying to kill my Wyn. Why would anyone want to do that? He's such a good man—a man of God. What kind of a mind would conceive of trying to murder Wyn, for heaven's sake?"

"I agree that we're dealing with a very sick person," I said. "As for motive, I don't mean to alarm you, but you have to be made aware that wherever there's a great deal of money, there is also a great temptation."

"Oh dear!" Patty's hand flew up to cover her mouth. "You and Detective Stern both believe that someone is after the Craig money. Gosh, the will's not even through Plymouth probate yet. Wyn hasn't had a chance to spend one cent. But if that's the motive, then it could only be . . ." Realization passed over Patty's face, turning her cheeks red, then white. Her voice sank to a whisper. "The Craigs are doing this? I can't believe it. I've met them all, and they seem like decent people, even if they did get nasty when the will was read. Especially that lawyer, Geoffrey's wife. Threatened to contest it, you know. Old Mr. Borer—such a dignified person, he is, with a voice like Moses on the Mount—assured her the will's unbreakable. 'We know what we're doing at B, B, and B,' he said. 'We're an old-fashioned firm, not a bunch of ambulance chasers.' Lord, the atmosphere in that conference room was worse than a church board meeting."

"What about the other Craigs, Bruce and his wife, and Jean Deluca? What were their reactions?"

"Bruce seemed okay with it, just tipped his chair back and whistled. His wife hoped they'd use their twenty-five-thousand bequest as the down payment on a house, but he was talking about a racing car. Arthur and Jean Deluca were as quiet as two church mice. She's a tense little person, isn't she? Stiff little smile, you know, but if looks could kill . . ." Patty stopped rattling on and looked aghast.

"I know it's a shock, Patty, but I feel you should be prepared for whatever the police investigation might bring to light."

"But you, Cass," Patty wailed. "You and the girls are praying— or whatever it is you do—for a holy vision, right?"

"Absolutely. And with all forces aligned against this person or persons unknown, we're sure to bring her to justice soon."

"It's a *woman*, then? Because only a woman would make poisoned chocolate brownies?"

"Well . . ." Did I feel a little jolt of intuition? "The male of the species can cook, too. Besides, those brownies came from a mix, not at all complicated to whip up. And that chocolate coconut cake that got Wyn at Thanksgiving was from a mix, too. Ergo, we can't say *for sure* it's a woman."

"But you suspect! Cass, you've had some insight, haven't you?" Patty demanded, grasping my hand tightly in both of hers.

"Hmmm. What did Stone want to know?"

"Who delivered the groceries. Was the bag of salad open or closed. Did I hear any strange noises in the kitchen, or see someone lurking about."

"*And?*"

"I never saw the delivery person. The box was left on my kitchen table while I was upstairs in my office answering parish requests and complaints. I don't remember if the bag was open, but I think it may have been, because I don't recall needing the scissors. Everything is so darned hard to open these days, I have to keep a pair of shears in the kitchen. And I didn't see any villains lurking about the parsonage. Oh dear, dear me." Patty took back her hands in order to wring them. "I'm so stupid, I'm no help at all."

"Patty, you are not stupid. Never, never think that being unsuspecting equates with stupidity. Now, you get yourself some rest, and give Wyn my warmest thoughts and wishes. I'm going over to Fiona's and see what she's discovered."

"Oh. With the pendulum, you mean."

"Yes."

"I wish now I'd taken Mrs. Ritchie's advice and—what did she call it?—*dowsed* our food. Do you think she'd give me a refresher on how to detect poisons? She said this cross of mine would do fine. I'll just explain to Wyn that it's a Celtic blessing of the food."

"Sure. Fiona will go over the basics with you again. Good thinking, Patty."

Chapter Eighteen

Fiona flung open her front door before I was halfway up the curved flagstone path. "Oh, Cass! Such great news!" From inside the house, I could hear a CD player. A familiar voice was belting out at top volume. "Come on-a my house . . ."

"You found the greenhouse!"

"Not that, dear. Oh, I may have done, but we'll get to that in a moment. Come in, come in. I have something to show you." Fiona was barefoot and wearing a crown of some kind of dried flowers. She began waltzing around with a broom through her crowded living room, nimbly dodging stacks of books and magazines and baskets filled with all manner of oddities. Omar Khayyám was hunched under the sofa, his cat eyes slitted with disapproval. *Is Fiona planning to fly off like a regular witch?* I wondered. *Without benefit of psychedelic ointment? Not a sign of that arthritis, either.*

A moment later I realized that actually Fiona was halfway between sweeping and waving a paper in midair. It appeared to be an e-mail message. "It's my little Laura Belle! She's coming to live with me again. Well, maybe not forever, but at least while her mother is in The Hague."

Laura Belle, affectionately called "Tinker Belle," was a dear little girl born out of wedlock to Fiona's niece, then a law student. Fiona had cared for the child for the first year and a half of her life. While the charming child with morning-glory eyes had been in residence, Fiona's messy quarters metamorphosed into a child-centered, apple-pie-neat little cottage. But after her mother, Belle MacDonald, had passed the bar exam and gone to work at the State Department, she'd whisked Laura Belle away and discouraged further contact.

"Belle's going to The Hague?" I was trying to get my bearings in this domestic drama.

"Yes, *yes!*" Fiona paused in her broom waltz long enough to thrust the e-mail into my hands. I read that Fiona's niece was thrilled to have been chosen to provide legal research support to the U.S. Government conferees at the International Jurisdiction and Foreign Judgments in Civil and Commercial Matters conference, which would require her to take up residence in the Netherlands. And *between the lines*, I read that Belle's parents, Fiona's brother and sister-in-law, were less than thrilled at the prospect of taking on the full-time care of Laura, now an active four-year-old, while Belle worked overseas for an indefinite period of time. So after being shut out of Laura's life for more than two years, Fiona had suddenly become the ideal candidate for full-time "nanny."

But what did fairness matter when Fiona was obviously in a state of complete delight? The only spell words the circle had ever said about Fiona's situation had been entirely open-ended—we'd sought only the best of all possible worlds to nurture Tinker Belle, however that might manifest in reality. The Universe of Infinite Solutions had come through with an unexpected but lovely answer once again! "For the good of all . . ." had worked out to be a boost for Belle MacDonald's ambitions, peace and quiet for her parents, and Fiona's little love returned to her heart.

"Miracles happen," I murmured. "I am *so* happy for you! Now do you think you could pause for a few minutes to share a cup of

tea and some news of the Peacedales? And don't you think, now
that it's December, you maybe ought to wear shoes and socks?"

"Don't nag, dear. I'm embarked on a magical cleaning, so naturally I needed to be barefoot and wear a crown. I have some of
your nice smudging herbs left over from our last crisis—what was
it? Oh, that clock man I had to shoot in the foot. Anyway, I plan
to smudge away any negative vibrations. I want everything to be
perfect when my darling arrives."

While Fiona slowly let her joyous feet touch earth again and
donned tartan sock slippers, I put on the kettle and made us an
aromatic cup of Lapsang Souchong, noting that the kitchen counters showed signs of a recent scrubbing. The Rosemary Clooney
CD finally warbled to a close, and a calming quiet descended.
While we drank the steaming brew in Fiona's thistle cups, I related my visit to the Peacedales, winding up with Patty's request
for a refresher in poison detection by pendulum. "Patty's going
to use her Celtic cross. She wants to call it a 'food blessing.'"

"Of course she does. Best not to alarm a husband, I always say.
Especially when Wyn's just recovering from two attempts on his
life. Not to worry," Fiona continued. "I'll zoom over for a visit as
soon as she's sprung from the hospital. I wonder if she'd like me
to smudge her kitchen? I'm really proud of Patty for deciding to
protect herself. I only wish the rest of you—"

"Now, Fiona," I interrupted. "What about my greenhouse? I
want to know what you've found. You know I depend on you."

"Oh, yes—that. It's the strangest thing, Cass. I dowsed over a
map of Plymouth, and the pendulum kept settling on Heather's
neck of the woods, can you imagine that? There are several other
mansions like the Morgan place in that part of town, not all of
them in good repair like Heather's. Do you think the greenhouse
might be a forgotten part of some decrepit estate?"

"Hey! Of course—that's it!" I yelled. Omar Khayyám, who
had been about to emerge from his refuge, hissed and backed
even farther under the sofa.

"What's 'it,' dear?" Fiona smoothed out the e-mail message on the coffee table and read it again. Clearly, I didn't have her full attention.

"Fiona! Think! Whose old mausoleum mansion is located near Heather, on the other side of Brian and Maeve Kelliher, your roommate in Manomet Manor?"

"Maeve, dear child, has got herself up into a walker now. Isn't she amazing!"

"Yes, it's *wonderful*. Now back to the greenhouse . . ."

The light dawned slowly over Marblehead. "Cass, you're thinking of Lydia Craig's place, the sagging porch and all. Who inherited that, by the way?"

"Wyn. He got everything except those modest bequests to nephews and niece. Old Borer, who's ninety-five if he's a day, of the law firm of Borer, Buckley, and Bangs, is the Craig executor, and I doubt very much if he checks around the old manse very often—or ever. If there was a greenhouse, it must be in great disrepair, judging by the rest of the Craig property. I'd be afraid even to tiptoe across that porch."

"So any of the Craigs might be aware of an abandoned greenhouse."

"If it exists in reality."

"Dear Cass, you simply have to have more faith in your visions. I think you're onto something important. Do you want to call Stone?"

"Well, yes, of course I will." *After I check this out myself*, I thought. "But first I ought to drive over to Heather's and get her to show me around the neighborhood. She probably knows that property very well. She grew up there, and I seem to remember her telling me that the kids used to call Lydia "Old Lady Craig" because she'd chase them out of her cracked tennis court. But once we find the place, I'll call Stone first thing."

"Uh huh. Want to investigate on your own, eh? Perfectly natural." Fiona looked around for her reticule, which was, as always, leaning against her easy chair. "Would you like to borrow my little pistol, dear? Just in case."

"No, Fiona, thank you all the same. We'll just be going for a little walk in the woods."

"You never know whom you may meet when you're poking around like you do. Personally, I prefer packing a little security. If I didn't have so much to get ready for my darling Tinker Belle, I'd go with you, dear."

"Oh, that's okay, Fiona." Truth be told, I didn't relish the prospect of tramping through the Craig property with Annie Oakley and her reticule.

It was only four o'clock, so I scooted directly from Fiona's to Heather's. Unfortunately, the cocktail hour had already begun at the Morgan manse, and Heather was trying her hand at mixing a Big Rita like the ones that had almost put out our lights at the Wander Inn. Dick was still seeing his four-legged patients. Acupuncture days always ran long. But Heather expected him shortly. A whiff of some delectable fish dish wafted in from the kitchen, where Captain Jack was at work, and I could hear an occasional squawk from his green-feathered companion.

Honeycomb was lying on a folded blanket under the bar in the conservatory, looking mighty pleased with herself. Trilby the bloodhound and Luke the Lab, were lying against the French doors, gazing dismally at the lacy snowflakes still falling, while a couple of greyhounds tussled with a stuffed bunny behind the potted palms.

After I'd delivered a report on the Peacedales and waved away a Big Rita, I said, "I suppose you don't want to go hunting through the Craig estate for a deserted greenhouse, do you?"

"Fiona found the greenhouse! Isn't she a treasure! I'm surprised it didn't occur to us to look there in the first place—it makes such perfect sense. I'll bet all the Craigs had a good look around when they went to pay court to their rich auntie. Jean probably thought, what with winter coming and her supply of poison hemlock dying back, that she'd better move a few plants to indoor quarters."

Something about that picture was bothering me. "She doesn't seem to care who she poisons on her way to that fortune, does she?" I said. "I mean, it's so whimsical and haphazard, and she doesn't seem the haphazard type. Well, will you go or won't you?"

"Hey, Cass. Look out the window. It's almost Yule, shortest days of the year. How about if we go bright and early tomorrow?"

"Okay, but what if the snow builds up in the meantime?" There really wasn't much danger of that. But I do dislike having to postpone an investigation once I've set my heart on it. Still, I wasn't quite prepared to tramp around the Craig place on my own.

"Do you want me to rent snowmobiles?" Heather took an approving sip of her mammoth Margarita.

"*No!* No snowmobiles, but I will appreciate your company. You know the lay of the land. I bet you already have an idea where the greenhouse may be hiding itself."

"Sure I do. Shall we say elevenish?"

"Shall we say tenish?"

"Okay, slave driver. And if you change your mind about the snowmobiles, let me know."

I got out of there before our simple plan could get any more complicated.

By the next morning, there was no evidence it had ever snowed. The sky was a clear, unpolluted blue, and the sun was shining, but the temperature, which had hovered around a melting thirty-four degrees the day before, was rapidly dropping into the twenties. I dressed for our tramp through the woods in long johns, a thick turtleneck, a hunter's cap with the earflaps down, and an L.L. Bean Rugged Ridge parka, as well as sheepskin-lined boots and heavy gloves. I could hardly move.

Heather, on the other hand, was lightly attired in a red ski outfit obviously made of some miracle fabric, ski boots, ear muffs, and slim mittens. She set off for the Craig place at a brisk rate— "the short way, off-road," she called it—and I lumbered after her, breaking through the branches like a fat brown bear.

"Did you say anything about this greenhouse notion to Stone or Joe?" Heather turned to inquire.

I paused to catch my breath and answer. "It's so tenuous. What would I say? That a greenhouse had come to me in a vision and Fiona found it with her pendulum somewhere near your house? So we're going to trespass on the Craig property to see if the greenhouse actually exists in this plane of being?"

"Yeah, I see what you mean. This is about where the Craig property begins." Heather indicated a line of fir trees that seemed to have been planted several decades earlier and now formed an effective barrier. We wedged our way through. "I think if there is a little greenhouse, it might be somewhere near the old stables, on the other side of the tennis court."

We trudged on. The tennis court looked as if an earthquake had roiled beneath the concrete. Dried brown stalks of weeds erupted through the cracks. In times past, the stables had been converted into garages, but even these were peeling and un-kempt.

"Oh, look there!" With growing excitement, I pointed to a ramshackle building with small-paned windows near an equally decrepit gardener's shed. "You were right on, Heather."

Heather ran lightly past the tennis court. I wallowed in the rear. We had found the place, but something was very wrong. It appeared to be completely deserted, the door hanging off by one hinge, and not a living plant inside.

"The ground is scuffed," I said. "Look there, and there. Some-one *was* here, but we're too late."

We looked inside. Bare, broken shelves. No space heater in sight. All the plants, if there were any, had been moved or dumped.

"What a pity it didn't snow enough for tracks," Heather said.

"We'd better get Stone and a forensic team in here to look for evidence that the greenhouse has recently been used, and maybe even some fingerprints, although the 'person or persons unknown' has been rather careful about that so far. But—"

"But they won't be able to follow the poisoner's trail," I finished Heather's thought. "What we need is a genuine tracker who can read what the earth has to tell us. And we know a skilled tracker. How I wish we could get him here before we have to call Stone."

"You mean Tip. Isn't he in Wiscasset, living with his uncle while he finishes high school?"

Tip was a young Native American whose mother had deserted him and whose father, an alcoholic, hadn't provided much of a home for the boy. I'd befriended Tip, and he'd become part of my spiritual family, the people we meet in life to whom we are naturally drawn, sometimes as if we've always known them. Much as I loved Tip and missed having him around, I was glad he now had a decent place to live and go to school. But I sure could have used his tracking skills right then.

"Yes, but he'll be back soon to spend Christmas week with his father. Too late to help us out here. But maybe he'll come to our anniversary gala."

"Okay, then. Stone it is. Stop postponing the inevitable." Heather handed me her phone. "I have him on my speed dial, number eight."

"Me too," I admitted. I pulled off my cumbersome gloves and punched Stone's cell number with freezing fingers.

I have to say that our favorite detective listened very patiently as I described what my vision had suggested, where we'd guessed the greenhouse must be located, how we were standing there right now, but not a poison plant was in sight. Then I think I heard a sigh, but it might have been the wind, which was at that very moment bringing a cloud cover over the sun.

"Okay. Even though there's nothing showing now, if you've

found a greenhouse where you thought it might be, I think I'll investigate your theory. Let me see who I can get to go over the premises. So stay where you are, Cass. I may have some questions." Stone added, "Did you say 'near the garages'?"

"Yes. Look for Heather. She's in fire-engine red, her stealth outfit."

Heather gave me a hurt look. "I can do stealth as well as the next gal, when stealth is called for," she declared. "I have a lovely camouflage outfit. At least I don't crash through the woods sounding like the running of the bulls at Pamplona."

We did as we were told, waiting patiently. Stone arrived within a half hour with two colleagues. My idea about the greenhouse proved not to be a wild-goose chase. The crime-scene specialists Stone had rounded up found plenty of evidence that the deserted greenhouse had recently been used, then cleaned, and they found one tiny scrap of hemlock that the cleaner had missed. By then, though, any tracks outside the door had been obliterated.

"Where could she have brought the plants?" Heather asked as we trudged back to her house for an invigorating cup of the captain's boiled coffee.

"Home, naturally. But I don't suppose Stone can get a search warrant based on our psychic flashes. We need some indisputable evidence pointing to Jean Deluca."

"What's her husband like? I always think you get a whole new insight into someone when you meet the spouse."

I hit my forehead with the palm of my hand. "Ceres! I should have found some excuse to meet him."

"Do I remember correctly that Deluca gives watercolor classes in his studio on Saturday mornings?"

"Arc you feeling a yen to paint sand dunes and seagulls?"

"Hey, aren't my candles works of art? I am definitely an artist in search of a tutor," Heather said.

So it was arranged that Heather would take up watercoloring

and give us a full report on Arthur Deluca. By the time she attended the introductory class, however, events had already taken a quirky turn. The wicked tricks had begun.

Perhaps, we reasoned, Jean Deluca had caught on to our surveillance and was taking revenge. Maybe she'd connected the dots between the circle's earlier forays into crime-solving and our recent interest in her—Phil and I shopping in her gallery, Fiona inviting her to tea, and now Heather signing up to take classes with her husband. The final straw, we decided, must have been Deidre's brainstorm—a trip to Assumption, her alma mater, to get some deep background on the Deluca family.

Deidre invited an old high school friend who worked in Assumption's office, Millie Murphy, to share a quick lunch and a friendly chat while Will held the fort at home. Over clam rolls on the wharf, Deidre tipped her hand and asked about Jean Deluca, said it was a minor investigation, and swore her friend to secrecy. Millie raised her eyebrows but spilled Assumption's gossip readily enough. Jean was no stranger to the office staff. Every time son Leonardo got into trouble, his mother stormed to his defense.

"Feisty little lady," Millie said. "Good thing, because that boy has got himself into many a scrape. But all of us here were eager to clear up any difficulties. Lee's a born charmer, as you may have guessed—surely he could sing the birds out of the trees. All his teachers say so. That makes it a double shame about the father, though. Always late with the tuition, and we have to keep sending letters, you know. Is this a money thing you're looking into? Credit report or something like that?"

"Yes, something like that," Deidre agreed, telling herself it wasn't really a lie. "I've heard that Lee loves the stage and was hoping for a part in *A Midsummer Night's Dream*."

Millie giggled. "The way I heard it, that play is all about sex and fairies. Naturally, it never got approved. It wasn't Principal Sheehan, though. There was a conservative group of parents who objected to the fairy queen consorting with a jackass." Her voice sank to a whisper. "Bestiality, if you know what I mean."

"It's Shakespeare, Millie. Thoroughly vetted by centuries of uptight English teachers."

"Well, when these parents demanded an open hearing on the drama curriculum, the drama coach, Sister Joseph, decided to present a stage adaptation of *Song of Bernadette*, a lovely, inspiring story, instead of *Midsummer*. But that Jean Deluca did kick up quite a fuss—what a mouth on her! Called Sister Joseph and Conan Sheehan some very bad names. No respect. The husband, now—the poor man was that embarrassed."

"So, did Lee Deluca get to read for some supporting role in *Song of Bernadette?*" Deidre asked.

"It's been postponed." Millie leaned toward Deidre confidentially. "Everyone connected with that production kept getting this stomach thing that's going around. Someone wondered if the lunchroom . . . something fishy about the haddock. But Principal Sheehan nipped that idea in the bud. Guess everyone in the diocese is skittish about lawsuits these days—all we don't need is a fuss over food safety."

Millie had proved to be a generous source of information. But when more strange and upsetting events began to occur, we wondered if the flow of information had gone both ways. Had Millie told Jean Deluca of Deidre's interest?

"I feel as if some evil pixie is playing pranks on us!" Phillipa declared when an unknown hacker penetrated her computer and erased not only her food files but also her poem records. This was right after Heather's Mercedes seized up with indigestion from sugar in the gas tank.

"'Pixie pranks' fits almost too well," I agreed.

"I'm just hoping the Computer Doctor can salvage some of my files. But even if he can work a miracle, I'm in terrible disarray over deadlines. I have a cookbook in the works, and all my restaurant reviews—I was several weeks ahead and breathing a huge sigh of relief."

"What about the poems?" We were sitting in Phillipa's office drinking some divine whipped hot chocolate she'd concocted, which she called Aztec Joy-Juice, while she gazed gloomily at the monitor of a computer gone amok.

Phillipa winced. "A dagger in my heart! But I have hard copy. It will take time—time I don't have—to re-key them, but it's doable. I just won't know to which journals I've submitted them. What a catastrophe! Oh, how I'd like to send an appropriate pay-back!"

"Yes, but even if you could, you can't."

"Spoilsport!"

I chuckled, using my demitasse spoon to scrape out the last drop of creamy, rich froth. "You're reminding me of Freddie, who always used to complain, 'What's the good in being a witch if you can't hex your enemies?' It wasn't easy being her mentor."

"She has a point, you know, Cass. What's wrong with *bad things happening to bad people?*"

"I know how you feel. But I believe, for us, it's against the universal law—*'harm none.'* And those who break the law are hurt the most."

What we didn't know then was that the chaos visited upon Phillipa and the inconvenience to Heather were only the start. Right after Joe and I celebrated our first year of handfasted bliss with our nearest and dearest at Yule, the tricks went from dirty to deadly.

But by then my psychic vision had cleared. Always a double-sided blessing.

Chapter Nineteen

From: witch freddie freddie13@hotmail.com
To: witch cass shiptonherbs@earthlink.net
Subject: *and they said it wouldn't last!*

hiya cass. are you up for some company on your first? if it's okay, adam and i might drive up there to help you two lovebirds celebrate. ☺☺

suppose i'd better bring my long johns. must be cold as a hunter's heart in new england right now.

cass, you oughta be proud—i've been taking courses in computer science and law at UGA. Passing's no prob, but it's, like, snail's pace, and i want that piece of paper pronto. also, o mentor, i haven't crashed the computer lab once. well, except for one teeny incident with professor lech.

hey girl, when you got the power, it's hard not to flaunt it.

speaking of which (witch), another poisoning in Plymouth is national news, baby! thought your neighborhood crime watch would have ex-spelled that culprit by now. tch tch.

see you at yule! oh by the way, we've got news—so get set for a wicked surprise.

hugs to all the witches. tummy scratches to Scruffy.
freddie.

Instead of chamomile-mint tea, I went straight for Joe's bottle
of Jim Beam. How often when people say 'oh, by the way,' whatever follows is far from incidental. I would act surprised, of
course. But in family matters, clairvoyants are usually aware of
the undercurrents, often trying not to know what they know.
Sometimes they even succeed in keeping the blinders in place.
But as surely as I knew that Becky's trial separation from Ron
would end in divorce this year, I also knew that Adam and
Freddie had fallen in love and her "wicked surprise" was their
engagement. The end of one marriage and the beginning of another.

Another aspect of being psychic is dealing with a pervasive
sadness. Sometimes it feels as if you're standing at some cosmic
window watching the world go its wrongheaded way and feeling
powerless to prevent the disasters. I poured a slug of Jim Bean
and added a couple of ice cubes. The pounding of Joe's hammer
in the bedroom was getting on my nerves, so I took my drink into
the living room, where the remains of last night's fire were still
glowing under a blanket of ash in the fireplace. I threw on some
kindling and a log, sat down in my favorite chair with my feet up
on the hassock, and watched the blaze catch the splinters of pine.
The hammering, now on the other side of the downstairs and
fainter, stopped completely. Ah, blessed silence!

"Having a little party?" Joe stood in the doorway with Scruffy
beside him. Both their heads were cocked at the same quizzical
angle. Cute. "May I join you? Although I do feel I should point
out that the sun hasn't risen over the yardarm yet. In fact, it's
only ten bells."

"It's your booze, sailor."

Joe went back in the kitchen and returned with a bottle of
Bud. "Little early for the hard stuff." Scruffy hopped up on the
window seat and scanned the front yard and the road beyond the

pines, giving us his noble profile. *I am the valiant canine guard whose powerful jaws all trespassers fear.*

"You are awesome indeed, but no cookie." Seeing Joe's perplexed expression, I tapped my glass and said, "This is purely medicinal. I'm coming down with an awful prediction."

"That so? Care to share the flash, swami?"

"Adam and Freddie are now an item. They're coming up to join us for Yule and surprise us with the news that they're mad about each other and are planning to marry."

"What's wrong with that? You love Freddie like a daughter, and now she'll really be kin. And even though I'm merely a mundane and not a Wiccan psychic like yourself, ever since I've known Freddie, I've noticed that she's been after your son with all of her formidable arts and talents." He took a long swallow of the Bud. "Do you think it's possible that you are expending a great deal of energy blocking out the truth before your real eyes?"

I took another mini-sip. This stuff was really strong. "It's possible. And, in fact, lover, you may have hit on the source of the psychic block I've been suffering from on the matter of these poisonings. I've closed the damn door myself. You're a pretty smart guy, you know that?"

"I know, but it's nice to be told. So what are you going to do to get unblocked?" Joe came over and sat on the hassock where my feet were propped. His blue eyes were warm with concern, and he smelled of freshly cut wood and some Danish aftershave. He stroked my arms, pushing up the sleeves of my flannel shirt. He kissed me softly on each corner of my mouth, then full on the lips—*Zing!* "Can I do anything to help?"

If I were a cat, I would have purred, but being merely human, I smiled. "Maybe. You're not using the bed right now for a sawhorse or anything, are you?"

He smiled back. "Allow me to give you a tour of how the new closet is progressing. And then, how about a massage with that jasmine-scented oil to get those psychic muscles back into shape?"

"You give the term 'home handyman' a whole new meaning."

I put my drink up on the mantel. Maybe later. I glanced at Scruffy. Having scanned the neighborhood and discovered no imminent danger, he'd settled himself into a deep-napping position, even his ears perfectly relaxed.

We tiptoed away to the bedroom.

Early on the evening of December twenty-second, we five held our Yule ritual. With her athame, Heather cast the circle of sacred space where we would work between the worlds. We began with the formal burning of the festive Yule log lit from last year's saved, blackened wood, encouraging the birth of the sun. Wearing sprigs of holly and ivy for protection, we performed a ceremony to guard us from the poison of evil. For prosperity and all good things in the year ahead, we lit bayberry candles and placed bundles of corn under the amazing tall fir tree, which was decorated with apples wrapped in gold and silver paper and bird ornaments as a symbol of spring. We invoked enlightenment for ourselves and those we loved.

Then the others arrived, and we began the merry part of the evening, the anniversary gathering.

"Some handfastings are only meant to last a year. The couple then decide whether they want to renew for another twelve months." Phillipa lifted her glass of champagne to Joe and me, the anniversary celebrants. Heather's Victorian living room was gloriously fragrant with evergreens and garlanded with holly and mistletoe. Strains of medieval music floated in from the front parlor where The Greensleeves Strollers were evoking a medieval mood.

Stone came over to stand by Phillipa's side, a tall, gentle man still obviously beguiled by his mercurial wife. She took his hand, and all her sharp features softened in the light of her smile. "We, of course, got married by a rabbi to mollify my family. Canopy and all. Haute traditional. 'To rejoice together forever,' *forever* being the operative word. Seeing you two now, looking as if you're still honeymooning, I don't suppose your handfasting included that traditional escape clause either?"

At that moment, I felt suffused with love and joy. Surrounded by my nearest and dearest, I was beaming so much sunshine it was difficult to speak—despite that nagging little concern about Adam and Freddie's future together.

"Traditional escape clause is the Wiccan way? *Not!*" Freddie declared. "When Adam and I get handfasted, I'm opting for the forever-and-a-day ceremony."

Was she looking a trifle less punkish, more mature? Instead of gelled peaks, her new haircut was practically a buzz cut, but it suited her in a subtle way. Her neck had taken on a graceful Nefertiti look, perhaps reinforced by the shimmering Isis earrings. Even my Becky, the traditionalist among my children, had nodded her approval and taken Freddie right into her arms when the couple arrived in Adam's Lexus.

Now my Adam was gazing at Freddie as if she were the incarnation of the Goddess herself, watching her mouth move as she spoke, waiting for the prophecy of his future to emerge. Was it Freddie's spells and potions finally kicking in, or some greater magic at work? Perhaps it was written in the Goddess's grimoire that these two should merge their considerable genetic gifts. For a moment I got rather dizzy imaging a baby waiting to be born, a child I could see in my mind's eye, but then Fiona's deep chuckle brought me back.

"Never fret, pet," Fiona assured Freddie. "When I tie the handfasting knot, it's in the realm of unending spirit, and may never be undone."

"Now you tell me," I said. "We had the Reverend Peacedale to make our marriage legal for a lifetime, never knowing that Fiona was tying us up for all eternity."

"Eternity is not too long," Joe whispered in my ear and refilled my glass. His fingers trailed across the back of my neck where my sage velvet dress scooped low. But then his cell phone rang, and he went off into a quiet corner to answer. *Bummer*, I thought. *I suppose Greenpeace will be sending him to some tropical clime while I'm abandoned here in New England to freeze my ass in January.*

I shook out my hands to rid myself of those negative thoughts and looked around the room to move outside of my own concerns. Tip was leaning against the wall looking longingly at Freddie. Did she even know he'd always had a crush on her? Seeing me watching, he came over and sat beside me on the Victorian fainting couch. We both needed a change of subject.

"I sure wished you were here two weeks ago," I said. "I was in desperate need of a skilled tracker to follow a trail over at the Craig place."

"Something to do with the poisonings?" His grin brought out the Asian cast of his gray eyes. I noticed that those eyes were now level with my own. I'd not thought he would grow up to be that tall, and as graceful and muscular as a dancer. He'd always been a magnificent runner, but now, with those long legs, he must be a wonder to behold.

"You bet. We're on the case, big time," I said. "Apparently the Craig greenhouse was used to house hemlock plants, which were then moved, and I wanted to know where and by whom."

"I suppose it's too late now?"

"After what I would call a cursory look for obvious footprints, Stone and a couple of his colleagues trampled all over the surrounding area."

"Hey, I could have a look around anyway. Never know! Maybe in a wider circle around the greenhouse."

"Would the sign still be there?"

"Depends who's looking."

"If anyone can find a sign, it would be you, dear. Are you still going out for track in Wiscasset? And what about the clarinet?"

"I've got a few running trophies. And I still play clarinet with the school band. But I have something else going now. I've been fooling around with Native music, too—flute, drums, rattles—you know. There's even a kind of fiddle. Sure wish I could find a real teacher, though."

I saw that Tip's eyes shone with the inner flame, so much like love. *He's finding his vision*, I thought. And I would help him with a good spell, if I could—*carefully, carefully*. Always allow the Universe to offer its surprise gifts.

"You should think about music school after graduation, even if you have to pursue Native music separately. But you'll find what you're looking for—I'm sure of it," I said. "And maybe even what I'm looking for. Is tomorrow afternoon okay? Come for lunch."

We agreed on a time just as Joe finished his call and returned to my side. I raised my eyebrows questioningly, and he shook his head as if to say, "Nothing important." For a moment, I saw him as a stranger, looking deliciously handsome in his blue silk turtleneck and navy blazer—love at first sight all over again.

"Do you still have that eagle feather?" he asked Tip, and they began to chat about old times. Joe had always been a good father image that Tip sought out when his own father proved a disappointing drunk. The old man was desperately ill now, in and out of the hospital with an ailing liver. I was always afraid Tip would leave school in Maine and come back to Plymouth to care for his dad. *And that could still happen*, my inner voice told me.

Before I could brood on this and on Joe's phone call—*who's he trying to kid?*—Heather and Dick graciously invited all of us into the conservatory, where dinner had been laid out on an improvised long table. I noted that Scruffy was having a companionable nuzzle with Honeycomb back among the potted palms. I'd been surprised when Heather invited that rascal. But she'd said, "After all, Scruffy was a member of the wedding."

Many of the other original wedding guests were here tonight for the reprise. Among them were our Druid friends, Maeve Kelliher, bravely standing with two canes, and her devoted Brian, a blond, bearded giant of a man. Although Wyn was still feeling too weak to socialize, Patty was here to represent him, conferring with Fiona on the finer points of dowsing. Becky was chatting with Deidre and Will. I missed my delicate Cathy and her partner, Irene, though. "Maybe in the spring," Cathy had said on the phone.

It was a beautiful celebration, with much loving worship of the sacred mistletoe. And an even more beautiful homecoming later that night—after all the toasting and dancing and laughing were through. Except for the part where Joe answered me rather evasively about that worrisome phone call. "Nothing we need to worry about tonight," he said. "Wow, that Heather really knows how to throw a party!" *Fast change of subject!*

I let it go in favor of falling into bed with my handsome bridegroom. But the magic year had passed—now he would have to be called "husband." We savored the joy of married love—knowing each other's bodies so well, just how to give the sweetest pleasure. Afterward I lay with my head on his chest while the feeling of ecstatic oneness ebbed like a slow tide from our limbs.

Just about the time I could tell where his legs began and mine ended—oh, that bucket of cold water—I *saw* where his thoughts were wandering.

"Greece again!" I cried.

"It's scary to be married to you, you know—no secrets." But I could feel Joe smiling in the darkened bedroom. "There's a shipment of genetically engineered soyameal coming into Greece from Argentina. Most Greeks don't want their cattle fed this stuff, but they don't know it's happening. Our goal is to stop the shipment, or at least to shine a big spotlight on what's going on. The activists team particularly asked for me—I speak the language, and I understand the country."

"Preserving the sanctity of the food chain—a worthy goal. But you won't have to leave right away, will you? Greenpeace is giving you a half-day off for Christmas, right?"

He chuckled. "That ship has already left Argentina, and we have to meet it in Greece. Apparently the Argentineans are not as generous as Scrooge in regard to the holidays. So I'll have to leave the day after Christmas, fly to Taranto, and join the *Esperanza*. They're sailing south after blockading other soyameal shipments in Chioggia and Ravenna. The ship's engineer had gone home for *Natale*, so I'll be replacing him."

"What will the *Esperanza* be doing, exactly?"

"We'll bring a ship into the harbor at Preveza to back up the activists—Greeks, Hungarians, Germans, Dutch, even some Aussies—who are going to throw themselves in front of the Argentinean ship."

"But you—you will remain safely on board watching over the *Esperanza* and replying to orders to cease and desist shouted in Greek from helicopters? Not splashing around in dangerous waters?"

"Of course, sweetheart. I swear it."

"So where is Preveza exactly? Is it far from Athens?"

"Prevaza is on the Ionian Sea. I don't know if there will be time for Athens this trip."

"The Ionian Sea! That's not at all like the Atlantic Ocean in mid-December, is it?"

"It's just a job," he said. But I caught that he was still smiling. Love, as well as clairvoyance, sees in the dark.

Chapter Twenty

Feeling a little wiped out the next day, I might have postponed our tracking expedition if Tip had not showed up at my door on the stroke of noon.

"Are you the lady who advertised for a tracker?" This was a traditional greeting between us that harked back to our first meeting, when I'd advertised for a handyman and discovered a needy little boy on my doorstop.

"I can't get used to how tall you are now."

"It's my Northeastern woodland heritage. We're not Kiowas, you know."

"Okay, Uncas. Let's have lunch and get going."

"Going where, sweetheart?" Joe and Scruffy had trailed into the kitchen, lured by the scent of simmering beef barley soup.

It's the boy! The boy who plays ball is back. Let's go outdoors for a game. After leaping up on Tip for an affectionate tousle, Scruffy nosed around the kitchen looking for his orange spongy ball.

Tip brightened, as always, in the presence of Joe. Having found the favorite ball, Scruffy danced around between them.

"Sorry, Sport." Tip took the proffered ball and tossed it gently onto Scruffy's faux-sheepskin bed. "No time for a game right now."

"I'm taking Tip over to the Craig place to look for a sign."

"Want us to go with you? Honor guard?"

"No, that's okay, honey. I know you want to finish that closet before you leave. You wouldn't want to abandon me with that mess in the bedroom, now, would you?"

Actually, I didn't want anyone else trampling on the evidence, if any. I served up soup, bread, cheese, and tangerines. At the last spoonful, I suited up in my winter-survival gear and hurried Tip out to my Jeep, leaving a very annoyed dog.

Not only was it the first day of winter, it was the coldest so far. My teeth were chattering like castanets as I clumsily followed Tip, who was moving delicately and slowly, his gaze intent upon the ground. He appeared to have forgotten everything in the world except his intention to find a track that did not belong to Stone's team. Stepping erratically and ever so carefully, he went from one sodden, leafy patch of ground to another in widening circles around the greenhouse.

"Here," Tip said quietly but in a tone of great satisfaction. "None of Stern's people were wearing these. These are Wellington garden boots. Small. Did you say this was probably a woman?"

"Yes. And Wellingtons fit with my vision. Wellingtons and a Swiss Army knife."

"She used a wheelbarrow, Cass." Tip added. "Parked it over here behind the old privet hedge. See the tire mark? Thought no one would spot the track that way. And see how this branch still has a few dead leaves on it? Tossed away, but not by the wind. I bet she used this branch to brush away footprints to and from the greenhouse. Hey, let's go."

Noting that the privet hedge still held some dried berries, such as had been mixed among Phillipa's dried cranberries, I wrapped a few in a tissue and put them into my pocket for later comparison.

After what seemed like hours of creeping around, suddenly we were practically running toward the old tennis court. *Uh oh*, I thought. *Will that broken concrete be the end of the wheelbarrow track?*

As if in answer to my unspoken question, "I've still got it," Tip cried, moving swiftly around the court's edge. "See how this muddy tire track just hits the edge of the concrete? Follow me." And I did. The track led us to the main road, Route 3A.

"Dead end?" I asked.

"Yep," Tip said. "Unless you want me to run after the Volkswagen that was parked here."

Volkswagen! More confirmation. "Could she have carried a little heater as well as potted plants?" I asked.

"That wheelbarrow was really loaded. Made it a cinch to track."

"Tip, you're a wonder. The Volkswagen is right, too. I'll have to call Stone, but I think I'll wait until I get home, because, frankly, I'm freezing. Would you be willing to show him the sign you've found? I bet he'll wish he had someone like you on his team."

A cloud passed over Tip's easy grin. "Sure. Tomorrow, though. So if I have to move back to Plymouth to stay, I should hit up Detective Stern for a job, right?"

Tip insisted on going home immediately even though I urged him to come back to our place for dinner, or at least to talk to Stone on the phone. "The old man's not getting around so good, and he's all skin and bone. I'm going to get a good stew into him tonight. Brought some venison from Maine."

"Don't ever tell Heather about the venison," I said.

Tip chuckled in that diffident way of his, half a laugh and half a cough. "I already got the picture last night when I was talking to Captain Jack. Said he never cooked for anyone so particular that a chicken had lived a good life before sacrificing itself for the dinner table. And she's just as fussy about fish. Can't even buy farmed salmon, the captain said."

"Well, you used to work at Animal Lovers, so you know where Heather's heart is."

"She always overpaid, I remember. It's a good heart," Tip said.

I couldn't reach Stone, who was in court and not expected back at the Plymouth Police headquarters that day, so I decided to try him at home later. Meanwhile I'd try to bring life back into my limbs with a hot soak in the upstairs bathroom's claw-and-ball tub—scented candles, lavender bath gel—the works! Joe was still immersed in finishing our extended closet, and Scruffy was giving me the back of his head for deserting him with Tip.

It was candle flame that did it. I was supine in sudsy, steamy fragrant waters up to my chin, practically half-asleep and gazing into the flickering light when I simply slipped out of myself into a cellar finished in "game room" knotty pine. Could this be the Deluca home?

Somehow I'd assumed the Delucas lived upstairs in that charming shop on the shore near Plymouth Center, but what I was seeing wasn't the shop. There were half-size windows on one side of the cellar that looked out onto a lawn ringed with pines. An elaborate computer rig and a spider's web of electrical cords covered the back wall. But I knew this must be Deluca's place, because I recognized the boy at the computer, Lee Deluca. And over in the corner, near the bulkhead door, standing neatly on a rubber mat, was a pair of green Wellington boots.

An older woman came down the cellar stairs and spoke to the boy. Not Jean—this woman had a wasp nest of knobby gray hair twisted in a mass over her slightly hunched shoulders. Lee turned and smiled brilliantly at her, and, as I looked beyond him, I saw a row of potted plants under the window. Although I strained to cross the room and look more closely at the leaves, moving in a vision, as in a dream, can be like trying to walk through water.

And it was water pouring into my nose that woke me. I'd slipped down into the bath a bit too far—hazard of the unexpected trance! Coughing and hacking, I was beset by a swarm of puzzles. Who was the gray-haired woman? Where was the cellar? Whose Wellingtons were those? As usual, my clairvoyant episode had brought more questions than answers.

Wrapped in an oversize bath towel, I padded into the blue guest room to call Stone. I could hear Joe still rattling around in our first-floor bedroom, cleaning up for his escape to the Ionian

Sea, the very name of which evoked in me an image of sun-drenched blue waters and mythic shores where columned temples perched on sparkling white cliffs.

Lucky bastard!

"Beg pardon?" Stone's voice. I was unaware that I'd spoken aloud.

"Oh, not you, Stone. That husband of mine is off to Greece right after Christmas. But obviously that's not why I called." The story I had to tell, about Tip's discoveries and my vision, wasn't delivered in precise chronological detail, but I certainly felt I had Stone's attention. And not just Stone's. I didn't need to turn around to know that Joe and Scruffy had come quietly into the room. Joe sat down beside me, listening to my fractured tale. Scruffy hopped up on the guest bed, the one near the window that was his favorite, where he often left one of his stuffed squeaky toys.

"I'm confused about the house," I admitted. "I got the impression that the Delucas lived at their shop—Arthur Deluca has his studio right there in a separate building. This was a different place altogether. I saw plants, but I couldn't be sure they were hemlock. Jean's son was there, playing with a sophisticated computer rig, and an older woman, frizzy gray hair, slighty stooped, came down the cellar stairs."

"'Over the river and through the woods,'" Joe hummed. "Try 'grandmother,' Cass."

"Yes, yes," I said. "Stone, Joe says maybe it's the grandmother's place."

"Okay," Stone said finally. "See if I've got this. Tip will be free tomorrow morning to show me what sign he found at Craig's, apparently a wheelbarrow and a set of small boot prints that we missed?"

"Not your fault, Stone. The boot person erased the tracks for quite a distance from the greenhouse. But you know Tip . . ."

"Yes. I remember. Next, you had a vision. Maybe the plants are at Granny's place?"

"Right. I just have to find out if Arthur or Jean has a living mom."

Stone cleared his throat. "Cass, we have our own sources. I'll look into all of this myself. Have faith, and let me handle it. But I do thank you for your, as usual, fascinating and useful input."

Joe had his ear to the phone, listening along with me. "Good advice," he whispered, "which I only wish you would take." His breath on my ear was a soft caress of air, a distraction I shook away for the moment.

"You're always welcome, Stone. Let me know what you think about Tip's finds."

"I will. But right now Phillipa wants to talk to you," Stone said before the phone was snatched away from him.

"Awesome! That kid is awesome. *And* you've had a vision! I'm up to my elbows in plum pudding at the moment, literally, but we'll get together right after Christmas." Phillipa said.

"Some of us will need to have a look at Granny's place. So when Stone locates the grandparents, you'll have to wheedle the information out of him."

Phillipa laughed her whiskey laugh—rich, deep, and irresistible.

Christmas was a love-filled, soul-satisfying holiday, with a magical sparkle of snowflakes falling on the Eve and obligingly melting on the Day. The sense of these days being 'time out of time' was very powerful. All the world seemed to pause and hold its breath, waiting for the sun's rebirth.

Naturally, the detecting business, too, came to a standstill.

Becky, who was at loose ends, not wanting to succumb to Ron's entreaties to spend the holiday with him, drove to Plymouth and spent Christmas with us. The strain of her separation from Ron was beginning to show in a permanent shadow under her blue eyes. Even her hair, normally a sassy chestnut brown flip, looked limp and mousy. I resisted asking her if a divorce was in her future—besides, I already knew the answer. Offering only the quiet support of simply being there and loving her, I urged her to stay in the rose guest room after Joe left on the twenty-sixth for his rendezvous with the *Esperanza*. So Becky was still at the house when the dirty tricks recommenced.

Chapter Twenty-One

Our wake-up call from the beatific Christmas season came when Fiona drove into a historic home in Plymouth Center. The victim was a sturdy 1770s Colonial that had withstood the Revolution and many other dangers. Fiona's big old Lincoln Town Car barely penetrated its unpretentious facade, merely crumpled the clapboards and cracked the windows. Her brakes had failed as she was driving down the famously steep hill near Plymouth Courthouse, causing her to zip along at ever increasing speed and lose control where the road turned.

Becky and I answered Fiona's frantic call, rushing to her aid in my daughter's Volvo. Thanks to the Town Car's airbag, Fiona was unhurt except for a sprained finger, but mildly hysterical. At one point, I thought she would faint, but a big warm hug and some deep breathing brought her back to herself.

We arrived in the nick of time. The damaged house fronted on a small square, grassy in summer, where four commemorative benches had been artfully placed. I persuaded Fiona to sit there while we waited. The officer who'd answered the accident call had been occupied in checking for injured parties, talking to the home's owner, and viewing the damage. Satisfied now that no ambulance would be needed and the house wasn't on fire or springing a gas leak, he asked to see Fiona's license and registration.

As she rummaged through her reticule to find these items, Fiona brought out a motley assortment of pamphlets, a pouch of corn pollen, a bag of butterscotch candies, lace-edged handkerchiefs, a tartan change purse, a tin of cat food, and her pistol, which she laid on the bench between us while she continued her search. After one horrified glance at the pistol and at the officer, whose attention, mercifully, was on his notebook, I swiftly moved closer to Fiona so as to camouflage the no longer concealed weapon. I found that there are two disadvantages to sitting on a pistol. One, it's cold, hard, and lumpy. Two, a person worries about getting accidentally shot in the ass.

Having located her papers, Fiona handed them over and began to repack her reticule. "Oh dear," she said. "Where do you suppose . . . ?"

I wiggled off the pistol, quickly stuffed it back in the reticule under the butterscotch candies, and held my finger to my lips.

After some time spent in completing the police report, arranging for a tow truck, and having an uncomfortable conversation with the historic home's owner, finally we were able to take Fiona back to my house and pour hot, sweet tea into her. Fiona's agitation was intensified because her brother had arranged that she collect Laura Belle right after the New Year. Fiona had been in a flurry of preparations when the accident happened. Her heart's dearest wish had come true, and now what would she do? The Town Car had got the worst of the collision. It was the luxury model of its day, and it would need extensive and expensive repairs.

"What will I do? I'm so afraid that my brother will change his mind. A thing like this could do it," she wailed.

"Fiona, we can work it out. Why don't you plan to use public transportation to meet me in Boston," my resourceful Becky suggested, "then I'll drive you back to Plymouth with Laura Belle and all her gear. Or if you're not up to that, I could drive you both ways. At any rate, I'll go with you to your brother's place, and we'll bring some temporary guardianship papers for Laura Belle's mother to sign."

For a moment Fiona looked hopeful. Then another worry crinkled her brow. "But my niece has already left for The Hague."

"Not a problem." Becky's voice had taken on a brisk, professional tone. "I'll send the papers overnight through Katz and Kinder to your niece's new office in the Netherlands. Guardianship is something you should have in case your grandniece needs medical attention while she's in your care. Also, we'll require a copy of her birth certificate and medical records in case you want to enroll her in pre-kindergarten."

"Oh," Fiona said. "You're the answer to my prayers, Becky. Goddess bless you."

"Prayers?" Becky glanced at me.

"In a manner of speaking," I said. "Sometime they're called words of power. Or meditations. What did you think we do? Voodoo?'

"Well, not with live chickens and all. But—"

"Cass, we're going to have to educate this lovely girl of yours," Fiona said. "My course in women's studies, the one you all took. The suppression of female authority and divinity. Taking back our old ways. Earth power. Tuning into the universe." She was beginning to sound like herself again. And the sprained index finger, now bandaged and sticking straight up, showed a definite attitude.

At first, we couldn't be sure—*was* this an accident? Possibly. But the mechanic who checked the brake system afterwards said the brake-fluid line had been cleanly cut, not all the way, but just enough so that it would rupture, probably as soon as the car encountered a serious bump or pothole.

"I insist that Fiona file a criminal complaint," Phillipa said. "Brake lines don't cut themselves. An evil prankster is at work here."

"Maybe you're right," I said. "But how? When? I can't see Jean crawling under Fiona's car, can you?"

The next incident brought me much closer to Phillipa's way of thinking.

One morning soon after Becky had gone back to Boston, an unexplainable sheet of ice covered my back-porch steps. Scruffy, dashing first out the door as always, went sailing off them as if he were a Frisbee taking flight. He landed in a bed of woody lavender, and whimpered in pain. I managed to keep my footing only by clinging to the new double railing Joe had installed in another round of do-it-yourself home improvement.

The temperature was ten degrees, true, but it was a dead, dry cold—there hadn't been a drop of moisture in the air or on the ground. Someone would have had to drench those granite stairs with water for a dangerous skim of ice to have formed. After I brought Scruffy back into the house and checked him for injuries—mainly a sore backside—I had another look around the stairs but could find no evidence of an intruder.

Then I remembered that just after three that morning, Scruffy had barked and run from window to window. Normally he doesn't disturb easily once he's really settled in for the night. I'd thought I heard a cat fight somewhere in the distance to explain his excitement.

"It's nothing," I'd said. "Go back to sleep."

My superior canine instincts say there's danger afoot, Toots. Better let me out to have a run at it.

"Oh, sure, let you run outdoors to get scratched up and sprayed by a couple of tomcats. Not on your life." At that weird hour, it wouldn't be easy getting back to sleep. I'd poured a shot of my Universal Antidote into an old Nyquil cup that I keep in the medicine cabinet and drank it down. My cure-all is a secret mixture of herbs and vodka guaranteed to restore a blissful calm to mind and body. As a precaution against further disturbances, Scruffy had been shut out of my bedroom to sleep on his kitchen sheepskin. He'd grumped a while but then he, too, had fallen back to sleep, and so did I.

I hate it when the dog gets to say, *I told you so*.

And I had to put up with Phillipa saying the same when I called her later that morning.

"But how can I file a complaint?" I wailed. "Did you ever hear of someone claiming that an icy doorstep was a criminal conspiracy?"

"What are you talking about, Cass? Clearly, these incidents are all connected, my dear. Including my wiped-out files, that bitch! Was Scruffy badly hurt?"

"He landed on his rump in a prickly herb bush. Nothing that my wintergreen liniment couldn't cure."

"You could have slid down those stone stairs yourself and cracked your head open. Have you got rid of the ice?"

"Luckily, I grabbed that new railing that Joe installed. I have to say it was a Goddess-send. A hair dryer and an old towel took care of the ice. Maybe I'll ask Tip to have a look at the scene. Where I see only a blank page, he reads an entire story."

"Best idea you've had. *Then* we'll file a complaint."

I couldn't reach Tip or his father all that day. Through several phone conversations, Phillipa and I were still arguing about whether I should file a complaint regarding the icy step when the next incident occurred.

Someone opened the gate to Heather's dog yard just at dusk, letting her several mutts in residence, who were outdoors for their last pee, escape for a wild romp on the main roads. She and Dick and Captain Jack had to race around trying to round them up before they were run over in the gathering darkness. In the past, Heather has sometimes had as many as a dozen resident canines, but, fortunately, marriage to Dick has restrained her largesse. Still, it was a difficult and scary business.

Not surprisingly, one of the new greyhounds, aptly named Flashdance, outdistanced all pursuers and got spooked by oncoming headlights on Route 3A. Seeing this gray ghost-animal motionless as marble in the road, the driver had slammed on his brakes, swerved, and hit a tree head-on. The driver appeared to get out of the crumpled mess rather well, suffering only a gash on his forehead requiring ten stitches and that ubiquitous neck injury known as whiplash. But as soon as he got out of Emergency and into a private room, he was in touch with a lawyer.

"And guess who!" Heather demanded. It was the next morning, still freezing cold, so all the dogs were now safely tucked up in their comfortable kennels, housed in what once was the mansion's triple garage. Deidre and I had driven over to hear all the details and commiserate.

"Well, I can guess. That Pryde person you wanted to foist onto me, right?"

"Heidi Pryde Craig, in the flesh, called me first thing this morning, said she was representing Timmy Finch. *Finch*, wouldn't you know. He's practically her cousin, or will be if Iggy Pryde of the pig farm ever marries Wanda of the produce-stand Finches. Of course I turned Craig right over to my attorney, Bartholomew Bangs. Deep pockets, that's what I am to her, I don't doubt."

The robust aroma of Captain Jack's coffee preceded him into the living room. Then the jaunty houseman himself appeared, carrying a large tray bearing the blue enameled pot, thick white mugs, and a stack of biscuits. Riding in style on his shoulder was the green parrot. Gone were the days of dainty Limoge cups and sterling-silver service at the Devlins'.

"Call me Ishmael! Wok! Wok!" the parrot croaked.

We chatted with the captain about last night's near disaster and admired Ish, whose beady eyes were fixed on the biscuits.

He fluttered a wing experimentally. "Belay that, you rascal," the captain said.

"Where are all the doggies?" Deidre wondered.

"Tucked up in their kennels, miss. Still cold enough to freeze flying fish. Got a pot of ginger jam there. Give it a try on them biscuits." The captain strode away whistling, taking the frustrated bird with him.

"We didn't know if you were bringing the little Ryans," Heather said. "Couldn't have them run down by a herd of housebound dogs."

"M&Ms is still at our house playing with their new toys. I wonder why no one ever thought of making kennels for kiddies? Well, I suppose playpens—"

"How is Bangs? Pretty staunch, is he, in the face of personal injury predators?" I asked. The coffee was as heartening as always, and the biscuits were drenched in sweet butter. I was beginning to feel rather buoyed up.

"The firm of Borer, Buckley, and Bangs has been rescuing the Morgan family for generations. High-principled but crafty old gentlemen. Never take a case on contingency. I think Bart Bangs may be more than a match for Craig," Heather said. "But what a needless mess this is! How could Jean Craig be so mean as to endanger the lives of innocent dogs!"

"Dirty tricks, her specialty," Deidre said. "Evil little woman."

"Childish," I said.

Suddenly, I felt my brain go *click, click, click* like a slot machine turning up the winning combination. Sometimes the clairvoyant moment comes right out of my mouth without passing through my brain. "*Childish!* It's not Jean. That last vision— Well, I don't think I read it right. I should have seen the truth right then. *It must be the son*, Leonardo—Lee."

"But he's just a child," Heather protested. "Fifteen? Sixteen? Puerile tricks, maybe, but the person we're after for the poisonings has to be able to whip up a batch of brownies laced with hemlock foraged from the wild. That requires some notably grown-up skills. Not to mention grown-up malevolence."

"When Deidre was nosing around at the school, her friend Millie, in the office, mentioned earlier 'scrapes' Lee had been in, that his teachers had been eager to have the matters cleared up because the boy is such a charming lad."

"Phil and I met Lee once in passing. *Passing* in the true sense—he could hardly wait to grab his mother's car keys and take off for some audition—the failed *Midsummer* thing. Jean declared he'd be 'a perfect Puck,'" I said. "But now I have a yen to encounter Lee again, preferably by himself, take his measure, see what my sixth sense tells me."

"How about another lunch with Millie?" Deidre suggested. "I could do that."

"Yes, we need to know more about those earlier episodes, the ones that were covered up. And also which courses he's taking," I said. But that would only be a background check. A strategy was forming in my mind to get closer, a plan I wasn't ready as yet to share.

"His curriculum? Poison 101, you mean?" Heather refilled our cups.

"Maybe not that, but how about Cooking 101? When Phil's show was hit by the poisoner, the audience, as I recall, included a bevy of students from a high school cooking class and their instructor, Miss Synge."

"I didn't know that!" Heather said. "It's plausible. But hadn't we better call Phil and Fiona, maybe set up a serious protective shield before Lee or Jean or whoever does even more deadly damage?"

Great minds . . . I was already punching in Phillipa's number on my speed dial.

"Yes," Phillipa replied at once, "but have everyone meet here, Cass. I can't leave my chutney—it's just reached the delicate stage of thickening."

Although Fiona was in the last throes of getting her cottage child-ready, she, too, agreed immediately. "I wouldn't want any of this nastiness to touch my darling."

I looked at Deidre questioningly. "If I don't get back, what can M&Ms do?" Deidre said. "She'll have to stay until Will or I turn up. They'll be all right. And besides, I want to be there when you tell Phil and Fiona that you're fingering the kid now."

We piled into our cars and drove to Phillipa's house to rev up our psychic posse.

Chapter Twenty-Two

"But we've been looking at Jean all this time!" Phillipa waved a wooden spoon in protest. Her kitchen was filled with the heady, spicy aroma of slow-thickening chutney. She'd served us her frothy, cinnamon-scented cappuccino, so I was now on caffeine overload. Actually I felt good—powerful, like Wonder Woman after the twirl that changed her into a superheroine.

Fiona leaned her round chin on her plump hand, her expression thoughtful. Only one pencil was stuck in her coronet of braids; this must be one of her calmer days. "Yes, we were looking *at*, when we should have been looking *through*, the mother to the son."

"What kind of banishing can we attempt against a child, though?" Deidre wondered. "I'm a tad uncomfortable with that. A lot of kids do mean things until they're taught differently. Just the other day, I caught Bobby trying to stuff Salty and Peppy into doll bonnets."

"Poor little pups. I'm not sure children should be trusted with helpless dogs. What did you do?" Heather asked.

"Oh, come off it, Heather. Children and dogs share some of the purest love that life has to offer." Deidre shook her mop of blond curls in protest. "I sat him down for a talk about the feelings that animals have, how they're real and not toys, that he'd hurt and embarrassed them. Soon he was crying and telling the doggies that he was so sorry."

"Because Bobby has a real little conscience," Fiona said. "Whoever poisoned Lydia Craig and the Luckey sisters has no conscience at all."

"I wonder if that's something you're born with . . . or without," Deidre said.

"Sociopath!" Phillipa banged her spoon on the chutney pot's edge for emphasis. "Dee, when you have another go at your gossipy friend in the Assumption office . . . No, she won't know."

"Know what?" I asked.

"'Nurture or nature,'" Fiona said. "Phil wants to know what happened to Lee when he was an infant, long before he began to accumulate school records. The 'nurture' proponents think this particular problem begins in infancy. The failure to form a loving bond with the parent results in an unattached child. The 'nature' people, on the other hand, call the youngster a 'bad seed.' It's all in the genes to them. And then there are the superstitious folk who believe such a child is a changeling, exotic and charming, but without human feeling because of being *other.*"

"Your pixie connection, Cass," Deidre suggested. "You've been trying to tell yourself to look for a faery child."

"I am *not* superstitious," I complained. "I don't even believe in the supernatural. Everything that happens, even the weird stuff, has a perfectly natural explanation. Somewhere."

"No, of course you're not superstitious," Fiona defended me. "You were being haunted by an archetype. The image of a small, dark, youthful prankster from the faery world. When you figured out *why* this image kept appearing in your mind, you solved the puzzle."

"As you told me I would."

"I try never to say 'I told you so,'" Fiona said. Phillipa's black cat, Zelda, padded into the kitchen and jumped into Fiona's lap. Fiona scratched her softly behind the ears, silver bangles tinkling.

"Let's not forget that film favorite, *Possession by the Devil*," Heather said. "Nothing that a rigorous exorcism can't cure, so they say. Preferably with a priest that looks like Richard Burton."

"Listen up, friends—this is an easy decision. Don't focus on the criminal's age. Let's just bind and banish *whoever it is*. In a nice white way, of course," Phillipa said.

We all looked at Fiona, who was now whispering in Zelda's ear.

"Sometimes I do think this kitty has the makings of a true familiar."

"Bind and banish, Fiona?" Phillipa brought Fiona back to the matter at hand.

Fiona looked up from stroking Zelda. "Do you remember the psychic wall we built between us and Quicksall? It was your spell, Phil, as I recall."

"Yes. And Q ran into an actual brick wall," I said. "I'm not prepared to go that far, I have to admit it. Always supposing it was our spell that caused the accident."

"All right, then, what about simple misdirection, throwing him off track? And protecting ourselves, of course," Deidre suggested.

"Water," said Fiona. "He will be thrown off the track if we cross water and leave him on the other side. Figuratively. From the microcosm to the macrocosm."

"Saturday. Esbat of the Wolf Moon. Rituals for protection of our homes are traditional. The perfect time," I said. "I'll gather together the herbs we'll need—anise and mistletoe—there's plenty of that still hanging around in Heather's house."

"Amber amulets," Deidre said. "I'll make those."

"Let's meet at my house, before dark this time," I suggested. "Weather permitting, we can cross that little brook that runs through Jenkins Park for the 'crossing water' spell. Then we'll go back for our regular ceremony of the full moon. I'll want to include Patty and Wyn in our circle of protection. Evidently the boy's caught on to our sniffing around and is having a little evil fun with us, but his real target must be Wyn. With Wyn out of the way, Lee's mother will inherit a third of the Craig millions. It could be a whole new life for Lee—expensive private school, Ivy League college, or maybe acting lessons at some exclusive New York school."

"I don't suppose you could get the Peacedales to wear amber?" Deidre asked "What if I paste an amber bead in the center of a cross . . . ?"

"If Lee took the trouble to Google us—and he probably did," Phillipa said, "all those *Pilgrim Times* news items about our amateur crime-solving would have popped up, including my personal favorite, 'Local Witches Hex Sex Killer.'"

"Well, as you've learned to your chagrin, Phil," I said, "he has plenty of computer expertise, including the art of hacking. And I think I've 'seen' his elaborate system, possibly at his grandmother's house."

"Yeah? You mean the setup by which that miserable kid crashed my computer files? Great Goddess, I wish Freddie were here to give her virus whammy to *his* computer, however she does that," Phillipa said.

"After all the time and trouble I've taken to teach that girl control and set her on the white way?" I protested.

"Oh, I meant to say . . . speaking of the grandmother's house, I got what you wanted from Stone, Cass." Phillipa smiled smugly. "There *is* one living grandparent, Bianca Deluca. Her house is on Summer Street, not far from the Duluca Gallery. Maybe you'd like to psyche it out before the Esbat. Not with me, though. Stone would have a bird."

"I'll go," Heather said. "I'm getting to enjoy these field trips with Cass."

"I wonder if it would occur to Lee that Jean Craig's share would be larger if the two nephews also were out of the picture?" Phillipa said.

"I don't think there's much that boy misses," I said.

*   *   *

Tip's father was in the hospital again. "Really bad, the old liver sickness," Tip said when he called. At such a worried time, I didn't want to ask him to look for signs of an intruder around my house, but it turned out he wanted to stop by anyway with a Christmas gift he'd made for me. Mine to him had been an official "Mountie" red and black winter jacket from the Royal Canadian Mounted Police store, and he'd been delighted with it.

Splendid in the new jacket, he knocked on my door that afternoon and was suitably greeted by Scruffy, all jumps and licks. His hair, dark brown and shining with russet highlights, was pulled back into a macho ponytail with a red bandana headband. His grin was irrepressible but didn't quite dispel the sadness in his gray eyes as he held out a long white box. I opened it to find a polished wooden flute in the form of an elongated woodpecker, with open beak and a red splash on top of its head. Jaunty red feathers decorated each end. Tucked in the box was a story, "The Sioux Legend of the First Flute."

"It's so beautiful." I was too near tears to say more, but managed to hug Tip's thin shoulders and plant a grateful kiss on his cheek. "And you made this? It's really a work of art."

"But mostly it's for the music." Tip took the flute from my hands, put his mouth on the mouthpiece, his fingers on the holes. A lovely, ghostlike tune emerged from the bird. Scruffy's ears perked up. He threw back his head and tried an experimental howl.

"Hey, old fella—that's a pretty good accompaniment," Tip said, laughing.

Scruffy dashed around the kitchen and soon produced his orange ball; Tip offered to take him outside for a few minutes. So I had to explain that although it was almost impossible with a dog who had his own pet door, I was trying to protect the "scene" so that Tip could have a look at it. I related the tale of Scruffy's alarm in the night, followed by an unaccountably icy step the next morning. Tip said he'd look, but he imagined the signs had been pawed to death.

After hurling the ball a good long way to occupy Scruffy, Tip set off to track in his halting, jerky, circular way, nose to the ground literally at times, searching for the beginnings of a trail. When Scruffy came dashing back with the ball, I clipped the leash on his collar.

Hey, you're ruining all the fun.

"We're working now, Scruff, tracking that intruder."

You should have asked me, Toots. Superior canine tracking skills at your service.

It was not until he got almost to the pines that I heard Tip give a high-pitched, Indian-style war whoop. I'd been afraid to move off the stairs, but now Scruffy and I hurried to where Tip was scrutinizing the needle-cushioned earth under the pines by the main road.

"See this?" Tip's voice was as excited as he ever allowed it to be. "Footprint. Small boot, like before. I bet if we go up to the road, we'll find that same Volkswagen track. And here . . ."

"What? What?"

"A bucket. Ice slush, I bet. She needed something that would stick and freeze fast."

"He," I said.

"He? Do you know who?"

"Will you keep this to yourself?"

"Hey, Mz. Shipton . . . don't you know the traditions of my race? Silent Injun?"

"I'm seeing a boy. I'm thinking it's Leonardo Deluca."

"Deluca? No shit."

"Tip!"

"Oh, sorry. I know Deluca. That is, at track meets, I'd come up against him on the Assumption team."

"And?"

"Well, let's put it this way. *Someone* from Assumption dumped *something* in our water bucket that took out half our team."

"Did you ever find out who . . . and what?"

"Nope. Lee kicked the bucket, so to speak. So much for the evidence. Me, though, I'd stuck to my own bottle of Injun Juice, so I was okay."

"Good for you. But what exactly is that?"

"I dunno. Paw mixed it up for me, but I think he started with cold herb tea, honey, lemon. Maybe some salt."

"So you figure Lee disposed of the evidence?"

"Yeah. Fast kid, though. His team might have won legit. So you're saying he's poisoning folks now?"

"Still," I said. "I met Lee once for a moment, but I'd like to have a closer look. Maybe you can help me. Do you know him well enough to stop by for a chat?"

Tip made a face. "Hey, whenever I'm home now, I avoid the kid. But in this case, you're sleuthing, right?"

"Right. Let's go. I have a feeling we'll find Lee at the gallery if we hurry." Actually, I could see him in my mind's eye, packing some things into a book bag in his room. Maybe, maybe . . .

By the time Tip, Scruffy, and I got to the gallery, I had concocted my story. I was looking for a match for Syllabub. "I thought two jugs would be nicer, one to grace each end of my mantelpiece," I explained.

Jean, who was dusting the pots, looked at me skeptically, though her little pasted-on smile remained in place. Perhaps I'm not the most convincing of liars.

But when Tip said, "Hey, Ms. Deluca, is Lee around? Like to say hi. We used to see each other at the track meets," the doubting look was replaced by a pleased smile that went all the way to her eyes this time.

"Oh, yes, he's upstairs studying. I'll call him. Tip, did you say your name was?"

"Yes, ma'am, but Lee liked to call me TeePee. Tell him Tee-Pee."

Jean picked up her cell phone and punched a single digit. I raised my eyebrows at Tip. He shrugged. "Sticks and stones . . ." he whispered.

"Lee, honey, there's a guy down here wants to say hello." There was a pause. "He says you'll know him by TeePee." Another pause. "Sure, sugar. I'll tell him."

"Lee's on his way," Jean said, still delighted. I wondered if Lee had many friends.

A moment later, the boy himself was in front of us, a bottle of Coke in each hand. A beautiful lad, probably quite small for his age, but well-sinewed in a graceful, softly curved way. A mop of dark curls, luminous brown eyes, and a heartbreakingly sweet smile. He reminded me, somehow, of Donatello's David.

"TeePee!" he said, accenting the second syllable a fraction, just this side of insult.

"Hey, Lee. How's it going? My friend here, Mz. Shipton, is shopping for a jug, so I tagged along to give you a shout."

"That so? No hard feelings, then?"

"About what?"

"About getting your ass whipped in track."

"Oh, Lee," Jean protested while she showed me several jugs that might be suitable companions to Syllabub. Cute little buggers, I had to admit. Most of my attention, however, was focused on the two boys, as was Jean's.

Lee mentioned some casual gossip about kids they both knew, but Tip didn't respond much to that, just listened and grinned. Then Tip changed the subject, talking about the hiking club at Wiscasset High and the track meets—was Lee still into the drama club? Lee said he was disgusted with the Assumption theater program, that he was going out for track again in the spring.

As Tip leaned against the wall, drinking his Coke, Lee eyed him up and down, measuring, I thought, the difference in their height. This year had brought a sudden spurt of growth to Tip that might not have been so obvious when the boys had competed in the same track tournaments. Tip mentioned being in the school band in Wiscasset. Lee looked down at his shoes—rather expensive trainers—not quite hiding a mocking version of his mother's smile. Then he looked up again and poured on the charm. They began chatting about hockey teams and movies they liked as if they were old friends.

"Hey, Lee. What about the Plymouth Players? Ever think of trying out for one of their plays?" Tip suggested.

"Yeah, if I didn't mind getting stuck with juvenile parts. I tried that. Bunch of old pussies."

"Lee!" his mother said sharply. "Do watch your language, dear."

I paid for my purchase, a fat little elf named Posset, and Jean began to wrap up the jug in green tissue. All the while I was thinking, *What excuse can I find to grasp Lee's hand?*

Chance favors the prepared witch.

As I turned from the counter with my wrapped and bagged elf in hand, I tripped over a stack of frames. The bag flew up, the package fell out, and by some miracle was caught in midair by Jean. Both Tip and Lee reached out to steady me—I marveled at their quick reflexes. But at the last instant, I twisted my body so that most of my weight fell against Lee's arm. At the same time, I grasped his hand.

Instantly, I was overwhelmed with the sweet fragrance of vanilla and the fetid odor of hemlock. If these were not real scents, I was experiencing a psychic phenomenon. But I wanted more. I might never get this opportunity again. Leaning on Lee, I looked straight into his eyes.

Talk about weird. Such a gorgeous face, but Lee's long-lashed dark eyes could only be described as soulless. Generally when I make eye contact like that, I get a sense of that person's spirit, but this was like gazing into a cavernous emptiness. I was reminded of those sci-fi films in which some horrid alien takes a disarming human form but then is unmasked in the last reel. *Shades of the changeling.* Then I thought of handsome, ageless Dorian Grey, and of the portrait in the attic that showed his true hideousness.

As if he read my thoughts, Lee gave me one quick, malevolent glance before tearing away his arm. I almost fell to the floor, but I caught the counter's edge and righted myself, with Tip leaning over me anxiously. "Hey, Mz. Shipton—are you okay?"

"Sure," I said, but that wasn't true. I was shaken from a glimpse into the mind of what might be a young Ted Bundy or Charles Manson. I took my rescued Posset in one hand, Tip by the other, and fled the scene.

Chapter Twenty-Three

"Yes, yes, yes," I said. Now I'm sure. I've looked into Leonardo Deluca's eyes, and I know who he is. Or maybe I should say, *what* he is."

"Okay, then. Let's do it," Phillipa declared.

We'd gathered early for the Esbat of the Wolf Moon, a moon we'd be fortunate to see if the prevailing cloud cover persisted into the night. But for now we had the pearl gray light of a winter afternoon. The air was very still; the temperature hovered just below freezing. The smell and feel of snow were in the air. Nevertheless, we bundled up and trudged out to the little brook that ran through Jenkins Park. Fiona, wrapped in a MacDonald tartan cape with an enormous hood, and lugging her green reticule, huffed and puffed with every step. But when we arrived at the brook, she drew herself up in her wisewoman glamour and took full charge of the ceremony.

The misdirection spell Fiona had unearthed from a dark, moldering *Book of Shadows* (oddly come to light in a box of books donated to the library sale) required us to leap over water, so we searched for the brook's narrowest place. We found that the brook thinned near the old cranberry bog hut that Tip had once used for his hideout. Still, the banks on each side were high, and jumping over it would be a tricky maneuver.

Fiona had brought a grainy newspaper photograph, printed off the Internet, of Lee starring in last year's drama club production of *Guys and Dolls*. Taking a card of thumbtacks out of her reticule, she attached the likeness to a tree. Then she threw her arms into the air and sang out a rhyming spell at the top of her voice. I looked around uneasily. Her chant would carry far in this cold, quiet air.

Water before me,
Evil behind me,
I leap to a place
Where harm cannot find me.

"You should have just let me make a poppet!" Deidre whispered, her eyes sparkling with laughter. Wearing her peaked red hood, she looked like a mischievous ten-year-old.

"Hush," I whispered back. "You know you wouldn't want to do anything voodooish and hurtful. Especially not to a youngster."

Then we were all watching Fiona with astonishment. Holding her cloak close in one hand, she sailed over the brook as if she had wings on her heels. "There we are," she said with a pleased smile. "You go, girls."

"Wow!" Deidre said.

"What happened to that crippling arthritis she had last year?" Phillipa said.

"Maybe our healing magic worked," I said. "Or maybe it was that Navaho blessing with sand paintings and corn pollen."

"Or maybe a little sex on the side with Mick Finn," Phillipa murmured. "Always a great joint lubricator."

"I don't think their friendship has progressed that far," Deidre replied in equally low tones. "Although there's plenty of scuttlebutt around the firehouse."

Heather didn't add her voice to our running commentary but simply followed Fiona, leaping easily in her own lithe way, the Goddess Diana, always at home in the woods.

That left us three, judging the distance somewhat hesitantly. An east wind stirred, pushing away the clouds. Occasional shafts of sunshine penetrated the woods like divine blessings. The little brook began to sparkle merrily—and possibly to laugh at us, as well.

"Oh, what the hell," Phillipa said, taking a running jump. She almost made it, but one foot slid relentlessly back toward the water. "Eeeeek," she cried out. Instantly, Heather grabbed Phillipa's black wool jacket and hauled her up onto the bank, a long scarlet scarf trailing behind her.

"Want to hold hands?" Deidre said to me. "Jumping buddies?"

"I wouldn't want to drag you into the drink," I confessed.

"No, listen . . . it's like in Peter Pan. 'Think lovely, beautiful thoughts . . .'" And with a surprisingly strong little hand, Deidre had me running with her, jumping, landing with no grace but not in the freezing eddies of the brook, either.

"Bravo!" Fiona clapped her hands. "Oh, golly, I do hope this works."

"Hey, Fiona, it's got to work," Phillipa said. "We actually managed to do this thing, with no little sacrifice to our dignity, so this is not the time to be a Doubting Thomasina."

"Must we jump that thing again to get back?" Deidre looked at the brook with dismay.

Phillipa and I laughed. To her and me, Jenkins Park had become as familiar as our own backyards, the home of our personal wetlands and endangered eagles, so we knew how to hike back to my house without any additional feats of athletic prowess being necessary.

"Come on," I said. "I'm feeling good about this. Let's sing."

As we shepherded our merry little band back to my house, the long way around the brook, we chanted, "All things come from the Goddess, and to her they will return. . . ." The winter sun set, gilding the Atlantic with secondhand rays of rose and gold. Seagulls rose and fell, catching the last light on their wings.

"There's hope for the full moon, then," Heather said. "Esbat of the Wolf."

We hurried inside to warm our freezing limbs and to begin our ceremony of house blessing and protection.

While the others were doffing their winter gear, Scruffy greeted me exuberantly, sniffing my pants legs and boots. *Hey, Toots . . . you're supposed to take me along when it's a hunt in the woods. You might have got lost without my superior canine skills to lead the way.*

"Sorry, Sport. How would you like to have a big delicious dental-aid bone in the bedroom?"

Ugh. Those things taste like plaster. Are you going to shut the door on me again?

"Not if you stay quiet and behave yourself." I took the bone out of its wrap and sniffed it. True enough, not much of an odor.

Grumpy dog trudged into the bedroom with his bland bone. I heard him jump onto the white chenille bedspread. He'd leave a powdery mess, but I let it go this time.

Heather uncorked the excellent bottle of sherry she'd brought while I lit the logs in the fireplace and tossed in dried sprigs of anise and sage for protection and a calm, meditative mood. After we'd sipped the sherry and thawed out our bones a bit, we began.

Each of us wore a sprig of protective mistletoe in our hair as I drew the circle with my silvery athame so that we might enter into the space between the worlds, the realm of magic. Fiona, enveloped in her wisewoman glamour, touched sticks of cinnamon and sandlewood to the fire, blew out their flames, and stood them in the old black cauldron on the hearth. Heather lit the candles, one for each of the four directions, and a white "work" candle she'd made, which was embedded with tiny crystals and silver runes.

Using an incantation composed by Phillipa, I summoned the powers of the east—air, greatness—of the south—fire, brightness—of the west—water, wellness—of the north—earth, oneness. I invoked female and male forms of the divine spirit of the universe.

The full moon obligingly shone in the living room window just as I was ready to draw it down into our midst. I asked that each of us, and the Peacedales also, would be protected from the evil that had entered our lives, and for the best possible outcome to our present dilemmas from the Universe of Infinite Solutions. We thought it best to leave these requests open-ended. Who could have imagined, for instance, that our call for an endangered species would have been answered by a pair of eagles, when the best we'd been hoping for was the red-bellied turtle?

One more traditional Wolf Moon ritual was performed, for healing the planet. Never let it be said that we sidestepped the big challenges.

Deidre distributed her newly created amber amulets. Then, carrying a silver cup of consecrated salt water, she sprinkled a few drops on each of us to purify our intentions. I looked longingly at my grandmother's old black walnut walking stick, a perfect banishing tool, but we had decided not to follow that path.

It was still early when I opened the circle, leaving plentiful time to go along with plentiful wine from Heather's miraculous wine cellar to put the "merry" in "Merry Meet, Merry Part." We feasted on a lentil soup I'd had simmering in the slow cooker, with garlic bread, both of which were good omens for wealth and health in the New Year. A chocolate sour cream cake (homemade and safe) stood ready for dessert—a little decadence is always welcome, too.

"Did you put chopped ginger in this lentil soup?" Phillipa demanded suspiciously..

"Great cooks are entitled to a few secrets," I said.

"So are witches," Fiona said. "Phil hasn't figured out the recipe for my scones, either."

Despite our best efforts at the Esbat of the Wolf Moon to divert evil from our circle, Deidre must have stirred the Deluca pot a tad too vigorously in her investigatory zeal. Either that or our white light had some holes in it this time. Perhaps spiritual protection can only do so much for those who persist in putting themselves in harm's way. But all we knew at the time was that Deidre's next lunch with Millie Murphy hit the mother lode.

"You're going to love this!" Deidre's excitement was palpable, even over the phone. It was good to hear a note of cheer when it had been sleety and miserable for days and my beloved was, I imagined, basking in sunshine on the Ionian Sea.

"What? What?" I asked. "I can't wait."

"Yes, you can. This has to be told in person, and I can't get out today. Will's on shift, and M&Ms is at the Mohegan Sun with her blue-haired gambling cronies. Golly, I wish my own mum hadn't moved to that Golden Oldies Village in Florida. She loves it, too—it's for retired music people."

Made her escape, I thought. "Sounds like a fun place, though."

"Oh, sure. Mum was a kind of early rock 'n roll singer, but more of a groupie, if you ask me. Maybe it's time for me to send out a call. Do you think the universe might zing back the perfect au pair? Will's been doing so much overtime, we could really afford it now."

"Sure. If you want to take a chance that your Mary Poppins will turn out to be Mr. Belvedere," I said. "Anyway, I'll be right over. Have you called the others?"

"Fiona's gone to Boston for the glorious reunion with her grandniece—accompanied by your daughter, as I heard it. Phillipa's taping her show. But Heather will be here. She's bringing a celebratory bottle."

"When did she not? Okay if Scruffy comes with me? He's

been housebound for so long in this weather, he's getting mighty cranky."

"Okay. I guess he can't help lording it over Salty and Peppy."

"It's a wolf pack thing. He likes to be alpha dog. We'll be there in a half hour or so, depending on the roads." I thought about my daughter driving back from Boston with Fiona and that most precious cargo, Laura Belle—and I said a small heartfelt spell for their safe return.

What is so dismal as a drizzly day in January? After a slippery, sliding, skidding trip to Deidre's, I was ready for a glass of whatever Heather was uncorking in her efficient way. The big surprise, though, was that she'd brought Honeycomb, who was now looking a trifle thick through the middle.

See you later, Toots! Scruffy tried to nudge Honeycomb into the kitchen for a tête-à-tête, but the golden retriever gave him her raised lip and low-voiced growl. Then she settled herself ostentatiously at Heather's feet.

Scruffy slunk away, overcome with canine gloom. *Hey, what's her problem? She used to be frisky, friendly, and fun.*

"She's in a family way now. It's a moody time."

"You're telling me," Heather said. "It's been a long time since I had a preggers female under my feet. Literally. Dick built Honeycomb this most marvelous whelping box, sanded smooth as satin, and filled it with paper to shred and herbs. Just lovely. And the ungrateful bitch won't go near it."

"Just give her a little while, and she'll get into her nesting mode and rip up those papers to feather her bed, don't you worry," Deidre said. Curled up on her blue sofa amid her embroidered pillows, she looked perfectly serene, like a woman with all the time in the world. How did she do it?

"Where are the kids?" Heather asked, pouring out an elegant muscat, a perfect antidote for the winter blahs, into the juice glasses her hostess had provided.

"Jenny and Willie are still in school. Be home in an hour or so. Bobby's under the kitchen table with the pups, playing African safari. And Annie's tucked up in her little bed for afternoon nap. It's what we call around here *'a magical moment.'*"

"Okay, so let's hear everything," Heather said. We sat forward eagerly.

"I took Millie Murphy to lunch at The Walrus and the Carpenter, my treat. She had two Manhattans, a lobster salad plate with steak fries, and a hot fudge sundae. Don't you think it's about time you gals gave me an expense account like a regular P.I.?"

"*Not*," we replied in unison.

"Phillipa would be appalled by that menu," I said. "But get on with it."

"Millie doesn't know everything, but I think I got all she does know. The first incident was actually in grammar school. The record was sealed, but Millie heard that it had involved an attack on deer at the Plymouth Play Pals Petting Zoo. How or why Lee Deluca got involved Millie didn't know, but she certainly didn't think such a sweet boy would hurt a friendly animal—it must have been some kind of weird accident."

"Monster!" Heather said. "Already I'm sick."

Ignoring this outburst, Deidre continued, "So later I just pretended I was Fiona and did a Google search on animal cruelty cases. I found something in the right time frame, two deer at Play Pals who were stabbed repeatedly with a palette knife. You know, like artists use? One deer survived, the other had more severe injuries, hamstrings cut, and had to be put down. Ugly! Two juveniles were charged, names withheld."

"And there was more, I don't doubt," I said. "What else?"

"The next incident was hateful but not cruel," Deidre said. "Several gravestones at the Gates of Zion Cemetery were overturned and black swastikas painted on many more. Lady of Lourdes Middle School students were accused and confessed, but they all swore their actions had been part of their initiation into an exclusive Hellfire Club created by Lee Deluca. The boys were expelled from Lourdes but allowed to attend a public school.

Their accusations against Lee could not be proved, however, and his teachers were convinced that Lee would never have instigated such acts."

"You'd think they'd begin to observe a pattern," Heather said.

"Sealed records are a mixed blessing," I said.

"The third incident happened at a school track meet. Several kids on the team playing against Assumption got sick and blamed the opposing team, which included Lee, for putting something in their water bucket."

"Tip was there that day, and he told me what happened." I related what Tip had said about Lee dumping the evidence.

"That wasn't the only sudden, unexplained illness," Deidre said. "Something similar happened at the intramural drama contest."

"Goddess only knows how many other crimes occurred that never got connected to Lee," I said. "And I think he's come to enjoy the power over others that poison gives him. Although he's obviously targeted his Grandaunt Lydia and Reverend Peacedale, I get the feeling he doesn't care who else gets sick or dies. That poisoning at Phil's show, for instance. Possibly just to try out privet berries, which turned out not to be as deadly as hemlock."

"What a little bastard." Heather made a little moue of disgust and refilled our glasses. The muscat was like a ray of liquid sunshine.

"Speaking of which, I've got another scoop," Deidre said. "Not from Millie. But I happened to mention to M&Ms that I was interested in the Delucas—those blue-haired ladies are a silver mine of secrets, you know."

"Yes, yes . . . give," we said.

"I knew part of this story but not the details, the timing. Arthur Deluca was still in Boston College when Lee was born to Jean Craig at the Florence Crittenden Home for Unwed Mothers. When Jean came home to her parents in Plymouth, she never brought the baby with her. Possibly she meant to give him up for adoption. But then something happened—

M&Ms didn't know what exactly—and the next thing the town knew, Arthur and Jean were married and had a new baby son. Arthur Deluca gave up his dream of pursuing fine art in Paris and became a typical Cape Cod painter, apparently without regrets."

"How the hell did your mother-in-law find out all that?" Heather asked.

"She and her friends simply put two and two together. When a teenage girl goes away for six months, then comes home to get married and, *abracadabra!* produces a mysterious baby boy . . . well. Also, I think one of M&Ms' cronies was on the FC Home's board of directors."

"A most interesting part of this little saga," I said, "are the number of weeks between Jean's ditching the newborn and her becoming a devoted mother. If you go for the 'nurture' theory, sometimes it's in the first few weeks of life when the die is cast for sociopathic personality. Anyway, my hat's off to you, Dee! This is some stellar detective work."

"So does that mean I'm getting an expense account?"

Chapter Twenty-Four

I'd rarely seen a lovelier little girl than Laura Belle at four. Her eyes were violet-blue, and her pale gold hair fell naturally into soft ringlets; her body was beautifully formed, with a slightly rounded "little girl" tummy and the kind of erect shoulder blades that look as if they might grow wings one day.

"Hello, Laura. I'm Becky's mom. I'm so happy to see you again."

She smiled shyly but did not speak. Omar sidled about her legs, on good behavior for once. With one hand, she reached down to touch his head, and he arched upward blissfully to meet her fingers.

Becky raised an eyebrow. "She hasn't said a word all day," she whispered when the child had followed her grandaunt into the now spotless kitchen. "Seemed to remember Fiona very well. All smiles. Never even cried when we left her grandparents at their front door, although they were shedding a few phony tears."

Fiona bustled about getting Laura Belle a cup of cocoa before tucking her into the newly freshened nursery, where once upon a time she'd been the reigning princess. The walls were stenciled with magical animals—deer, owl, fox, otter, and turtle. Fiona had wanted to add bats, spiders, and snakes. "The bat is a symbol of rebirth, the spider spins the web of fate," she'd declared. "And as you know, snakes are a repressed emblem of female power."

"Tell that to the thought police," Phillipa had warned her. "I shudder to think what a social worker would say if your fitness as a foster parent were ever called into question. Being a Wiccan and all."

"Are you out of your mind?" Deidre had screamed at Fiona. "Do you want to give the kid nightmares and neuroses?"

So, fortunately, Fiona had allowed herself to be talked out of adding pictures of these maligned creatures, and the nursery had retained a conventional look.

"How'd it go? Any problem with the papers?" I noticed Becky was wearing her serious navy-blue-from-head-to-toe court outfit.

"Of course. That's to be expected. We had to sign an agreement that we'd take Laura to her therapy sessions every week and some other minor matters. In return, we have temporary guardianship, to be relinquished only to her natural mother, all medical rights and records, and, of course, the child's birth certificate. Do you know who her father is?"

"No. Should I?" To tell the truth, this question had never crossed my mind, but now that it did, my sixth sense began to kick in. I "saw" a black-robed individual, perhaps a judge. A flash like this vanishes so fast as to make you wonder if it happened, which is why so many clairvoyant hits go unrecognized.

"Maybe not. But perhaps Fiona will want to share that with you some time," Becky said. "Come on, you can help me unpack the car. That child has every toy known to F.A.O Schwarz. Have you seen her stuffed Lion King family?"

"That's why I'm here, to help. And I'm so proud of you, Becky, for taking this on. It means a lot to all of us," I said as she and I suited up and trudged out to the Volvo.

"I like Fiona. I was glad to do it. But, Mom, how's Fiona going to get to those therapy sessions in town without her car?"

"Oh, the car will get fixed soon. Meanwhile, I'll see to the transportation. Or one of us will. It's a condition of the guardianship, and we don't want anything to go wrong. By the way, what kind of therapy sessions are these?"

"Speech. Ask Fiona."

When Fiona had tucked Laura into bed and all of the cartons of clothing and toys had been deposited at least inside the door, Fiona brewed a pot of reviving Lapsang Souchong. "I don't know what happened to my little darling." Fiona filled three thistle mugs with the steaming brew. "But she doesn't seem to want to talk right now. When she was with me before, she had just begun to speak She called me 'Fifi.' I would dearly love to know what went wrong."

"Fifi? That suits you, somehow. Not to worry, Fiona," I said. "She's yours until her mother returns to the States, and we'll work on this together."

"What are you going to do about a sitter?" practical Becky asked. "Aren't you going to miss being able to come and go freely. And you do have a part-time job at the Black Hill Branch Library, if I remember correctly."

"Deidre and I are working on a sitter swap," Fiona said. "Laura Belle and Bobby are nearly the same age, you know. I suppose it's too much to call for a Wiccan day-care center."

"Perish the thought," Becky said. "There would surely be complaints of Satanism."

"Deidre wants to send out a call for an au pair," I said. "Let's see what that brings."

"What's a '*call*,' Mom? You mean, like, work a magic spell of some kind?"

"Eh . . . it's more like a prayer, dear."

"Nonsense, Cass," Fiona said. "Tell Becky *yes*, it's spellworking, plain and simple. Is there something you'd like us to call for you, Becky dear? I owe you so much."

Becky gazed thoughtfully through the frost-laced, small-paned windows of Fiona's little cottage. "If only I knew myself what I wanted . . ." she said.

"We can handle that sort of query, too, dear." Fiona patted

Becky's hand reassuringly. "You'll want clarity to see the possibilities ahead. Wisdom to choose the right path for your personal karma. Strength to follow wherever it leads you."

Becky looked at me. Another raised eyebrow. "Have I heard something like that before?"

"Excellent motto for a Wiccan thirteen-step program," I said. "Good one, Fiona. I'm going to start following you around with a notebook."

A surprise was waiting for us at home—a demented woman. The moment we got out of Becky's car, petite Jean Deluca sprang out of her leafy green Volkswagen, which had been parked in the shadows. The pasted-on smile had become a cruel smirk as she hurled herself at me with hands held out in front of her like chipmunk claws. With great presence of mind, Becky jumped in front of me, using the briefcase she was holding as a shield to block whatever injury Jean was intending to inflict.

"Witch! Bitch!" Jean screamed, trying to dodge around the briefcase, which Becky kept shifting so adroitly that I wondered if she'd had some previous experience in using it as a defensive weapon. Perhaps some martial arts course for female attorneys?

"I know all about you, Cassandra Shipton. You and your devil-worshipping friends fancy yourselves crime-solvers, and now you're out to ruin my family. Tell me where I can find that little blond sneak so I can scratch her eyes out." Jean huffed and puffed. "The one you sent to dig up dirt on Lee. Did you think that fat tart, Millie Murphy, could keep it to herself for two minutes?"

"Maybe we should have a quiet talk about this," I suggested while I danced out of range. "For your son's sake."

In a flashing motion, Jean bent over, grabbed a handful of gravel from the driveway, and hurled it at me. I ducked most of the barrage, but the stone that got through stung my cheek.

Inside the house, Scruffy had begun barking wildly and throwing himself against the living room window. I prayed he wouldn't dive through it, which had happened once when the UPS man was delivering my PC. (The monitor case was a bit dented, but the computer worked okay.)

With a quick shift of her little body, Jean tried again to dart around Becky to get at me. Becky shoved her back against the car none too gently. "Mom," my daughter cried out, "for heaven's sake, get in the house and call nine-one-one. This woman is deranged and dangerous."

"Oh no you don't!" Jean scrambled into her car and locked all the doors, as if she fancied that we were the attackers. "Stay away from us or else I'll make you sorry," she screamed out the partially open window while she started the engine. Suddenly the Volkswagen jumped forward as if it had been shot out of a cannon. It seemed that Jean intended to run down my daughter. With a leap I didn't know I was capable of, I pushed Becky out of the way, and we both fell into the foundation plantings near the back stairs.

Jean gunned the motor and sped out of the driveway. In a moment, she had disappeared around the pines and onto the main road.

"Good grief! What was *that* all about?" Becky pulled herself and me up from the bushes, and we brushed ourselves off.

"It didn't go well, did it? I wish she'd been calm enough to discuss what's been going on. I can't imagine that she wants the boy to go right on poisoning the heirs and anyone else who gets in his way." The barking inside had now reached the level of frenzy, so without further explanation, I hurried onto the porch to unlock the kitchen door.

Scruffy zoomed out of the house like a streak of light. *Help! Help! Murder! Let me at 'em.* I'd forgotten about our new porch pet door. He bolted through it lickety-split, intent on chasing down the intruder. Luckily she was far away by now. "Whew! I didn't know he could still run that fast," I said. "He'll be limping back soon enough, poor baby. He was going crazy locked in here while we were being attacked."

"And I was going crazy *out there!*" Becky complained, falling into a kitchen chair. She examined her navy blue hose, where an inch-wide run snaked from her ankle to where it disappeared under her lawyer-lady suit. "What in the world got her so revved up? Who is that crazed character, anyway? Maybe we'd better talk about a restraining order. Or at the very least, a criminal complaint."

I examined my face in the little shell mirror beside the back door. My cheek was still smarting from the gravel pellet, but the skin was merely scratched. "Hell hath no fury like a mother defending her young,"

"So I noticed when you tackled me and threw me into the bushes. Out of harm's way, I guess. I could use a shot of something, couldn't you?"

"Joe keeps a bottle of Jim Beam in the parson's cupboard. It's that hidden cabinet in the pine paneling beside the fireplace. Or we could have a glass of wine. There's a bottle open in the refrigerator. A nice fruity white called Fat Bastard."

"Oh, you're kidding." Becky pulled herself out of the chair and opened the refrigerator door. "No, you're not." She laughed and examined the bottle's label. While she was filling wineglasses, I punched in Phillipa's number on my cell.

"Listen, Phil. No time for long explanations. Jean Deluca was here, out for blood. Millie Murphy told her about Dee's interest in the Deluca boy. Plus, I guess she researched our press clippings on the Internet."

"I can't believe it. Why would she want to confront you? It's like an admission of guilt—someone's guilt."

"Who can figure? So I want you to tell Stone everything we know *and suspect*. Maybe it's crazy. Maybe there's no evidence. But it's about time for Stone to take a cold, hard look at the kid."

"It's more than about time," Phillipa said. "He's in the living room right now watching some Chaos Theory thing on the Discovery channel. A perfect moment to shake up his orderly investigation. Is Becky staying the night, I hope? How are Fiona and the kid doing?"

"Yes, Becky's here. Fiona and Laura Belle are just fine. I've got to go now."

Becky handed me a glass. I sipped while I punched in Deidre's number. "Dee, take all possible precautions. Jean Deluca is hot on your trail, and it won't take her much time to find out where you live. She's behaving like a madwoman. Look out for a green Volkswagen."

"Shit! How'd she find out?"

"How? Your old school chum. We should have foreseen that one. If Millie would blab about Lee to you, she'd blab about you to Lee's mother. Is Will home?"

"Nope. Night shift all week."

"Go lock the doors and windows. I'll talk to you later."

"Okay, that's out of the way," I said to Becky. "I guess Fiona and Heather can wait until tomorrow. Shall I make us a sandwich?"

"Absolutely. I'm starved."

The mere mention of food seemed to make Scruffy materialize out of the night. He scratched at the bare place on the wood frame, and I opened the door. The dog was panting as if his little heart would give out at any moment. He threw himself onto his kitchen bed, tongue lolling out of his mouth, sides heaving. *Boy, am I pooped, Toots! I almost caught that green monster, though.*

"Scruffy," I said sternly. "You know you're not supposed to chase cars for any reason. Now look at you! You'd better have a long drink of water." I brought the water bowl over to where he was sprawled across the sheepskin, breathing heavily. He put his nose into the bowl, then flopped back without drinking.

"Honestly, Mom. Will you please stop fussing over that dog and tell me about the nutcase?"

I took the remains of a roasted chicken out of the refrigerator and began to cut slices off the breast. Lettuce, tomato, mayonnaise, sourdough bread.

Scruffy showed signs of reviving. *No rabbit food on mine, Toots.*

While I put together two hefty sandwiches and a dish of chopped chicken for the dog, I told Becky about the Delucas and how I had come to suspect the son, Leonardo, of the Plymouth poisonings.

"Good Lord, Mom. If only you'd leave this sort of notion to the police to investigate. I mean, why did you send Deidre, of all people, to ferret out school records? You must have known it could only get her into trouble. You'd think she'd have enough on her hands with four little ones, never mind some clandestine operation that borders on being illegal."

"Yes, you're probably right. But when sharing gossip becomes illegal, who shall escape jail? And I doubt any detective would have got the goods on sealed records and family scandals as surely as Deidre. It needed a woman's touch."

Becky's sigh of exasperation was a response I'd heard often over the years. What her life needed, I decided, was a bit more irregularity to stir her out of the maturity rut she was sinking into. Maybe I would add a pinch of spice to Fiona's promised ritual for Becky.

We ate, we finished the wine, we went to bed exhausted— Becky in the rose guest room and Scruffy in my room. He flopped on his other bed, the L.L. Bean bolster bed with the built-in pillow. I changed into a flannel nightgown, lay down, and, looking at Joe's empty pillow, sighed. *Oh, where is my wandering husband tonight?* Too tired to read the book Fiona had pressed into my hand, *Secrets of Psychic Karate*, I turned out the light and a moment later was soundly asleep.

I was awakened by a hysterically barking dog and a strong, steady pounding on the front door, the one we never use. Incredibly, it was only half-past midnight. Becky came trailing down the stairs, barefoot, wearing an oversized pink T-shirt.

She was yawning but not too sleepy to take charge and direct activities. "Don't you dare open that door, Mom. That crazy gnome-woman must have come back. Maybe she went home for a gun. And don't let Scruffy out, either. Best thing would be to close him into the bedroom while I call the police."

"Let's see who it is first," I said. "Might be one of my friends, you know."

"Pounding at the front door?"

"Stranger things have happened. I'll just peek through the bay window. Don't hit those buttons yet, please, honey."

I snapped on the outdoor light, and we all peeked through the window. Scruffy pushing under my arm, growling, and Becky's chin resting on my head, we formed a curious totem pole. On the front step, a woman with a matted wasp nest of gray hair was pounding on the door with a sturdy cane. Apparently she'd driven up in the black pickup truck now parked behind Becky's Volvo. "Open up! Open up! I will talk with you, *strega* woman."

"Don't do it, Mom."

Let me out . . . let me out. My teeth are sharp and my jaws are strong. Scruffy jumped at the front door, snarling.

"Okay," I agreed, and took hold of Scruffy's collar. I hauled him into the bedroom and shut the door. Fortunately, I'm inured to canine obscenities.

"I believe that's Lee Deluca's grandmother. Let's hear what she has to say. Maybe she wants to give the boy up before he kills any more innocent people."

Becky shook her head as if in disbelief. She put the cell phone she was carrying on the antique sea chest that serves as my coffee table and picked up my grandma's black walnut walking stick. The door groaned a little, but I got it open. "Yes? Would you like to come in?"

"I am not stepping a foot inside your cursed house. I'm here to demand that you leave alone my grandson and my daughter-in-law, who is *pazzo*. She screams at me that it is you and some friend of yours who are trying to keep Leonardo out of college by false accusations, maybe even force him to stay in a juvenile detention place. If you don't stop attacking our family, I will stick a knife in your heart." She tapped her own heart and her old black leather handbag, where I imagined she kept the family stiletto sharpened and ready for the occasional vendetta.

"Okay. *Calma, calma*." A useful Italian phrase I'd learned from Lucrezia, who'd been Heather's interim housekeeper and was now in witness protection. "I understand your concern. I'm a mother myself."

"*Maledetta la Madonna!*" the old woman cried, and flicked her finger against her teeth in a gesture that needed no translation.

But I went right on, hearing myself talking coolly as if I were someone else. "Your grandson has often been in trouble, isn't that so? The family wants to protect him. That's perfectly natural. But if the boy is doing something wrong now—terribly wrong—you'll want to save him from getting in any deeper. And the only way you can do that is to stop him from poisoning anyone else."

Becky was right behind me. "Mom, I'd feel a lot easier if you'd let me call the police. This isn't right."

The old lady hawked and spit on my front step. "I have warned you. Now it's your grave." And she stomped off. It was then that I noticed she was wearing bright green Wellington boots.

"The idea was that it would be too tiring for me to drive all the way back to Boston tonight when I could spend a restful night at Mom's and get a fresh start in the morning," Becky said with a moan. "How will I be able to sleep now? I'll be waiting for the third mystical sister to show up with the final curse on you and your firstborn."

I was fixing us a cup of cocoa and thinking about those boots. *Probably he borrowed them from Granny. After all, how many boys own gardening boots? He's small for his age, so they probably fit well enough. And what about those plants I saw in my vision? Is that where Lee stashed the hemlock?*

"Mom," Becky said. "Have you heard a word I've been saying?"

"Of course I heard you, honey. And I'm really sorry that these little upsets had to happen tonight of all nights. Do you want to have your cocoa in the living room or take it upstairs with you?"

"Oh, it's all right. But I do worry about you. Is this what your life is like? I thought you'd be different after you got married. Settled, you know." She gave me a kiss on the cheek, then backed away, the better to see my face. "I didn't realize that you actually got hit. You'd better put an icebag or something on that bruise—it's right under your eye. Want me to take a photo while it's fresh? In case you decide to make that complaint."

"No, thanks. I don't want to make matters any more complicated than they are."

"You have a point there." She picked up the mug of cocoa. "But, frankly, I'll feel better when Joe gets home to look out for you."

"Please keep in mind that I took care of myself for many years, my dear, and that grown-up women do not need keepers. But for your information, Greenpeace is wrapping up the soyameal thing in Greece, and Joe's managed to stay out of jail. He's even resisted the urge to visit his mother. The last time he called, he said he'll be able to get home soon."

"I'm so relieved. Let him deal with the crazies, I say. Thanks for the cocoa. I'll take mine upstairs. See you in the morning, then."

When I finally got into bed myself, a freezer cold pack held against my face, Scruffy was barely speaking to me. Instead, he grumped and muttered, tossed and turned. *No one truly appreciates the fierce dedication and keen intuition of dogs.* Finally, he stalked out to the kitchen for a long drink of water. I took up Fiona's book again. Under the present circumstances, maybe this was one I ought to read. By the second page, just as the author was averring that psychic force always can be generated by profound meditation, I literally passed out with the book on my chest. It had seemed like too much trouble to reach over and shut off the light.

I woke in terror.

Someone had switched off the light and was standing beside the bed!

Much as I wanted to scream my head off, no sound would come out of my mouth but a pathetic squeak. How I wished I had a neat pistol like Fiona's! What use was Grandma's rifle hanging over the living room mantel? The only weapon I had to hand was the book. I whipped it up into the air, ready to smack the intruder on the head. But something made me hesitate a moment.

Why had Scruffy trotted amiably into the bedroom to greet the figure looming over me?

"Oh, for Goddess's sake, Joe! You gave me such a start. Why didn't you call?"

He switched the light back on. "Darling, I did call when I grabbed that last-minute cancellation in Ravenna. Then when I got to Boston, it was three in the morning—why call just to wake you up? So I just jumped in my rental and tore on down here. But didn't you check your messages when you came home?"

"I never even went in my office to look. Long story, and it can wait until later." Gazing into those ardent blue eyes, I lost my train of thought entirely and simply held out my arms. His embrace surrounded me with warmth, his scent filled my senses, and I was lost. A kiss like that makes me forget my own name.

"*Jesu Cristos*, sweetheart—what happened to your face?"

"I ran into a cabinet," I murmured. No point in ruining the mood of the moment with tales of the mad Deluca women. I could handle those two.

Scruffy stalked out of the bedroom. *Too much thumping around in here. I'm dog-tried from chasing off that green monster, and I need my sleep.*

After the dog left, Joe closed the door and shut off the light again. I heard him slipping out of his clothes and tossing them on the chair. Somehow, although I'd had practically no sleep at all, I wasn't the least bit tired.

When his naked body slid under the covers next to mine, it was like a flash of sweet fire searing my flesh everywhere we touched—which was everywhere we could. Lovemaking is another entrance to that space between the worlds, the magic place.

Chapter Twenty-Five

If I'd gone into my office that night to check the answering machine and e-mails, I'd have discovered that my computer had been invaded by a merciless virus lurking in one of those e-mails. But such a catastrophe surely would have cast a pall on that romantic reunion with Joe.

The next morning was soon enough! As I began to realize the full scope of the calamity, I felt much more sympathy for Phillipa's similar losses. Hadn't I been a bit too cavalier about her predicament? After all, I'd reasoned, she had a hard copy of the cookbook manuscript her virus had deep-sixed, and how arduous could it be to rewrite the restaurant reviews?

"What a disaster!" I wailed as I tried to access missing or blocked files. There was no one except Scruffy to hear my tirades, and he disappeared upstairs the moment I threw the first instruction manual across the room. Becky had already driven back to Boston, and Joe was making an emergency trip to Home Warehouse for remedial electrical equipment. The new track lighting in the cellar kept blowing fuses.

A flock of customers had ordered my herbal products and paid by credit card, and now I wouldn't even know who, what, or where. "And it's January!" I moaned. January is the month when everyone wants to shake off the winter blahs and make a fresh start. It was a big time of year for rejuvenation teas, sensual message oils, and wishcraft incense. "Oh, Sweet Isis, where is Freddie when I need her?"

The monitor kept flashing weird error messages. *bad command or file name . . . invalid file specification . . . fatal application error . . . illegal entry, you are being closed down . . . permanent loss of data . . . file is locked . . . incompatible file format . . . invalid drive/directory . . . abort, retry, fail?* Phrases calculated to chill the heart of any novice in electronic communication.

I tried to e-mail Freddie or Adam, but my e-mail service was completely clogged with hundreds of incoming messages from "*mystery chef*" with the subject line, "your goose is cooked."

For what seemed like hours, I was clenched like a pretzel over the computer. Finally, with great effort, I yanked myself away. Either I could shoot myself with Grandma's rifle and end this misery or go for a head-clearing walk outdoors, trying to achieve detachment and perspective. All right, I am not the stuff of which Zen masters are made, but I could try.

As I looked out my office window, the deceptively warm-looking morning sunlight was in full glory, shimmering on the waves like sequined velvet. Which reminded me of my luxurious green hooded cloak, a gift from Joe. I wrapped myself up in all its good karma, like the blessing of love. Taking Grandma's walking stick in hand, I opened the back door to the glacial chill of an east wind off the Atlantic.

In an instant Scruffy bounded down the stairs from his retreat. *Hey, Toots! Wait for me! Wait for me! I ought to be leading the way and scouting for danger.*

"All right, you can come with me, but there will be no squirrel detours today." Scruffy's leash always hung on the hook by the back door; I hooked it to his collar. "And don't go down those stairs too fast. They may be icy."

I found the stairs already sprinkled with a pet-friendly melting agent by my thoughtful and energetic husband. Just thinking of

Joe brought a throb of pleasure as I remembered our passionate embraces of the night before. What drug is greater than the fulfillment of love and the sweet oblivion afterward? A flush traveled through my body. I wondered if it was a hot flash or plain, old sexual heat.

Come on, come on faster. Let's get a move on. Gotta see what's happening in the woods. Scruffy sniffed the air eagerly.

Preoccupied with libidinous thoughts while trying to manage a long cloak and a leashed dog without falling on my head, I hardly noticed the slight figure standing between the pines up near the road. It was more like the sudden consciousness of a malevolent vibration somewhere in my environment. The boy must have stepped into our line of vision just at that instant, because Scruffy reacted with a mighty tug at the leash, nearly taking me off my feet.

Changeling! Leonardo Deluca was standing between the pines. As I moved closer, the dog thrusting ahead and barking, I saw that the boy was smiling at me, as cold as the January sunshine that glistened through the icy trees. I was aware of a piercing ray catching me in the eyes. Intense light at that particular angle has a curious effect on me. It bounces me out of time and place. *This is not the moment to lose myself in a trance*, was my last thought before I fell down right on my knees on the frozen leaves covering the ground.

No longer was I crouched in my own front yard. Instead, I found myself looking down an earthen track between darkly massed trees. At the end of that slope, water rippled in the sunshine. Several boats were moored at that shore, most of them half-filled with frozen water. They looked like wooden canoes, with rough, hand-hewn surfaces. A car came over the ridge of the hill. The motor revved. The car headed straight for the water. It was a green Volkswagen. I couldn't see the driver or the passengers, but I could hear their screams. The scene faded slowly; the sparkling water was the last thing to dissolve, like the smile of the Cheshire Cat.

Scruffy must have done his best. When I came out of the vision, he was whining mournfully in my ear, nuzzling me as he would have done to a wounded canine companion. *Hey, Toots! What's the matter with you? You've got me really worried now. Want to lean on me a while? I'm a strong, tough Shepherd de Brie. My ancestors pulled milk carts to market, you know.*

"Yeah, yeah!" I said. "Just give me a minute to recover my wits. I'll be up in no time."

Nauseous and disoriented, I did lean on Scruffy to stand on my feet again. I may even have pulled on his fur, but he stood staunch as a champion. Then I remembered the peculiar presence of Lee Deluca. Gone now. Leaving me with a vivid impression, a shimmer of evil intention. Why had he come? Perhaps to let me know that my problems were caused by him and not a routine computer malfunction. Yes, he would want to take credit. And now what was he up to? What was the meaning of my vision? Where was that scene happening or due to happen?

Joe drove in the driveway. His abrupt stop splattered the driveway's gravel. Jumping out of his Rent-a-Wreck, he ran to where I was still leaning on Scruffy. "What's going on here, sweetheart? You look dazed, and you're leaning on the dog. Did you fall?" His sea-muscled arms went around me, holding me close and safe. It was good to feel sheltered by a man, but I knew it was a lovely illusion. So many dangers that must be faced alone.

That furry-faced person is pushing me out of the way now. No respect for the loyal protector. You'd better tell him how I saved you again.

"It was more like a swoon," I explained to Joe. "The sun was in my eyes, and it brought on a vision. The next thing I knew, I was on my knees and Scruffy was trying to revive me." I reached down to pat Scruffy, whose head was wedged between the two of us. "What a good dog you are!"

"Sunlight does that? Maybe you should start wearing dark glasses," Joe suggested as he helped me back up the stairs and into the house. The moment I stepped foot in the kitchen, my PC woes washed back over me in a tide of misery. I groaned, and

Joe hastened to settle me comfortably in the kitchen rocker, then set about making a fresh pot of coffee. Scruffy sat beside me with his head resting on my knee.

Don't you worry, Toots. I'm here. A dog's reminder that life's necessities are truly few. I was okay, and I had friends.

"The most terrible thing has happened to my computer." I tried not to wail. "Some hacker got into it and erased all the files—my accounts, my records, my current orders—the works! Even my e-mail is clogged with hundreds of messages from someone calling himself the 'mystery chef.' Oh, Joe, I think it's that Deluca boy. He knows I'm onto him. When I came out of the house with Scruff, the boy was just standing up there by the main road, grinning at me. If I believed in the devil, I'd call him the devil's child."

"Wait a minute . . . let me get this straight. This weird kid ruined your computer program while standing outside your house?" Joe took our coffee mugs out of the strainer and put them onto the kitchen table.

"No, I mean he must have done his dirty work on the computer last night, then turned up this morning to let me know it was him. I could swear he was gloating."

"That's one sick kid," Joe said. "I'd like to get my hands on him."

"He is that," I said. "But not *your* hands, my dear. Let's be legal here. Stone's hands will do fine."

"Since when did you fret about legalities?" The coffee sputtered to a finish, and Joe filled our cups. He handed me the one that said *The Sybil Is In* and took *Have You Hugged a Whale Today?* for himself. They were, of course, gifts from Phillipa.

"The fact that this is a child makes me very nervous," I confessed.

"What makes me nervous is that this child is a sociopath," Joe said.

He hadn't asked me about my vision. Joe was always a bit cautious about questioning my clairvoyant episodes, as if they were some ecstatic religious experience I might prefer to keep private. I'd learned to tell him anyway, for the sake of whatever insights he might add. Also, I need to put the details of an episode into words before they fade like a dream. "Speaking of sociopaths . . ." I began, and described the locale, the Deluca car poised at the top of the incline, the screaming inside.

"Where do you suppose you were?" Joe asked.

"That's what I'm trying to figure out. It's nowhere I recognize. It might be Myles Standish Forest. That place is so huge, there are probably hundreds of vistas I've never seen."

"And, more to the point, who was in the car?"

"That's what scares me most," I said. "The voices were high-pitched, young." Suddenly I had a mind's eye glimpse of Lee dressed as the Pied Piper, playing a merry tune on a recorder and leading children into the yawning mouth of a Stygian cave.

Looking out my kitchen window, I saw Patty's black Buick Regal had pulled into my driveway. It was just after three. She was carrying her knitting bag as well as her handbag, so she probably planned to stay for a chat. Good. A distraction would be welcome.

At a loss to know how to occupy myself without herbal orders to fill, and distraught over the customers I was losing during the current computer crisis, I was brewing a pot of Wisewoman Tea, my special blend. Its strong, spicy aroma might soothe my wounded spirit. If I weren't a highly evolved Wiccan on the white path, I'd really enjoy hexing this hacker!

Patty, however, was in worse shape than I. "You have to help me," she said as soon as she got in the door. She dropped her bags and clutched both my hands. Her little heart-shaped face was looking anxious and vulnerable.

"Of course I will, Patty, if I can. Sit down here and tell me all about it." I disengaged myself gently and took down another cup and saucer from the shelf.

"Oh dear. What's that banging under the floor?" She looked about fearfully.

Tempted though I was to tell her that Beelzebub was stirring in his subterranean chamber, I said, "It's only Joe. He's rewiring my workroom. In the cellar."

"Oh, he's back. That explains it, then," she said. I poured the tea and waited. "I never thought I would, but I have really grown very fond of Loki." She took a real handkerchief—lace-edged— out of her handbag and wiped her eyes. "The poor little thing!"

"Oh, Great Goddess. Is he all right? Did something happen to Buster—I mean, Loki?"

"Close call, I fear. Heather Devlin will be so cross with me. But you know that Loki is an independent fellow, and he was moping so at the window, watching the birdies in the feeder, I decided he needed a breath of fresh air. I'd been talking to this pastor's wife from Britain, and she said the animal-rescue people in England wouldn't allow her to adopt a cat unless she agreed to give the animal access to the outdoors so that he wouldn't get depressed. Can you imagine? A completely different point of view from cat people here. Well, that set me to thinking."

Patty took out her knitting, obviously an aid to deep thought. It seemed to be a heavy moss green chest covering of some sort, like a bulletproof vest. I wondered if it was a present for Wyn. A single lock of brown hair fell over her broad forehead as she studied her work and picked up the stitch. I had faith Patty would eventually get to the point. I waited, semi-patiently.

"Now I admit that I may be carrying this pendulum thing too far, but I have been dowsing Loki's food as well as our own. I don't know if I'm doing it right, but so far, so good. 'Must you bless the cat's food, too?' Wyn asked me, but I just said, 'Yes, animals have souls, too.' Then, this morning, quite early, I allowed Loki to go out. He'd been scratching at the windows in a positive fever to get at something, and I thought, well, what's the harm? Better to let the cat do his yowling outdoors than to have Wyn wake up and have a bird. So to speak. Loki is still a bit of a sore subject. And I'm forbidden to mention Saint Francis's rapport with animals again."

"Sometimes women go right ahead and do the things they're forbidden to do," I said.

"Oh, do they, dear?" Patty's hazel eyes looked at me earnestly as if this was an insight that had never occurred to her. "Well, there's so much divorce these days, isn't there?"

Touché, Patty.

"That was about five. I got up myself at seven and went downstairs to make breakfast. The temperature was close to freezing, and I began to worry about Loki. Perhaps I shouldn't have let him out after all. I looked out and couldn't see the cat on the porch or anywhere nearby. So I got the coffee going, put on my coat and boots, and went out to call the cat. Oh, I feel so guilty, Cass."

"Are you ever going to tell me what happened?"

"That's what I am doing, dear. I found the poor little thing under the porch, drooling and heaving. Beside him was the remains of some raw beef burger on a piece of waxed paper. It looked as if Loki had dragged the thing in there. A private treat. Now, you know Loki is not a great traveler."

"I certainly do. You should have called me, Patty. Either Joe or I would have helped you with Loki. Where did you take him?"

"To the Wee Angels Animal Hospital, of course. Dr. Devlin is such as dear man. I took that burger with me, too. While I was waiting for news of Loki, I dowsed it. Well!"

"Your cross went a bit erratic, did it?"

"Good heavens, yes! A whirling dervish. So I gave the burger to Dr. Devlin to have tested."

"Oh, Patty, I'm so sorry. What did you find out? And how's Loki?"

Patty sobbed into the moss green thing. Then she blew her nose in the lace-edged hanky. "Heather Devlin came rushing in when she heard I was there with Loki. She insisted on taking that sorry burger meat to the laboratory herself, went speeding off in her Mercedes. An hour later she was back. Dr. Devlin said, 'How did you do that? I never get results so fast.' She said, 'Never mind that, the burger was laced with nicotine.' Then he tells me Loki is terribly sick, and he can't guarantee his recovery."

"Loki is a tough old guy, a real survivor." As I put a consoling arm around Patty's shoulders, a scary thought occurred to me. "Patty, have you been home since you took your cat to the hospital? Have you dowsed the food in your refrigerator?"

Patty's hand went to her mouth in an expression of horror. "No, I stayed at the hospital for a while, then I went to tell Heather what happened, but I didn't mention that Loki was *outdoors* when he got sick. She insisted I stay for lunch, although I really wasn't a bit hungry. Afterwards, I came here. You see, I was so afraid that Wyn would look, you know, pleased to be rid of Loki, that I . . . well . . . Lord, I'd better call and warn him not to eat anything."

"Patty, it's three-thirty. By now he's probably eaten breakfast *and* lunch." Even as I spoke, I was punching in Patty's number on my cell. It rang, and I handed it to her.

"Oh, Wyn, Wyn . . . are you all right? Yes, of course I'm coming home. I've been with Loki at the vet."

There was a pause, during which a fat tear ran down Patty's cheek.

"No, dear, I wouldn't dream of giving up the cat. I love Loki. You're all right, then?"

Another pause. "What did you have for lunch, dear? Good. That was okay, then. Yes, all right, I'll be home directly." She punched END and handed me the phone.

"He said he decided not to have a hamburger, he's watching his cholesterol. So he had two doughnuts and a hunk of cheese instead."

"I wonder about that hamburger," I said.

Patty looked at me with an odd expression. "When I left home this morning," she said, "there was no hamburger in the refrigerator."

"Uh oh. I don't suppose you took my advice about keeping your doors locked?"

"It seems so unchristian."

"Okay, Patty . . . I'm going home with you now. We'll call Stone. I'm sure he'll want us to pack up that meat for him to have tested. I have an idea that this was another attempt on Wyn's life, with a more reliable poison. I hate to say this, but actually it's a good thing for you that the poisoner couldn't resist trying it out on the cat. I don't suppose nicotine is very hard to obtain. It's in nicotine patches and things like that. He may have even grown a tobacco plant. Anything he needed to know could be found on the Internet. Pack up your knitting, and let's go."

"Who? Who are you talking about, Cass?"

"Lydia Craig's grandnephew, Lee Deluca."

"You mean, a young person did this?"

"Yes, that's what I've *seen*, and by now Stone Stern knows all about my suspicions."

"You mean 'seen' as in a vision, Cass?"

"Yes, I guess so."

"Oh, capital!" Patty enthused. A wan smile lit up her face for the first time that afternoon.

It turned out that Lee Deluca had slipped up for the first time in using ground beef. He'd bought it at Angelo's, and the checkout clerk, a young man who'd also gone out for track, remembered the small, fast sprinter from Assumption buying ground beef. That was the good news. The bad news was that, while Patty and I were having tea, Lee had emptied his mother's cash register and disappeared. By the time Stone was ready to question the boy, Jean Deluca was in her hysterical mode, filing a missing-persons report and threatening to sue everyone in the county of Plymouth who was hounding and harassing her son.

As Phillipa related the scene to us, Stone had talked to Jean very gently and got nothing but verbal abuse. The detective then turned to Arthur Deluca, who'd accompanied his distraught wife to the police station. Stone explained that nicotine poison had been found in the ground beef that the cat had consumed and that more poisoned meat had been waiting for the Peacedales in their refrigerator. Jean Deluca screamed that there was no connection between this so-called poison and her son, and they couldn't prove differently in a thousand years. The ground beef her son had bought at Angelo's had been purchased at her request, and the family had eaten it for their dinner. Stone had been going to ask permission to have a look at the plants in Arthur Deluca's mother's basement, but thought better of it right then. It was of prime importance not to tip off Jean as to where evidence against her son might be found.

Nor was that the end of the bad news. Although Stone was able to lift Lee's fingerprints from his locker at Assumption, they did not match any found in the parsonage kitchen. When the detective tried to obtain a warrant to search Lee's grandmother's house, Judge Paradise could not be convinced by the evidence of past misdemeanors (the records of which were sealed) and a tenuous motive that the young person who attended Assumption with her own son, Ted, could be responsible for the series of poisonings that had been plaguing Plymouth. And Judge Lax was reluctant to search an innocent old lady's home for nebulous evidence against her grandson. If the press got hold of the story, the judicial branch might be accused of insensitivity toward senior citizens. Now that the boy was missing, his mother was screaming blue murder that someone ought to pay for falsely accusing her child and possibly causing him to harm himself.

"Stone is tearing out his hair," Phillipa said. "I would never urge you to do anything illegal, you know that, but if you gals *could*, for instance, stumble across a more convincing piece of evidence, something to persuade those candy-ass judges to sign a warrant . . . Well, I'll say no more. Besides, the oven bell just rang, and I've got to take out the madeleines."

"Madeleines?"

"This happens every time I read Proust. I even bought the damn pans. Let me know what you come up with . . . preferably after you've done it. Bye!"

I pondered this challenge, and how my good friend Phillipa was dumping the quest for evidence on me while she covered herself with a cloak of deniability. I would sooner storm a Medici castle than break into Bianca Deluca's immaculate ranch house on Summer Street. I needed to concoct a ruse. I needed a crafty think tank. I needed confederates.

I called Deidre and Heather.

We decided this was no time to involve Fiona, who only had temporary custody of the beloved grandniece. We would go it alone, without our mistress of the invisible glamour and trigger-happy finder.

But how?

Chapter Twenty-Six

"**P**erhaps it would be better *not* to break into the old lady's house," Deidre said, sticking a needle firmly into the Bettikins doll she was sewing together. Not yet attired in peasant dress and apron, the doll appeared to have actual breasts and a V-shaped cleft between her thighs. *Inverted chevron, symbol of the Goddess*.

We'd met at Heather's. The day being too raw and miserable to enjoy the conservatory (or "dog playroom," which it really was) we were lounging in the library, my favorite room in the Morgan mansion. On one wall shelves were stocked with leather-bound volumes of nineteenth-century travels and adventures that had belonged to Heather's great-great-grandfather, the redoubtable Captain Morgan. On other walls were Heather's collection of arcane and recent volumes about candle-making, candle-burning spells, and the ways of animals, plus Dick's holistic veterinary texts. The sweet little fireplace was surrounded by tile portraits of historic naval leaders. A small, brisk fire sparked cheerily, and the decanter of excellent port on the library table, liberally poured by our hostess into crystal glasses, was adding to our bonhomie.

"No one said 'break in,' Dee." Heather curled herself up in a dark leather chair and sipped her port, which was the same ruby shade as her tunic and tights. "We need someone to have a look at Bianca Deluca's house *legitimately*. I don't suppose she ever orders a pizza delivery?"

"With a name like Deluca, who needs Domino's," I said. "I bet she hurls her own pizza dough into the air to create perfect circles that fall neatly into their pans."

"Okay, what about an Avon lady, then, or a Fuller Brush person?"

I chuckled. "Bianca wears the traditional black dress and scowl of the Mediterranean matron, so, naturally, no makeup, and her hair in a gray tangle, like a hank of yarn or a hornet's nest. Her back has that matriarchal hunch. Come to think of it, she's reminiscent of the witch in 'Rapunzel.'"

"Oh, wash out your mouth with soap," Deidre said. "I resent all those 'ugly old witch' stories and would personally like to rewrite them to feature dirty old men instead. Makes a lot more sense for a guy to lock up the nubile maiden in a tower, I'd say. Want me to drop in with a basket full of senior-citizen gifts— Geritol, Metamucil, Viagra, and what-you-will—from the Chamber of Commerce?"

"Do they really do that?" I asked. "How nice."

"Ha!" Deidre said. "Don't hold your breath. Although I must say you gals are almost at the right age to collect your baskets."

"Dee, you can't go near Bianca Deluca," I said. "When she banged on my front door in the middle of the night, she was mumbling about a blond bitch investigating her grandson—and she meant you, honey."

"What about me?" Heather asked. "I could get away with it, I think. Some historical pretext. I do belong to the Plimouth Historical Society, you know."

"Of course," I murmured. "And everything else. I bet you're even an Odd Fellow."

Heather ignored me and continued. "I could say I was collecting oral history from Plymouth seniors. I bet old Bianca has a tale to tell. And while I'm in there, I'll get her to show me the cellar where Lee has his computer. I guess I probably couldn't walk out with *that*, but I could take a leaf off one of the potted plants you believe are down there."

"Hey, that just might fly," Deidre said.

"Or, here's another idea." I found that I didn't want to be left out of the fun investigative work. "You have a chat with Bianca about her history, and while she's in the kitchen making espresso or something, you surreptitiously unlock the outside door that leads into the cellar. Then I duck in while you two are upstairs. I'll have a look at those plants myself. Or anything else of interest."

"And that's not a break-in?" Deidre tossed the Bettikins back into her workbasket and took out a Bobbikins, the Brownie Shoemaker. She held it in the air and gazed at it reflectively, as if considering alterations.

"Good Goddess," I said. "I hardly believe my eyes. Isn't that male doll anatomically correct? Haven't you been receiving letters from irate parents?"

"The subscribers to the Deidre's Faeryland catalog are a fairly broad-minded bunch, but it's true that not all the Puritans are in Plymouth. You'd think they'd be more upset by eunuch dolls, wouldn't you?" Deidre's busy little fingers stitched quickly and efficiently while she talked. She was wearing several needles threaded with bright yarns, woven through her Irish sweater like a row of medals. She grinned impishly. "Money back if not satisfied, my dear. If the parents can yank my dolls out of the arms of the kids who got them. But never mind *that*, hasn't your hacker already researched our circle's past crime-solving endeavors on the Internet? Is there a chance that Bianca will recognize Heather's name?"

"I think I was still Heather Morgan then. The woman who calls on bellicose Bianca will be Mrs. Devlin. Listen, Cass, if you want, I'll try it your way—white-light myself and unlock that cellar door. But be warned that if you get caught, I'm going to say I've never seen you before in my life. Because I'd like to get out of there without having a stiletto stuck between my ribs."

"Fair-weather friend," I said. "By the way, how are those art classes going with Deluca?"

Heather raised her eyebrows and shrugged her shoulders. "I've learned nothing except how to paint a sand dune at all times of the day and in all seasons. Arthur Deluca seems to know a lot more about mixing shades of gray or beige than he does about what's going on in his own family. Definitely out of the loop. And anyway, I've been expelled."

"Expelled! Really? You?" Deidre grinned. "The Vassar valedictorian?"

"Hell hath no fury like the mother of a defamed son."

"At least Lee hasn't crashed your computer yet," I said. "And that reminds me, before I leave here today, may I use your e-mail to write Adam and Freddie about the sad demise of my system? They may be trying to contact me and can't get by the '*mystery chef.*' In fact, I guess I'd better write to Becky and Cathy as well."

Which I did. Brief but brave notes to multiple recipients. Subject line: "*Mother is out of order.*"

When Heather called Bianca Deluca to make the appointment, there really was an ongoing oral history project she could cite—"Plymouth Old-Timers in Their Own Words"—although it tended to seek its material from Yankee old-timers rather than from the Italian population. I could just imagine the patrician tones in which Heather introduced herself as "Mrs. Richard Devlin of the Plimouth Historical Society."

Distraught over her grandson's disappearance though she might have been, Bianca agreed to allow Heather an hour or so in which to explain the importance of the "In Their Own Words" project, and jot down a few preliminary facts about the woman's life history.

"Not very much time to get the house tour and unlock the cellar door. I'll have to play it by ear. Then, if I do succeed, you'll have to work fast," Heather warned me. "Friday. Three P.M. Be out back where you can see the cellar windows. I'll wave or something. Watch yourself, now. All we *don't* need is your getting caught at this."

What happened on Friday came in two versions, mine and the story I heard later from Heather.

Between the backyard of Bianca Deluca's house on Summer Street and the backyard of her neighbor's house on Billington Street were several scraggly pines and an overgrown privet hedge (another possible source of Lee's privet berry poison?) By two-thirty, I was at my post, lurking under the cover of the evergreen branches, hoping not to be spotted by either resident. I'd planned to synchronize with Heather, but it didn't seem like a good idea to be carrying a cell phone while sneaking through someone else's house. I'd have to keep it turned off, so what good would that be?

It was a raw, wet day, with an off-and-on icy drizzle that threatened to become snow by nightfall—which in January would be only a couple of hours later. I was wearing Joe's navy wool pea coat because my new Rugged Ridge parka was purple—a dark shade but still eye-catching in winter. The parka would have been much warmer. I was thoroughly chilled, peering through the freezing drips and drops.

Finally, at a quarter past three, I thought I saw a hand waving from the cellar-level window. I skulked around the edges of the backyard in the afternoon shadows until I reached the cellar door.

Cautiously, I turned the knob. The door opened. I would congratulate Heather on a job well done, I thought, as I stepped into the room. It was very like the room I had envisioned—not so much a cellar as a lower-level workroom, finished in light oak paneling with a tile floor. A bank of sophisticated computer equipment took up the wall near the stairs, and tall plants were arranged on a old table under the two windows near the door overlooking the backyard. In my vision, however, I hadn't seen the sagging, overstuffed sofa against the wall at one end of the room or the laundry area at the other end—washer, dryer with a heaping clothes basket perched on top, and an ironing board set up for use. Nor had I seen the plywood door that probably led to the real cellar stuff.

It was just after I'd taken in this *mise-en-scéne* that I heard an ominous sound. The door at the top of the stairs opened. I glimpsed heavy shoes, thick cotton stockings, and the black hem of Bianca Deluca's dress. It was the work of one desperate moment for me to open the plywood door, leap through, and shut it with a click I hoped would not be heard over the woman's footsteps. I found myself in a place dark as a cave, but I could make out the shape of a furnace and an oil drum. Crouched behind the oil drum, where a number of unsavory webs and bugs made for a creepy, crawly cubbyhole, I thought, *Where the hell is Heather?*

From my miserable hiding place I heard Bianca humming something Puccini-ish. "O Mio Babbino Caro," I thought. After a while I heard the slap of the iron hitting the ironing board. Again and again and again and again. If that basket I'd seen was filled with ironing, I would be here for some time. And I began to itch mightily down the back of my turtleneck sweater. Between smacks of the iron, Bianca continued to hum *Puccini's Greatest Hits*.

Had Heather come and gone already?

It was an eternity later, or maybe a half hour, when I heard the doorbell ring upstairs—a booming sound, reminiscent of Big Ben at noon. Bianca stopped ironing and clumped up the stairs, speaking loudly in Italian, and from the tone, I guessed she was swearing at this interruption. Possibly she'd just got herself into the swing of ironing and regretted being torn away from her task. *Don't tell me that's Heather just showing up now.* I glanced at my watch. Four P.M. *Oh, thanks a lot, good buddy.*

Unclenching my body after crouching for ages behind the oil drum was not an easy task, but now I was really anxious to get out of there. Slowly, I opened the door to the workroom/laundry.

I would settle for a leaf of each of those plants. I tiptoed across the tile . . . softly . . . softly.

Then I heard Heather's voice. She was caroling on about what a lovely home Bianca had and was it okay if she just looked around. Bianca said, "I go with you. This is only the basement downstairs. You want to see the basement, too?"

I shuddered to hear Heather's clarion, clear voice insisting that she wanted to see every corner of "this charming home." There wasn't time to reach the plywood door at the other end of the room. Looking around frantically, I saw nowhere else to hide except behind the sofa, although I'd have to shove it slightly away from the wall. Maybe Bianca wouldn't notice that the sofa had moved a foot into the room. I wedged myself in back of the sofa with my cheek on the floor and my rump in the air, the better to see the feet of whoever was in the room.

Heather's faux-alligator boots stepped merrily across the tiles toward the plant table and the outside door. Older and slower, Bianca was still laboring down the stairs.

"Psssst," I hissed. "Get her out of here."

"Oh, Sweet Isis," Heather murmured, then, in loud tones suitable for the elderly, "How very special this is! And I see you have quite a computer setup here. What a commanding view of your backyard, too! Must be lovely in the summer. Now let's press on to the kitchen. I know you don't want to dilly-dally."

The boots turned swiftly and headed back toward the cellar stairs.

"Something wrong with that couch," Bianca said. "Out of place."

"It looks good that way. So modern not to have everything plunk against the wall," Heather said.

"Move it back for me, missus, will you? My back, from ironing, you know."

"Oh, of course, Mrs. Deluca. I'd be glad to help." Heather took hold of the couch and shoved it into my ribs. My rump fell to the floor as the couch plastered me against the oak wall. Its feet scraped against my outstretched hands, my waist, and my toes. I expected my flesh would be permanently indented by the grooves in that paneling.

"A place for everything, and everything in its place, I agree. And as fast as possible," my untrustworthy friend was saying loudly.

"I'll never play the piano again," I whispered.

"Did you hear something?" Bianca asked uncertainly. "Wall groaning?"

"Oh, you know how old houses are. I expect it's just settling a bit," Heather said. "Well, now, shall we go upstairs and have a look at your elegant living room?"

"This house is new, missus." Bianca's heavy shoes were headed my way but stopped when, I imagined, Heather took her arm and piloted her back up the stairs, continuing to make lively conversation on the wonders of Bianca's split-level ranch.

I almost didn't want to get up and feel how bruised I'd been by Heather's crushing sofa maneuver. Still, the thought that Bianca might come back to see why her wall was making pained noises gave me sufficient energy to get myself together. But I'd be damned if I'd leave without examining those plants.

Ficus lyrata, Dracaena, Dieffenbachia, Maranta, and BINGO! I pulled a plastic baggie from my pocket—every crime-scene investigator's basic equipment—and nipped off a branch of the hemlock without actually touching it. I tossed one last, longing glance at the computer—wouldn't it be fun simply to smash the hard drive a few times with Bianca's iron! But, in a major triumph of good sense and maturity, I gave up thoughts of revenge and tiptoed out the cellar door. By now, it was dark enough to sprint across to Billington Street and into my Jeep.

I looked forward to having a few crisp words with Heather! But first things first. I drove right to Phillipa's house, told her about my misadventures, and left the sprig of hemlock for Stone. "Keep it in strict quarantine," I instructed. "Don't even touch it."

"You mean, then, that I shouldn't chop this up into tonight's mesclun?"

"Don't even joke."

"Okay, all joking aside, what do I tell Stone?"

"Tell him Heather went to see Bianca on an absolutely legitimate excuse—the Plymouth Old-Timers oral history project—and just happened to notice the hemlock plant."

"And just happened to have a plastic bag open as a branch of it fell off?"

"Yeah, that's good. You'll manage. The main thing is that Stone now has a perfectly good piece of evidence to demand a search warrant."

"I don't know if he'll see it that way—and I know he won't believe the story you've concocted. But I'll try," Phillipa said. "Want a cup of cappuccino? You're looking a tad fatigued."

"No thanks. You're observing the stresses and strains of being a psychic P.I. I'm going home to put wintergreen liniment on my bruises. Do you suppose Joe will believe that I ran into a sofa?"

On the way home I called Heather on my cell. "I hope you've got a damned good excuse," I said. "The cellar door was unlocked, so naturally I thought you were already in the house and keeping the old lady busy upstairs. *But you hadn't even got there yet!*"

"*You* were supposed to wait until I arrived. We had a little accident here, and I was delayed. Ishmael got out of the house, and we needed to lure him back. It took ages, because despite his partially clipped wings, the little bugger got himself rather high up in a willow tree. We had to wave handfuls of goldfish crackers under his beak. You could have knocked me over with a witch-hazel wand when I realized you were behind that sofa. You have to admit I saved your ass there."

"Bruised it, you mean."

"But, did you get the hemlock?"

"Yeah. I took it straight to Phil."

"Okay, then—wasn't that worth a few bruises?"

*   *   *

Going home without delay was a wise decision on my part because there was a surprise waiting for me. Well, two of them, actually. Freddie was in the kitchen, and Joe was cooking dinner.

Where were you, Toots? It's the hamburger girl again! Scruffy danced around ecstatically. *The furry-faced guy is doing something fishy that smells good.*

"Freddie!" I screamed in the time-honored female squeal, and we fell into a girly hug. "Am I glad to see you! But what in the world are you doing here? Joe, why didn't you *call* me?" I turned to kiss Joe, who hugged me with one arm while lifting the cover from a pan of rice pilaf. I sniffed the aroma wafting from the oven appreciatively, recognizing a Greek influence on the baked bluefish—tomatoes, onions, herbs, olives.

"I did call you, sweetheart," he protested, "but you must have left your cell phone in the car when you were—where did you say? Shopping with Heather?"

"Oh, hey, Joe, I hope you didn't fall for that one," Freddie said. I pinched her arm. She took the hint and launched into an excited explanation of her own presence.

"When we got that "out of order" e-mail, Cass, you sounded so desperate, I just jumped in Adam's Lexus and started driving. Oh, don't worry about your son—I doubt he'll miss his car, or even me. He's up to his cute buns in a massive program that's just about to run for the first time. Hush-hush government stuff, too. Some military nerds are hanging around, like, with their guns flapping. You wouldn't believe it. Was I glad to have a reason to split! And, besides, Adam and I have to keep you up and running so that we won't have to support you in your golden years, you know what I mean?"

All this spilled out in the usual Freddie fashion, accompanied by hand gestures and grimaces by way of emphasis. Perhaps she had been in a hurry. Her hair, instead of midnight spiked with gel, was more her natural dark brown, which I liked infinitely better. She was wearing only three earrings in one ear instead of five and the usual dangling gold pentagram in the other. And no nostril ring. Her amber eyes were heavily accented with mascara and eyeliner—the Egyptian goddess look that I have to admit suited her. Instead of a micro skirt and thigh-high boots, however, she was dressed in faded jeans, a simple black sweater, and jaunty Western footwear.

"Oh," I breathed, "do you think you really can do that? Get me up and running, I mean?" There was an open bottle of wine and three glasses on the table. I poured some wine in each glass and handed them around.

Freddie went back to the task I'd interrupted, tearing up greens for a salad. Beside her on the counter a paring knife flipped over toward her hand. She picked it up casually and began to peel a cucumber. "I sure as shit can, even if I have to re-build the whole program. Remember that your former appren-tice witch is now Iconomics' top troubleshooter. A job for which my particular skills, and a few tricks you taught me, Cass—yes, you did, too, so don't shake your head—keep me, like, on the in-side track."

"I don't doubt that you're a wonder." Dinner being well in hand, I began to set the table.

"And when I've got Cass Shipton's Earthlore Herbal Prepara-tions back in business, I have another project in mind." Freddie grinned wickedly. "I'd like to try my hand at tracking down that 'mystery chef' hacker. Maybe give him a taste of his own poison."

I winced—that was entirely too close to the truth.

"Cass suspects a link between the dirty tricks being played on her and her friends and the Plymouth poisoner," Joe said, taking the fragrant pan out of the oven.

Fish! Fish! Fish! Scruffy nosed his empty dog dish meaning-fully.

I took the hint to spoon in some dog chow and add a chunk of the delicious bluefish, skipping the olives, stirring to cool it more quickly. "And that's just why we have to be super careful with this vengeful kid," I said.

"Kid! You know who it is!" Freddie's face lit up. "All right! So

Cass has zeroed in on the perp, and we're going to zap him good. You go, girl!"

"It's not that easy. Suspicions we have—evidence we have not. Except . . . I did get a frond off a plant in his grandma's house that's definitely poison hemlock. I took it straight to Phillipa to give to Stone."

Joe and Freddie arranged the fish, rice, and salad on the table, and we sat down to enjoy them.

"So, was this hemlock frond something you picked up on your 'shopping trip' with Heather?" Joe raised his eyebrows and held my gaze with his sternest expression. "What did you do? Break in? I guess I can't let you out of my sight for a moment without you getting into some illegal escapade."

"I don't think you're the one who should talk," I said tartly. "Since we were married last year, you've been in jail three or four times, whereas I . . . I have managed to stay clear of the law."

"Cass has magic on her side," Freddie said, "or else some really stressed-out, overworked guardian angel. You just gotta get with the program, Joe—then you too can weasel out of tight corners."

I couldn't get Freddie to tear herself away from my deadhead computer until long past midnight. The next day, with the resiliency of youth, she was up with the birds and back at it again. Barely taking a few sips of black coffee, she seemed to get herself energized simply by dealing with the devastation that Lee Deluca had inflicted on my computer. "I have to start from scratch," she explained to me. "Reinstalling the program Adam designed, and cleaning out your e-mail as well. After I get through, you're going to have, like, a born-again computer. And I've installed some awesome firewalls that the CIA wouldn't think were too shabby. Speaking of which, by the way, one of those military nerds offered me a job working for the government, ha ha. As if I'd leave my honey all alone at Iconomics."

"I've always worried that either the government or some gambling consortium would get you in their clutches. With your psychokinetic abilities, you'll always need to keep a low profile. Okay, no more lectures. I guess you're ready for breakfast, right?"

"Yeah, I'll have a bite. But I'm looking forward to the real fun now—Revenge of the Super-Witches, I'm calling it."

"Dare I ask? We're not into the negative stuff, you know."

"Haven't I had that drummed into my little head! No, this is a return zinger I'm sending to the '*mystery chef*.' Pure skill, not black magic. Hacker 101."

"You mean shut him down?"

"His computer will be, like, turned to stone by Medusa-me."

"And he won't be able to send the virus back to us?"

"I'll leave no tracks to follow, I promise. Stop worrying, Cass. But first I have to find his password, with a little help from this program." Freddie took a disk out of her leather satchel; the buttery-soft bag looked new—Italian and expensive. *Adam's gift*, I thought.

"What's this badass into?" Freddie asked. "Also, I need his birthday, his parents' birthdays and anniversary date, his phone number, his social security number—you know what I mean?"

"He won't be that obvious, but I'll find out what I can. Maybe from Deidre through Millie. Lee Deluca's sights are set on the theater. He's an actor, or he wants to be." I sighed. Right now Lee's whereabouts were unknown, but if he connected somehow with his home computer, wouldn't he guess what had happened? Maybe that would smoke him out, though.

"If you were after his password, what would be your best guess?" Freddie asked.

"Something Shakespearean." I felt a word skittering around the dark recesses of my mind, never quite emerging into the light. It would be better not to focus on the question, simply allow the answer to surface on its own. "If I think of anything specific, I'll let you know. So, okay," I said reluctantly. "Do your worst."

"I like to think of this as my best," Freddie said.

* * *

Instead of showing up with a search warrant and a team, Stone Stern, that gentleman detective, merely had a quiet talk with Bianca Deluca about Lee. Amazingly, she listened without hysterics to his pitch that parting with the hemlock plant would "prevent your grandson from compounding his problems, and protect yourself, too, ma'am, from accidental poisoning."

Then, with an elaborate Mediterranean shrug, Bianca declared that there was no poison plant in *her* cellar, the detective was *pazzo*. She offered to take Stone down to see for himself, and she allowed him to take a leaf from each of the plants. Which later proved to be *Ficus lyrata*, *Dracaena*, *Dieffenbachia*, and *Maranta*. But no poison hemlock. As far as we could determine, the lone survivor of the Craig greenhouse had disappeared with Lee Deluca. Perhaps he still cherished the notion that if he could only get rid of Wyn Peacedale, his mother Jean would inherit her share of the Craig millions and Lee's future would be assured. Or perhaps he'd destroyed the hemlock and moved on to nicotine, so easily obtained in patches.

Motive we had, but *means* still eluded us. And so did Lee.

Chapter Twenty-Seven

Lee Deluca was a resourceful boy. When nicotine didn't work, he moved on to another, tastier poison for Wyn's sweet tooth. And I was a witness.

Now that Loki, a.k.a. Buster, had recovered his health—that canny survivor was leaner and meaner than ever—Patty asked me to give her a hand in getting the stubborn Maine Coon cat home. Maybe all she really needed was moral support, because Heather's husband, Dick, personally put the struggling cat into his carrier.

"You know, I'm a champion of acupuncture for pets," Dick said, "and I've known it to work miracles with advanced arthritis. Dogs tolerate it well, and some cats, but I would never, never recommend acupuncture for Loki. Even getting medicine into him required the help of two orderlies."

"He's a devil, isn't he," Patty said proudly, peering through the barred front of the carrier. Loki spit and tried to claw her.

"Oh, cut that out, Loki," I said. "You've lucked out with Patty, so treat her with love and kindness, please." I deliberately emptied my mind and pictured my forehead pressed against Loki's.

It's a training matter, Tabitha. A feline can't be too permissive. Caretakers lose respect for him.

"Oh, boloney, Loki."

"Does Mama's little sweetie want bologna?" Patty cooed.

"Now, now—no people food, Mrs. Peacedale," Dick said sternly. "Loki's tummy needs to be soothed by a bland diet. Just the dry food I've prescribed."

What does this guy know about feline cuisine? Loki hissed disdainfully. *I require real nourishment. Poached salmon! Braised chicken liver! Fresh beetle on the half shell!*

After Dick's final admonishments not to cater to Loki's taste whims, I offered to take the cat carrier for Patty, placing it in the rear of my Jeep as far away from the front seat as possible. I had no intention of exposing myself to a blue streak of feline profanity all the way to the parsonage.

"Oh, he's back, then," Wyn said when we opened the carrier in the Peacedale kitchen.

After giving the pastor a disdainful look, Loki checked the saucer on his Lion King placemat. He turned up his nose at the dry food Dick had prescribed, gave an insolent wave of his tail, and stalked away upstairs.

"Loki does love the sunny windowsill in my office. It's right over the radiator, and I've made some lovely cushions," Patty said. "After such an ordeal, he'll need a lot of warm and comfy catnaps."

I thought I saw Wyn make a slight gagging motion. He opened the refrigerator and took out a bottle of pink juice. The label read *Naturally Nice Organic Pear and Papaya*.

"Wait!" Patty ordered in a surprisingly peremptory tone. "I just put that bottle in the refrigerator to chill, and I haven't blessed it yet." Grabbing the bottle, she placed it on the kitchen table, well away from her husband, and tried the top. "It's been opened," she whispered. Whipping out the Celtic cross from beneath her beige twin set, she dowsed the juice in a very competent manner, visibly slowing and calming her demeanor, despite her earlier anxiety. Fiona had taught her well.

The cross hung quietly over the bottle for several heartbeats and then began to swing in a figure-eight pattern, speeding up suddenly into an erratic zigzag. "There! See that?" Patty screamed. In a nanosecond, she was on her way to the sink to dump the juice.

I grabbed Patty's arm. We almost lost it on the floor as we scuffled for the bottle. "No, no," I explained. "Dowsing is all well and good, but now we have to verify that the juice is poisoned, and with what."

Wyn couldn't have looked more perplexed. "Will someone please tell me what's going on here?" he demanded. "What the devil's got into you two?"

At that, Patty sank into a kitchen chair and put her hands over her face. "This burden the Lord has placed on my shoulders is too much for me to bear." Although still clueless, Wyn patted her shoulder in a comforting manner.

"Don't blame the Lord, Patty," I said. "Blame that sociopathic kid. Now, tell me you're not still leaving your door unlocked!"

Instantly, she looked guilt-ridden. "To tell the truth, Cass, I don't think we even have keys to the parsonage. Do we, Wyn?"

Wyn was staring at the *Naturally Nice* bottle with some dismay. "Do you mean to say that this stuff is poisoned, too? It's that damned money!" He rubbed his forehead as if trying to erase some distressing thought from his mind. "Keys? Keys . . . Let's see. I think we put them away somewhere in my study for safekeeping."

"Wyn wouldn't have locked up anyway while I was still out of the house. How would I have got in?" Patty said.

"Patty, find the keys. Keep the doors locked. This is the third time someone has entered your kitchen and tampered with the contents of your refrigerator. Someone who wants Wyn or both of you dead. So get real, will you!" I would have said more, but I saw that Patty was close to tears.

Gingerly, I opened the bottle. "It smells so very sweet," I commented.

As a matter of caution, I immediately called Joe and everyone in the circle.

"Don't ask any questions now, Joe," I'd ordered. "I'll explain later. Just don't drink anything from open cartons or bottles in the fridge. And for Goddess's sake, warn Freddie, too. How's she doing?"

"She's chortling to herself in your office, that's how she's doing. It's unsettling that one so young can sound so wicked."

"Good. She's making progress, then. Gotta go call everyone."

"Okay. Wouldn't it be easier if you installed some kind of permanent conference-call arrangement on your cell phones?"

I made believe I hadn't heard that, hung up, and punched the next number on my speed dial.

"Hey, getting into this place would be like trying to penetrate an active missile site," Phillipa said. "Stone has installed a state-of-the-art alarm system that gives us barely three minutes to punch in the code before it blows its top. Twice my dear husband himself has messed up the number sequence, and squad cars have come squealing into our driveway, much to his chagrin."

"Phil, I do want you to explain this whole alarm-system idea to Patty at another time—it's exactly what she needs. But right now I've got to call the others."

"Well, let's phone-tree then. Who do you want me to call?"

"Great. You get in touch with Heather and Fiona. I'll call Dee." I was glad to assign my friend to those most liable to go ballistic at hearing this new twist.

But as it turned out, the real uproar was at the Ryan house. "He was here!" Deidre screamed in my ear. "Can you imagine the nerve? If Will hadn't been so groggy from fatigue, we'd have had the little bastard. But I just couldn't hold him by myself. I guess I did mark him—just a scratch, though."

"A scratch where?"

"Where? Oh, on his cheek. It was an accident."

"Did it bleed?"

"Well, yes, I guess I took off a layer of skin. Maybe it was more of a gouge than a scratch. Welled up red, and drops of blood ran down his cheek. Surprising. I mean, I keep my nails cut short."

"He'll probably accuse you of child battery. Did you call the cops?"

"You bet. But he's not exactly a wanted criminal, you know, just a missing kid, and by the time they moseyed over here, Lee was long gone."

I worried about Jean having her usual maniac response to an attack on her son. Perhaps those displays were fueled by guilt at abandoning him as an infant. At any rate, I decided not to lay that worry on Deidre right then. "What was Lee after? Have you any idea? Do you want me to come over?"

"Yes. I could use some protective vibes right now. I'll save my story until you get here."

"Okay. I'll bring sage for smudging," I said. I packed up a Wiccan emergency kit: dried sage and rosemary, sandlewood incense, sea salt, kava tea. I also tucked the suspect bottle of juice in my car and raced over to the Ryan place. Glancing at my watch, I was truly surprised. I felt as if I'd lived a century already that day, and here it was only eleven. I still had lots of morning left to soothe Deidre and drop the juice off at Phillipa's on my way home for lunch.

Jenny answered the door. "Mom is lying in the living room with a cloth over her head. Daddy's gone to the police station. I'm taking care of everything," Deidre's oldest greeted me with grown-up aplomb, her brown braids swinging officiously as she led the way to the jonquil yellow kitchen.

Instantly, Deidre appeared in the kitchen door, a wet washcloth in one hand and little Annie in the other. "Jenny, you go upstairs now, dear, and keep Willie and Bobby out of trouble in the playroom while Aunt Cass and I have a quiet cup of coffee."

"Let me make the coffee," I offered, "and you talk."

After installing Annie in her bouncing chair, Deidre sank into one of the kitchen chairs and gazed out the window at the cheerless backyard—drifts of frozen mud, patches of dirty snow, a deserted jungle gym. The brilliant winter sunlight served only to emphasize the scene's bleakness. Deidre's usual cheery mien was now a cold mask of anger, and her pale blue eyes were icy. "Will had just woken up—some big fire in Carver last night—so I took the opportunity to run to Angelo's for a few things. Guess I got home just in time. Lee Deluca was at the door talking to Jenny. Apparently Will had flopped on the living room sofa, turned on the ESPN channel, and fallen back to sleep. That evil boy was dressed in some kind of white uniform, holding a wire sixpack of bottles. He was offering one of them, a cherry-colored stuff, to Jenny."

"Uh oh," I said.

"Right," Deidre agreed.

Annie gurgled and tried to swallow her fist. Absently, Deidre handed her a zwieback and continued her story. "Jenny said, 'Look, Mom, this dairy guy is offering us a free sample of Maraschino Milk.' I recognized Deluca instantly from that school photo Millie had showed me. So I grabbed him by the jacket and pulled him into the house. He's not a very big guy, shorter than I am, if you can believe it. Millie said how charming and handsome he is, but to me he looked like an evil elf."

"Of course," I murmured. "The pixie connection."

"'What poisonous tricks are you up to this time?' I demanded. 'Hey, lady,' he said, 'I'm just giving out free samples, like your girl said.' 'If you're trying to hurt my family, I'll kill you myself,' I said. But he was wiggling free of my grasp. Quite a muscular little scoundrel. So I screamed for Will, but by the time he got himself out of his coma, Lee had run off and taken the bottle with him. Oh, I am so shook!"

I hugged her, feeling how small and delicate Deidre was, reminding me of my Cathy. I reached for the Light of Universal Energy to surround us both. This was a time when I really felt its warmth; it was like love turned luminous. "We are safe. You did wonderfully," I said. Of course, I could have wished she'd got hold of that Maraschino stuff, but at least we still had the *Naturally Nice Pear and Papaya*. "I've just come from the parsonage, where there was a similar crisis." I poured the coffee I'd made and I told her about the new attempt on the Peacedales.

"There's one thing that worries me the most," Deidre said, making a face at the strength of the brew. She added another half-teaspoon of sugar and stirred.

"What?" I took a sip. To me, the coffee was just right.

"When Lee Deluca ran off, he looked back at me for an instant with the most malevolent grin you can imagine. He touched his cheek and looked at the blood on his hand. Those skin things really bleed profusely. So then he said something weird. 'You shouldn't have marked my face, lady. I play a mean Richard the Third, so watch out.' What do you make of that?"

The murdered princes in the tower, I thought. This was a threat directed toward Deidre's children. I should have told her right then and there, but it seemed to me, looking at her anxious blue eyes, usually so mischievous and merry, that my spunky friend had had enough for one day.

"That changeling fancies himself a Shakespearian actor," was all I said.

I left the bottle in Phillipa's care. She, too, gave it an intelligent sniff. "Ugh. Smells sickeningly sweet."

"'That's what I thought, too. Lock it up someplace until you can put it into Stone's hands. Any sign of Lee yet?"

"Stone and Billy Mann are making that kid their priority. Hopefully they'll get their hands on him before he finds yet another way to eliminate the Peacedales."

"Yes, the little fox is quite adaptable. I wonder what concoction is in this, don't you?" Right as I said that, I had an idea of how Lee might be traced. Instantly, I rang home on my cell. "Let me speak to Freddie," I said.

"*Freddie!* Oh, goodie!" Phillipa's smile was like megawatts of sunshine, softening her sharp features into beauty. "She's here to rescue your computer, isn't she? That blessed girl. Do you think she'd have time to have a look at mine, too?"

"Hi, Freddie. Listen up, hon. Don't send that virus. Repeat. Don't send that virus."

"Hey, Cass, are you having an attack of the mundanes? I've got this thing all ready to unleash on the Bad Seed. His computer will be toast. Burned toast. I'm going through your copy of *The Complete Plays of Shakespeare*, trying all the main characters' names. Have you come up with anything."

"Puck," I said absently, surprised at the word coming out of my own mouth. Sometimes being clairvoyant simply means getting out of the way, letting what you know in your unconscious mind emerge without thought barriers.

"Is that with a P or an F?" asked Freddie.

"Did you know that the hacker boy's disappeared? What I'm thinking is, the kid may come back at night to get stuff off his computer. I don't know. Information, maybe. To read his e-mail. Or maybe he'll contact his computer from elsewhere. Is it possible for you to get into his computer without his knowing about it and trace his activity, maybe even lift his correspondence?"

Freddie laughed. "If he turns it on and you're right about the password, it's a cinch. Or if you have any idea of what his favorite sites might be, I could set up a phony one to hook him good."

"I have no idea, but my guess is that Deluca might be tempted by scholarships to theater schools or, better yet, casting calls for a production at some South Shore amateur theatrical company."

"Any special play?"

"*A Midsummer Night's Dream*."

"That's Shakespeare, with the fairies and other fey types? What a blast! I'll get a worm on the hook in case he logs on. Say, did you know that your Indian kid is here?"

"Oh, Tip . . . good. I'm on my way home. We'll all have lunch together."

"Cass . . . his father died this morning at Jordan Hospital."

"I'll be there in ten minutes." I tried to think good thoughts for S. E. Thomas's journey to Summerland, but I also couldn't help feeling relieved that now Tip could get the education he deserved without interference from his dad, who'd always wanted to drag him out of school and into some dead-end job for minimum wages. So finally the old man had drunk himself to death. Good and bad, so inextricably woven together that the one would always contain aspects of the other.

There was something inflexible about Tip's reaction to grief. He stood as straight as a soldier at attention and allowed himself to be hugged, never for a minute breaking down. But I could see in his eyes all the pain and guilt of a difficult relationship that now never could be mended. "Maybe I should have stayed with the old man instead of traipsing off to Wiscasset," he said. I did my best to explain that Tip had a right to live his life and develop his talents in his own way; it was as nature intended.

Although I wanted him to stay with me, Tip stalwartly insisted on going home and "getting ready for the family." Later, I was surprised to discover how many relatives there actually were when they all gathered at S. E. Thomas's funeral. But not his ex-wife, Mary, Tip's mother. One of the great-uncles had to escort Tip's younger brother to their father's funeral. The sibling's given name was Little Bear, Lib for short, just as Tip was Thunder Pony. But the boy now preferred to be called Chris, the name he'd been given at the Catholic school in Bangor where Mary had deposited him like an unwanted bag of clothes in a missionary box. From what I could observe, the boys were distant and shy of one another, set as they were on different paths, but before the weekend was over and Chris returned to his school, some of the old sibling camaraderie surfaced.

Big, red-haired, fair-skinned John Thomas, Tip's uncle, his father's brother, who had appointed himself Tip's unofficial guardian in Wiscasset, had taken care of all the arrangements—and paid for them, too. The Reverend Peacedale officiated—Tip's suggestion—and Tip himself played a haunting tune on the Native American flute he'd designed and made. His hidden grief soared movingly through the music and brought tears to other eyes as well as mine. Except for family, though, the funeral was sparsely attended, just a few wasted drinking buddies of S. E. Thomas's. So I was glad all five of us were there, plus husbands. More heads for Patty to count.

Tip introduced us as "the medicine women, my friends." Fiona seemed especially pleased with that. She was still carrying the bag of corn pollen she'd brought home from Arizona, a pinch of which was used to bless and heal us as the occasion arose.

Just before the service, Stone leaned over and whispered to me the results of the test on the *Naturally Nice* juice. It was found to contain a killing amount of sweet, odorless ethylene glycol—the chemical used as antifreeze. How, then, did both Phillipa and I decide that it "smelled" too sweet?

"Psychic noses," Phillipa explained it. "Every sense must have its extrasensory counterpart."

"Ah, yes," Heather said. "I often smell a rather distinctive scent of tobacco in my study—very pleasant, really, with a touch of molasses—although no one's smoked in the Morgan house since old Captain Morgan passed away to Summerland. And when I catch a whiff of that pipe smoke, it's sure to be accompanied by an idea or impulse that seems to have no relation to *me*. 'Out of the blue,' as they say."

"Maybe Captain Jack's been hanging around the study, enjoying a pipe while browsing through your great-grandfather's collection of old sea stories," Deidre suggested.

"Captain Jack has given up tobacco, he tells me, to spare Ishmael. Apparently the bird cannot tolerate secondhand smoke."

"Coughing a phony little cough, is he? The one that the Health Police have developed to perfection?" Phillipa asked. She'd given up smoking only a few years ago and was still bitter about it. Occasionally she still enjoyed a puff or two when no one was around.

"If you're going to sneak a smoke, it's better not to have a clairvoyant friend," I told her. "Especially one with a psychic nose."

Chapter Twenty-Eight

Although I still had worries about Adam's future with Freddie as his wife and the mother of his children, I had to admit that having my former protégé for a daughter-in-law might prove to be a blessing after all. The one I admitted this to was Joe, in the privacy of our bedroom.

"But aren't you proud," he had said, "that he's chosen an amazing gal who's something like his mum rather than some cheerleader chick with designer nails and a registered sterling-silver pattern?"

"Yeah, I suppose. And she is, as you say, amazing. And not just for reprogramming the Earthlore Herbal Preparations Web site, which required finding the original program in my office, a monumental task."

"Where was it?" As I was lying on my folded arms, gazing out the window at the leafless world of winter etched against the rising full moon, Joe began to massage my back. I felt myself melting into liquid pleasure.

"Mmmmmm. In a folder labeled, for some strange reason, *Genesis*. But that's not all. She's constructed the most wonderful fake Web sites to lure Lee Deluca. I'm trying to detect whether he's sneaking home—or rather, to his grandmother's house—to use his computer. If he opens his e-mail at all, it will, in a very few seconds, install a secret gizmo to allow us to delve into all his files. Oh boy, do that shoulder again, will you? It's heaven."

"Muscles are a little tight right there."

"Not any more, lover."

"What's the lure?"

"The first one is a theater thing. Freddie found a legitimate amateur theater company called the Provincetown Troubadours and created a fictitious casting call for a phony production Lee will find irresistible—*A Midsummer Night's Dream.* It looks completely authentic and links to what appears to be the Troubadours' home page—simply a work of genius. The second one is a link to a site called 'Poisons in the Kitchen, A Guide to Dangerous Substances Commonly Found in and around the Home.'"

"Yesterday morning, when Freddie picked up a Post-it notepad, a pen slid right across the kitchen desk into her fingers." Joe said. "She didn't even appear to notice that anything unusual had occurred."

"That's not surprising for Freddie. I just hope she's more careful at Iconomics."

"How would you like to roll over?" Joe kissed the back of my neck, an electrifying zinger. Relaxation turned to anticipation.

"I thought you'd never ask."

"What are your plans now?" I asked Tip. After the onslaught of Thomas relatives had departed, I'd insisted he have dinner with us, and he'd agreed readily enough. "You'll be finishing the school year in Wiscasset, won't you?"

"Nah. Got too much to do, so I'm going to complete *this* term, anyway, in Plymouth. Uncle John laid down the law on that one. As soon as I get things closed up properly—sorted, stored, dumped, and like that—I'm back in the Wiscasset system. Two more years, and then I can fly free as an eagle, Uncle John says. Unless

I want to work with him at the shipyards. Good wages and all. But I'm thinking of studying music, you know. Especially primitive music. I think that's my path, the one I should follow."

"What about your dad's house?" Joe asked.

"Soon as the court says I can, Uncle John is going to arrange for its sale. He's already had a real estate lady in to evaluate the property. Lib and me will split the money. Only Uncle John is going to put it away for us, so that Mom . . . well, so Lib's share will be there when he graduates from high school. That should give us a start at college. If my dad ever knew that little house of ours is on a piece of land that's actually worth something, he'd have sold it a long time ago."

And drunk away the money, we all thought but didn't say.

"You may find some colleges offer scholarships to Native Americans," I suggested.

"Yeah, my guidance teacher in Wiscasset said that. She's going to do a search so that we can apply for early admission. Hey, they haven't found Deluca yet?" Tip asked. "What's he up to, anyway?" We'd finished dinner and dessert. Tip glanced at the fruit bowl, and I passed it to him. This was a kid who used to eat raw potatoes in lieu of apples.

Hey, how about another bite of meatloaf? Scruffy was resting his nose on Tip's moccasins, sensing the easy touch.

"You've had quite enough, fella." Tip grinned at me and peeled a banana. Tuning in to Scruffy was something special we shared. "Unless you're fond of banana."

I beg your pardon—do you think I'm some kind of monkey? Scruffy growled in disgust.

"Deluca knew he was about to be questioned in the hemlock matter, and other incidents, so he's made himself scarce," Joe said. "It wouldn't surprise me to learn that his mother and/or his grandmother have him in hiding somewhere locally."

"Fiona's on the case," I said. "She's our champion finder."

"What about that program Freddie set up before she left?" Joe asked. "If Deluca takes the bait, it will prove your theory. Put a watch on Grandma and you'll have him nailed."

"Freddie showed me how to check her little traps, but so far, nothing. I'm pinning my hopes on Fiona. In fact, I thought I'd drive over there now. If nothing else, it's such a pleasure to share her joy in her grandniece. I suppose Fiona's guardianship won't last forever, but that's all the more reason to revel and celebrate. Do you want to come with me?"

"You don't mean that," Joe said. "You ladies probably do better on your own. 'Mysteries of Isis' and all."

"Wouldn't surprise me if we were tuning into the Mysteries. Most of what we do dates back to ancient times, perhaps even to prehistory. So I believe, but there are two schools of thought on that."

"You believe in the old gods—or should I say goddesses?—because you're an incorrigible romantic. Are you sure you're not part Greek?"

"With a name like Shipton? I'll own to being romantic, though."

Tip was beginning to look uncomfortable. "Don't worry," I said, "we're not going to get mushy. Come on, I'll give you a ride home on my way to Fiona's."

"Aren't you going to call her first?" Joe asked.

"I'm betting she already knows I'm coming. Think of it as a little drop-in test."

"I had an idea you'd be turning up. I've got the kettle on," Fiona said when she opened the door to her picturesque, fishnet-draped cottage. Laura Belle was clinging to her great-aunt's colorful striped skirt, smiling shyly. She was wearing a sweet flannel nightie with sparkling stars scattered over a violet-blue background, a perfect match for her eyes, and holding a soft stuffed spider under one arm. I raised an eyebrow and glanced at my hostess.

"That's Grandmother Spider, who brought fire to the Choctaws and taught them spinning and weaving," Fiona said a bit defensively. "Laura Belle loves her spider, and Aunt Fifi is going to tuck them in together, warm and snug. Say good night to Aunt Cass, sweetheart."

Is the child speaking at last? I stooped down so that we were on the same level. and gazed into her morning-glory eyes. Everything about her was delicate and flowerlike. Rosebud mouth. Camellia-petal skin. But, alas, still the silence, the gentle smile. Laura Belle merely gave me a soft hug and kissed my cheek, the spider dangling over my back. I'd forgotten how sweet little girls smell and almost envied Fiona. Wouldn't I be thrilled to have a little girl like this to love? I had to shake myself to remember I'd already lived that mother part of life with my own little girls, two of them, now all grown-up, grown away. And a son, too. Nostalgia had me in its sweet, enclosing grip. *You can't go back to where you were, you can't go back to who you were,* the little voice of reason insisted.

"Shall I make the tea while you tuck her in?" I asked.

"Good idea. Everything's ready." Fiona scooped up her charge, silver bangles jangling, and sprinted up the stairs, very spry for a formerly arthritic old lady.

Fiona's little kitchen, once a galley of gruesome grease, had undergone a magical transformation indeed. Every shelf gleamed with neatly arrayed dishes and goods. Pots of rosemary, sage, and mint thrived on the windowsill despite the waning winter sunlight. Every surface was tidy, only a bowl of shining apples and a cookie jar in the shape of a troll sitting on the countertops. A tray with thistle-pottery teapot, mugs, and a plate of poppyseed cookies was laid out on the diminutive wooden table, now scrubbed to the golden grain. I measured Lapsang Souchong and filled the teapot from the steaming kettle. *I really ought to have a go at my own kitchen*, I thought as I carried the tray into the living room. *Whoever thought Fiona's housekeeping would put me to shame?*

"My little Tinker Belle falls asleep as soon as her head hits the pillow," Fiona said. "Oh, good, you've got the tea ready."

"Still not talking?"

"Yes, not talking. But she will, she will. I have faith, and I have spirit." Fiona filled our cups and passed the cookies. We sipped the steaming brew cautiously. "You're looking for something and you need help?"

"Right. I'd like to find out where Lee Deluca is hiding. Freddie set an Internet trap for the boy, but there's been no response so far."

"And you can't zero in on him yourself?" Fiona asked.

"You know I don't have conscious control over my visions. They come and go in their own good time."

"Well, when you're ready, that will change. But I do understand, my dear. It can be so dreadfully upsetting. A walk on the wild side."

"So . . . will you help me?"

"Of course, but before I try dowsing, how about if we apply a little common sense to the problem?"

"What do you mean?"

"Where did you find the hemlock greenhouse?" Fiona's smile just bordered on smugness.

"Lydia Craig's place . . . Oh, of course. Why didn't I think of that? It's been deserted ever since she died. Lydia probably hid a key near the door, and Lee figured out where. What a perfect hideout!"

"Well, not ideal. The water must be turned off so the pipes won't freeze. Still, he'd know the layout, and it must be full of cubbyholes that a kid would have ferreted out. You'll suggest this to Stone?" Fiona asked.

"I guess I ought to. I'm tempted, though, to have a look around myself first."

"Wait until morning, and I'll go with you. I can leave Laura Belle with Deidre. Maybe I can help to spell the boy out of hiding before he does more damage to himself and others."

"Laudable, but unlikely," I said. "Shall I pick up you and

Laura at eight, then? We'll drop her off at Dee's and have a good look 'round the Craig place."

Our plan unwittingly set a dangerous sequence of events in motion. What happened later almost turned me off amateur investigations forever.

"Fiona and I are going out early tomorrow, Joe. I'll be home by lunch, though."

"Shopping?"

"Sort of." My amazing, lovable husband had that rare quality of not being suspicious. Either that, or his head was so full of his own concerns that there was no room for doubting what he was told. Which gave me a slight twinge of guilt, but nothing that reason couldn't overcome.

Deidre was the elected babysitter, and Phillipa might feel the need to report to Stone. But Heather was right there in the neighborhood, so I decided I'd ask her to go with us. While Joe was watching some show about Phoenician shipbuilding on the Discovery channel, I ducked into my office to call. At the same time, I booted up my computer and checked up on Freddie's Troubadour trap. Nothing yet.

"What's up, Cass? Another *Mission Impossible?*" Heather greeted my late call.

"Eight-thirty tomorrow morning, Fiona and I will be on our way to the old Craig place. Want to join us?"

"Why didn't I think of that?" Heather demanded, echoing my own reaction. "You're guessing that Lee's hiding out there, aren't you?"

"Not me. Fiona. She didn't even dowse it."

"Let's face it, she's a phenomenon, a force of nature."

"Yeah, Mary Poppins meets Miss Marple. And we've got her. Are you in?"

"Always. Dress warmly. There's been talk of one of those Cape blizzards, and you know we share the same weather patterns."

I worried that my going out "shopping" in a blizzard might alarm Joe, but as it happened, he slept late and never heard me as I prepared to slip out the door at seven-thirty.

But Scruffy did. *Hey, hey, I need to pee.* He danced around the kitchen, making a case for urgency. I grabbed the leash off its hook but didn't bother to clip it to his collar. At this hour, he'd attend to business and not run off after squirrels. True to form, he sniffed the bushes around the garage and chose his spots with care.

The fact that I had car keys jingling in my other hand, however, had not escaped his attention. *A ride, we're going for a ride! Let's open the windows and feel the breeze in our ears.* He trotted confidently toward the driveway. It took some fancy footwork to whisk the dog back into the house and shut the door on his crestfallen face. By then I could see through the glass pane in the door that Joe had woken up and wandered into the kitchen.

I waved gaily and ran down to the Jeep. The skies, although a strange shade of yellow-gray, seemed clear enough. But I noticed flocks of noisy gulls were flying off the ocean to the inland ponds and lakes—never a good omen.

In the haunted shadows of two looming catalpa trees, the decrepit Craig mansion now sported a FOR SALE sign, offered by local Realtor, Fanny Finch, and a dayglo pink notice, *ESTATE AUCTION VFW HALL February 1st, Bertie Pryde, Auctioneer.* "The Finches and the Prydes, a finger in every pie," Heather commented. "Bangs tells me that Lydia directed the firm to sell all her property, the proceeds to become part of her estate. She didn't fancy having her relatives rifle through her belongings in the guise of retaining items of sentimental value. I wonder how she'd have liked Bertie Pryde messing around with her prized possessions."

"What about letters and personal papers?" Heather and I busied ourselves looking under all the obvious flowerpots and rocks near the front door.

"The firm sent a junior partner to sort through Craig's papers, unenviable task. I wonder if there were any love letters. Rumor has it that an early romance was thwarted by Lydia's parents. Maybe that's what soured her," Heather said.

Fiona stood aside, assuring us that we were wasting our time. She felt certain we'd find no key in the usual hiding places.

"If Fiona can't locate the key, Lee probably pocketed it when he moved in here," Heather said.

"Shhhh. Let's be very quiet. Voices carry in this cold, still air. Maybe we can locate an unlocked window. We should at least try them," I said. "I won't give up so easily."

"Let's stay off the porch, though. It looks as if it's rotted through," Heather said. "I hope Bertie has a good insurance policy covering his movers. I wonder if Fanny Finch will be able to sell this old derelict. Talk about a 'handyman's special.'"

Fiona fished in her green reticule, mumbling to herself. "Stones and rocks, dials and clocks, open minds will open locks."

Heather and I glanced at each other nervously, as Fiona, cackling wildly, pulled what looked like an ancient multi-tool knife out of her reticule. Only this set of tools looked like none other I'd ever seen. She held it aloft with a gleam of triumph in her eye.

"Are those lock picks? They are, aren't they?" Heather demanded. "Ceres help us, I'll have to take you along if I ever decide to raid a laboratory again."

"I've had these since the sixties, my dears." Fiona's eyes sparkled with merry memories. "Sometimes they worked to break into government buildings and burn draft records." She twirled through the set expertly and selected one tool that looked like a miniature harpoon. "Rather an old-fashioned lock. This should do it." Removing her purple mittens, she hunched over the door intently, still murmuring her incantation, "Rocks . . . clocks . . . locks," to herself. We were so quiet I could hear ourselves breathe, each breath turning to mist on the chilly air. One fat flake of snow fell, then another. Perhaps we would get that storm after all.

Click, click, click. "Eureka," Fiona whispered, and turned the elaborate marble knob. The massive oak door swung open readily enough, squeaking on ancient, unoiled hinges. Tiptoeing as softly as possible in our heavy winter boots, we stepped into the entry, filled with hulking Victorian hall pieces, as ugly as gargoyles. The living room we could see beyond promised more of the same, cave-dark, with heavy drapes closed and smelling of dust, mice, and mildew.

"Shall we stay together or split up, do you think?" Heather whispered.

"Stay together," Fiona commanded, suddenly pulling herself up into a wisewoman glamour. There was a sense of illumination around her in that shadowed place, especially around her hands, which she now held in front of her like a Hindu greeting. "I will dowse the way."

When Fiona gets herself into a full glamour, we naturally follow her lead, as we did now. We checked out the two front parlors, where heavy sofas were swathed in sheets, then the library. I noted that the huge oak rolltop desk showed signs of having been thoroughly cleaned out, not a piece of paper remaining. The books had been packed and labeled with lot numbers and Bertie Pryde's logo. None of the other rooms we'd seen appeared to have been sacked yet, the mantels and side tables still laden with dusty ornaments.

We advanced through the dining room and butler's pantry to the kitchen "on little cat feet." Fiona put her finger to her lips and pointed out a candle and a pack of matches on the counter, then a bucket of water in the sink. She examined the fireplace with care and pulled out a shred of a white paper bag with greasy stains, giving it a knowledgeable sniff. "Takeout clams," she mouthed in triumph, and pointed her finger at the ceiling. Heather and I looked up at the sooty white expanse as if seeking the handwriting on the wall.

"No, no," she whispered. "Upstairs. Let's go upstairs to see if he's been sleeping in any of the beds."

"The Three Bears search for Goldilocks," Heather murmured in my ear.

"Yeah, maybe so, but this house is strictly from *Great Expectations*," I whispered back. "And that's just what Lee Deluca has, extremely great expectations."

There was no way to climb the stairs quietly. Although they were carpeted in a tarnished-looking red, every step harbored its own special squeak. Fiona, however, seemed to have the knack of still-walking like a deer hunter through the woods even while wearing her bulky MacDonald-tartan cape and lugging her green reticule.

We entered each room with trepidation, as if Lee might jump out at us from a bathroom or closet. I had to keep reminding myself that this was just a boy, probably an unarmed boy, and we were three mature women.

Lydia Craig's pale green bedroom appeared untouched since her death, the prim mahogany four-poster neatly covered with a crocheted bedspread yellowed with age. Next to it, an almost pretty sitting room, with delicately flowered rose wallpaper, was equally unused except for the small white desk, which had obviously been emptied, as had the rolltop downstairs. Like the kitchen, these rooms were less dusty than the others, suggesting that they comprised Lydia Craig's true "apartment."

Unfortunately, I hovered too close behind Heather, and when she stumbled over a chaise longue, we both pitched forward. Fiona threw up her hands in a gesture of despair.

In the next moment, we heard a series of sounds down the hall. The twang of a shade snapped up too fast, the slide of a heavy window thrown open, the rustle and thump of someone jumping over the sill. We hurried to follow the obvious sounds of whoever—but it must be Lee!—was escaping the house. The room we sought was two doors down from the sitting room. Cold air was blasting in an open window. Outside it was the porch roof. We raced downstairs, lithe Heather in the forefront, her bronze braid swinging as she bounded ahead, but we weren't quick enough. Lee had jumped to the ground and disappeared around the corner of the house.

"Oh, Sweet Isis," Fiona groaned, holding her side. "He was here all right. Did you notice the tumbled blankets on top of this bedspread?"

"I'm thinking now," Heather said, "that it might have been better if we'd brought the police into this, asked *them* to search the house."

"I was rather hoping we could get a line on Lee informally first. Maybe get him to incriminate himself."

"Stone could have waltzed in here with Bertie Pryde and had a quiet look around. After all, the boy is an official missing person," Heather said. "Neville Borer is Lydia's executor, and I doubt he would have gone for his client's grandnephew camping out in her property."

"We've screwed up, ladies," Fiona pointed out. "I fear you're still going to have to tell Stone, Cass, that the boy was here. And now he's gone."

"Maybe he'll sneak back," I said, but I didn't believe it. As a safe house, the Craig mansion was blown.

"Hey, look at it come down now!" Heather drew our attention to the increasing fall of snow, as the world around us turned to dancing white flakes. "Perhaps we'd better get out of here before this gets too deep for safe driving."

"Oh, I'll have to get Laura home, then, while the roads are still passable," Fiona said. "And cancel our therapy session for tomorrow, praise the Goddess. We've been bumped up from speech therapy to a husband-and-wife team of psychiatrists in Quincy, Wacker and Wacker. Elective mutism, they call it. They want to try anti-anxiety, social phobia drugs, but I want to try time and love."

"Laura's awfully young for mind-altering meds."

"It will never happen. I know I agreed to seek therapy for my little Tinker Belle, but I draw the line at pharmaceuticals. A magical banishing line, that is."

Magical banishing line? I wondered just how Fiona would accomplish that, but, occupied with negotiating slippery roads, I resolved to question her later.

Heather's home was nearby; I let her off first. Sorry as I was to miss brunch with Captain Jack and his wonderfully bracing boiled coffee, I didn't want to worry Joe. So we hurried away to collect Laura, then get Fiona and her charge home before the gathering storm shut down Plymouth. Afterward, I supposed, I'd better call Phillipa and let her juggle the hot-potato news about Lee Deluca.

Joe had left a note on the kitchen table.

Gone to Home Warehouse for a couple of decent snow
shovels and some more ice melt. Don't worry, pet-safe
stuff, and will drive carefully. Love you. J.

After a perfunctory greeting, Scruffy pressed his nose against the bird-feeder window in the kitchen and studied the weather disconsolately. *Paw-freezing white stuff all over. No good place to pee.*

"Nevertheless, you'll have to go sometime. I'll take you out in a few minutes."

Why can't I have indoor accommodations like some other canines do?

"Because you're not a Chihuahua, you big horse." Time to make that unpleasant call to Phillipa.

"So *I* have the fun of telling my husband, the police detective, that you guys have spooked the suspect out of his hiding place and Goddess knows where he is now?" Phillipa summed up the situation in a chilly tone.

"Yeah, I guess that about says it all. Sorry. Don't be cross. Who knows what kind of problems might have arisen with an official search, maybe complaints about roughing up a missing boy. Whereas with Fiona and her lock-pick kit . . ."

"Surely you jest. Fiona has a lock-pick kit? Does Joe know what you've been up to? Oh, just a moment. Call waiting. Let me see who it is real quick and get back to you and your fascinating life of crime."

But Phillipa was gone a few heartbeats more than she should have been. Then she was back, her voice betraying a trace of nervousness. "Stone says the blizzard is sporting gale-force winds, many roads are impassable, and he doesn't know when or if he'll be home. Where's Joe?"

"Goddess knows. He went to Home Warehouse to buy snow shovels. Two of them."

"Ah, togetherness. But wait, there's more news. Just to add a little extra wrinkle, someone's reported that a huge old catalpa tree over at the Craig place has crashed into the mansion's roof."

"Uh oh . . . it bodes ill for the estate auction," I said. "I wonder where Lee Deluca will hole up now. He'll need a decent shelter in this storm."

"Might run for Grandma's. Keep checking that computer trap Freddie left for him."

Sure! At that moment I lost both the lights and the phone. Obviously, computer entrapment would have to wait until power was restored. I still had my cell, of course, but I'd need to be careful not to use up its charge. *Where was Joe?* I looked out the window at the fiercely swirling snow—a white, inscrutable world.

As soon as I turned on my cell, it rang. "Hey, sweetheart, I'm having a bit of a problem here. Are you all right?"

That Rent-a-Wreck wouldn't be worth a damn in the blizzard. "No lights, no telephone, but I'm okay. Where are you?"

"Owl Swamp Road near the old Grange Hall. The car skidded into a drift. I'll have to dig it out."

"Did you get the new snow shovels?"

"No, they'd sold out of the kind I wanted. I've got a shoebox in the back of the car, though. I'll use that."

"Look in the trunk. Maybe you'll find something sturdier.

Listen, honey, I've got the Jeep, four-wheel drive and all. Let me come and get you."

"*Absolutely not!* I'll be fine. Better, if I don't have to worry about you."

"Are you wearing your watch?"

"'Takes a licking and keeps on ticking.'"

"Right. I've got just noon. I'll turn my cell on again at twelve forty-five and call you, okay?"

"Okay. Synchronizing watches now."

"And, honey . . . please get home safe. Soon. Watch out for traffic while you're shoveling. Drivers won't be able to see you."

"I'll be fine. You stay inside until I get there."

If only he hadn't gone out in the storm to buy, of all things, snow shovels. *Well, here's another nice mess you've gotten us into, Stan.* I put on my heaviest winter gear, my new purple parka. Scruffy joined me at the door, heavy-pawed. I Velcro-strapped him into his fleece-lined slicker, which I only use in really rotten weather.

Speaking of Chihuahuas, Toots . . . don't you realize that a full-sized, heavy-coated French briard like moi *doesn't need to be tied up in one of these silly things?*

"Just shut up and wear it. The bright yellow complements your sandy fur. I bet if Honeycomb were here, she'd be most impressed. Now your job, as I see it, Scruffy, is to blaze a trail to the garage."

Hey, Toots—it's up to my ass out there.

"Oh, go on, you protein-packed sissy."

To his credit, Scruffy soon got the hang of forging through the heavy drifts, and I followed in the path he had broken through. We trudged out to the garage for Grandma's old snow shovels, kept waxed just as she'd taught me. Not lightweight plastic, they were smaller and heavier, but they worked just fine and had for decades.

I used one of the shovels to clean off the back stairs to the kitchen door, feeling elated, in full pioneer mode, almost reluctant to go inside. Then I realized it was a minute past time for my phone appointment. Hastily I tried my cell. No answer! Well, perhaps Joe was in the midst of jockeying his car out of the drift.

After giving Scruffy a brisk toweling, and cleaning the ice off his paws, I assembled storm supplies: flashlights, kerosene lanterns, candles, and my battery-operated radio, items that no self-respecting resident of the South Shore would be caught wanting. Yes, I was prepared. The only thing I had left to do in order to earn my Superwoman merit badge was to set about making soup in the kitchen fireplace.

I was kneeling down arranging a nice crisscross of kindling when I heard stamping on the porch. Scruffy did his friend-not-stranger *woof*, and I looked up to see Tip grinning through the glass pane in the door. That boy had certainly sprung up tall!

Pioneer woman or not, I suddenly felt relieved not to be alone. I flung open the door, nearly as effusive in my greeting as Scruffy. Tip was leaning the snowshoes he'd been wearing against the porch wall next to my shovel, and he had a second pair slung on his back.

"Did you advertise for a handyman, lady?"

"Tip, am I glad to see you. But I thought you'd be busy packing up stuff at your house."

"Naw, I got time now. What with the special circumstances, Uncle John got me permission to transfer to Plymouth for the rest of this year so's I can keep an eye on the house until we get it sold. Then it's back to Wiscasset for my junior year. But now I guess we'll be snowed in for a while. Where's Joe? I brought him these snowshoes," He shrugged them off his back and held them out, grinning. "They were Paw's, and Joe isn't much taller, so they should fit. I'll just take this shovel and clean up the paths."

"Joe's stuck in a drift somewhere between here and Home Warehouse. Which reminds me. Hang on a minute while I try the cell again. We just lost our lights and phone. And don't worry about those paths yet. They'll only fill up with snow again. But I could use your help when it stops."

Still no answer from Joe, but no need to panic yet, I told myself. Maybe his cell needed a charge. Tip insisted on shoveling out the garage so I could get the Jeep out later. I messed about in the kitchen, making a fire and setting on it my old black cauldron, which I filled with beef, vegetables, herbs, and water, thankful that we weren't dependent on a well run by an electric pump as some residents were.

When Tip came back to the house, I told him that Joe wasn't responding to my repeated attempts to call him. I would leave Tip to watch the fire while I took the Jeep out to find Joe. I knew just where he was. Coming out of Standish Plaza, he would have cut across by Owl Swamp Road to Route 3A. He should have gone by Route 44. But a little storm never daunted us pioneer types.

"Hey, Cass, I don't think that's such a good idea," Tip said. "The plows can't keep up with this storm, and the roads are a mess."

"Now, don't *you* start." I leaned over to stir my cauldron, feeling primitive and powerful.

Smells mighty good, Toots. Scruffy tried to position himself on the hearth rug, but I hefted him off. "Not here, big fella. You go lie on your bed, away from the fire."

"Well, then," Tip said, "I'm going out to clear away more snow from the sides of the garage door. Give the Jeep room to turn." He was gone before I could stop him.

The world without power had gone quiet except for the vicious wind howling off the Atlantic. What a surprise, then, when I looked out the window at the sound of a familiar motor and saw my Jeep cautiously edging out of the newly shoveled driveway. Seeing my face slack-jawed with unbelief, Tip had the chutzpah to wave when he drove by. I glanced at the small hook by the back door where I hang my car keys. Gone, of course. The boy was nervy enough to have taken over my rescue mission.

The dumb soup didn't keep me busy enough. I wrung my hands and paced the kitchen. It would get dark early. I'd call Deidre. When not on duty, Will often earned extra income by helping the town maintenance crews plow the roads. Maybe she could reach him, have him check Owl Swamp Road for Joe and Tip, the traitor.

Deidre didn't answer. Phillipa didn't answer. Fiona?

My finger was poised to punch in Fiona's number when my cell at last rang. "Hi, sweetheart. Everything is fine. Great idea to send Tip with the Jeep. He's just finished hauling me out of the drift, and we're on our way home."

I was relieved, angry, and nearly speechless.

"Thank Goddess. But that boy stole my car!" I complained.

"Now, now. He explained that to me. Sometimes guys have to take things into their own hands and do what they believe is right."

"We'll see about that."

"Love you."

"Yeah. Love you, too." I poured myself a medicinal brandy and went back to stirring the soup.

Chapter Twenty-Nine

For a few days, the roads were closed to all but emergency vehicles. Plymouth was shut down, many homes and businesses without power for nearly a week, but I was lucky, it was only two days before the electric and phone lines were restored on our street. Gradually, we all got in touch again, and I walked over to check on Patty, too. Lee Deluca had not surfaced anywhere, and no more poison attempts had been made. It was almost peaceful. A lull in the continual agitation of the past weeks.

I found Patty in good spirits, all smiles, with Loki weaving himself around her legs in a proprietary manner. She served tea and cookies by a cozy fireplace cheerily glowing with one of those fake logs that has a peculiar smell.

After we'd drunk our tea and Patty took up her knitting, some shapeless peach garment, she said, "Terrible thing, this storm. Treacherous walking, you know. Personally, I'm always careful to wear my galoshes with the ribbed tread. But, alas, Mrs. Pynchon went out into the driveway wearing shoes with slick leather soles, hurrying to give the paper person a piece of her mind for depositing the *Pilgrim Times* in a puddle of melting snow. Slipped on the frozen snow and cracked her ankle, poor dear. Crutches being too dangerous on icy walks, she hasn't even been able to attend services. Wyn paid a call, of course, and tried to pray with her, but she was not receptive, he said, to accepting her mishap as the Lord's will."

"Well, who is? It's human nature to accept the misfortunes of others better than one's own. But here's what we believe, Patty," I said, noting the impish grin she was trying to suppress. "Thoughts are things. Whatever you send out into the universe comes back to you threefold. Not that it's easy monitoring one's innermost impulses." I felt somewhat hypocritical delivering this Wiccan mini-sermon, remembering how I'd once had just such an evil thought toward Wyn Peacedale when he'd kicked Scruffy in the backside for dumping on the church lawn. But that was before we all got to know and like each other better. Possibly Wyn's broken leg had had nothing to do with me, anyway.

" 'Do good to them that hate you, and pray for them that despitefully use you,'" Patty quoted. "I try to be a good Christian, Cass. I even brought Mrs. P. some homemade brownies to perk up her spirits." Now Patty was grinning shamelessly. "I wonder if she dared to eat one, don't you?"

"Brownies!" I squeaked. "I hope you made them yourself."

"Hmmmm. Yes. Easy enough with a mix. I don't think that evil boy had any problem turning out batches of the things. I understand he was enrolled in a school cooking class, and his grandmother is famous for her pastries."

"His computer is located in her basement room. I wouldn't be surprised if he concocted his deadly treats in her kitchen."

"Bianca Deluca is quite active at Holy Family," Patty said. "She's over there almost every day, assisting in one parish project or another, from flowers to fetes."

"So with Grandma at the church organizing a rummage sale, Lee would have a clear field to play around in her kitchen."

"Play, indeed!" Patty sniffed.

"Detective Stern has talked to Bianca Deluca about giving up her grandson for his own good. He thought he got through to her, that she'd help to bring him in for questioning."

Patty laughed merrily, but her laugh had an edge to it. "That Bianca! *Omerta* is her middle name."

"You know her?"

"Oh, yes indeed. Jean introduced us at the Interdenominational Gospel Day. Jean's a member of Wyn's congregation, as was her aunt Lydia, even though the boy's been brought up Catholic. Lydia Craig was not pleased about that." Patty counted stitches, a lock of hair falling across her broad, fair forehead.

"From what I hear, Lydia Craig was never much pleased about anything her niece and nephews did or believed that departed even slightly from her own views."

Patty looked up from the indefinable peach garment—a shawl perhaps? "You could have knocked me over with an angel feather when she left all that money to Wyn."

"But you're adjusting to the notion of being rich?"

"The Lord moves in mysterious ways . . . blessed be the name of the Lord." Patty surveyed her handiwork more closely. "Money in Wyn's hands will be used for worthy causes, because basically he's a really good person. I believe that's why the Lord has spared Wyn from all those close calls with the poisoned desserts, the deadly salad, and the damned *Naturally Nice* juice."

"You may be right, Patty. It *is* rather miraculous."

"I owe you so much, Cass. And Heather. Especially for convincing me to adopt Loki. Such an unusual personality. I always wondered if animals had souls, and now I'm convinced not only that they have souls but that they connect us to the Holy Spirit in an utterly pure way. So I'm hoping, when the Craig will is probated, that Wyn will make a nice contribution to the Animal Lovers Shelter."

"Amen," I said.

It was the first of February, Imbolc, the Wiccan end of winter. The aftereffects of the Cape blizzard had reluctantly melted away, leaving the land rutted and muddy and the roads potholed. But the skies were clear blue again, and there was a whiff of something hopeful in the air. Could it be, as this Sabbat promised, the first stirrings of spring? We'd gathered at Deidre's to abolish the season of darkness and sweep away all negative influences. It was also an occasion for promoting fertility, but our hostess and priestess Deidre said she'd had quite enough fertility for the time being.

"Not for you, dearie," I'd said. "For you, we're calling the Universe of Infinite Solutions to bring you the ideal au pair. And fertility doesn't necessarily mean more babies, you know. What about creative inspiration?"

"Yes, let's focus on that," Phillipa had agreed. "Although you, Cass, might already have enough fertile ideas to keep us busy in the foreseeable future."

When our ceremony was concluded and the circle had been dispersed, it was time for the merry part of the meeting, with an excellent sherry provided by Heather and delectable almond moon cookies baked by Phillipa. But the merriment was somewhat muted by our mutual sense of foreboding.

"Where is he?" I asked Fiona. "You've always been our finder, and we need to find Lee Deluca." Weeks had passed without a clue to the missing boy's whereabouts. On the good side, no one had been poisoned, or threatened with poison, during the hiatus.

"That poor boy has ruined his whole life with impatience and greed," Fiona said. "And to tell you the truth, I have tried to dowse him out of hiding, but for some reason he's been able to throw up a very creditable cloak of invisibility. Maybe he *is* a changeling. And I'm not infallible, you know."

"No! I can't believe you mean that," Phillipa said with one of her wicked smiles.

"Yes, and what about the Plymouth Police Department?" Heather chided. "Foiled by the 'cloak of invisibility,' also?"

"Don't be a smart-ass. Every year thousands of young persons disappear off the face of the earth, and Goddess Herself can't find them, let alone an understaffed police force," Phillipa said. "Stone thinks that the Deluca boy, with his interest in the theater, may have headed to New York and lost himself in the crowd of young theater hopefuls."

"He's one slippery fish, all right. Squirmed right out of my hands, too," Deidre said. "A Pisces, naturally. Born on the Ides of March, Millie told me. I'll never forget how chilled I felt— Well, all I can say is, I've heard a lot about the 'evil eye,' but that boy really has a look that's everything I conceive *mal occhio* to be."

"I've seen that look. 'Soulless' is how I'd describe it."

"So how come many of his teachers described Lee as 'enchanting'?" Heather asked.

"They never encountered his anger," I said.

"Or scratched his pretty face," Deidre added. "That gives me an idea. Do you remember when we needed to find that bombmaker, Thomas Gere, and we called him back to us? Why don't we try that with Deluca?"

"One of Hazel's spells, as I recall," Heather said. "She had some innocent name for it. 'Recipe for Bringing Home.' What a hoot she must have been. I wish I'd known her. I remember I made special candles. Onion-skin yellow, in the old way."

"Heartsease. *Viola tricolor*. Sweetgrass, too. And cinnamon oil." I assembled herbal supplies in my mind.

"But do you also remember that we were all very sorry when Thomas Gere reappeared?" Phillipa reminded us.

"Oh, never mind that," Deidre said impatiently. "I can't stand the suspense. Let's do the damn spell. I'll make a poppet again, like I did then. A likeness to hang in the rafters with sweetgrass?"

"We wrote down his name and burned it in the candle flame," I recalled.

"Well, we hardly need to consult *Hazel's Book*, then," Fiona said. "You girls remember that spell very well."

"All except the gory results." Phillipa was still the bringer of evil omens. We should have listened. But, no, the very next night we five gathered at my house and retired to the newly refurbished cellar workroom. Joe's track lighting, while excellent for emergency appendectomies, was far too bright for spell-working.

We settled for my old green-shaded, single-bulb, shadow-swinging light.

Heather had created a marvelous yellow candle, studded with dried forget-me-nots and a few shards of yellow onion skin. From her friend Millie, Deidre had obtained a yearbook that showed Lee among his classmates. Using this likeness, she'd made a tiny poppet, which we secured to the cellar rafters with a braid of sweetgrass. On a square of parchment, Deidre lettered in charming calligraphy, *Leonardo Deluca*. I folded it, inserted a sprig of heartsease, and scented the paper with cinnamon oil for its attractive power.

Phillipa relented enough to compose a rhyme. We joined her in chanting:

Longing fills you, breath and bone,
Heartsease draws you ever near . . .
When the Goddess calls you home
All life's roads will lead you here.

Deidre burned the folded paper in the candle's flame, dropping it neatly into our working cauldron. Humming to herself, Fiona added a chant, the age-old rule of spell-working, "'To know, to dare, to will, to keep silent.'"

This should do it, we agreed. And Deidre was feeling especially pleased with herself for having come up with the idea of bringing Lee home.

Chapter Thirty

Lee Deluca came home all right, just long enough to borrow his family's car and embark on a vendetta. For some unimaginable reason in his twisted mind, he focused on Deidre. Perhaps it was her investigation of his early delinquencies. Or the scratch that marked his cheek, which had somehow festered and not healed adequately, leaving a crescent mark on his left cheek.

I'd been printing out my Internet orders for herbal products—thrilled to see that my new Psychic Visions dream pillows and Aphrodite's Bath baskets were selling so well—when I got one of those nanosecond flashes that I ought to check out Freddie's computer traps. It had been a long time, and with Lee on the run there was little chance that he'd be interested in the fake casting call, but maybe the other link—"Poisons in the Kitchen"—would still be intriguing.

I consulted the carefully noted step-by-step instructions Freddie had left me for penetrating Lee's computer. As I typed in his personal password, "Puck," I considered that my efforts might be considered illegal by some, but I dismissed the thought instantly, like brushing away an irksome fly.

Eureka! I was in! I could scroll through Lee's files and open whatever I wished. Some of the file titles were rather obscure, so

I realized I might have to go through them one at a time in order not to miss anything relevant. But there were hundreds. So that would take me hours. Why couldn't I simply dowse them the way Fiona would? Worth a try.

I printed out several pages that listed the file documents in his PC. From the bedroom, I fetched the gold eagle pendant that Joe had given me to commemorate where and why we'd met. I held it dangling on its gold chain over the list of Lee's files. It hung there unmoving. I closed my eyes and brought all my spiritual power to bear on the eagle. My eyes flew open as I felt the pendant begin to swing in lazy circles over the printed page, not unlike our own eagles soaring in Jenkins Park. Then, gradually, the circles turned into a horizontal track to first one and then the other file. The names read FAM HIST and SCHOOL REC.

I hung the pendant around my neck and tucked it inside my flannel shirt. Then I opened FAM HIST, which proved to be the genealogy of the Craig family. But what was most interesting was the list of names typed underneath the chart: Lydia Craig, Rev. Peacedale, Geoffrey Craig, Bruce Craig, Bruce Craig, Jr., Shirley Craig. Could this be a cold-blooded inventory of everyone who stood between Lee and his aunt's money? If not, why would Wyn's name be noted on the Craig family page? If Wyn died, the money would be divided between Geof, Bruce, and Lee's mother, Jean. Geof had no children, but if Bruce died, would his share pass to his children Bruce, Jr., and Shirley? A trust, perhaps? I would have to ask Heather, with her direct pipeline to the firm of Borer, Buckley, and Bangs.

Did Lee intend to poison all of them so that the whole five million would belong to his doting mother?

With a little thrill of fear, I brought up SCHOOL REC. Not "recreation," but "recipes" from Basic Cooking 101, were typed into this file. The recipes were indexed by title. Scrolling down through Eggs Goldenrod, Sloppy Joes, and Gingerbread Cookies, I clicked on "Brownies," and found not a cooking-class recipe but a recipe titled "Mom's Brownies Plus." What followed were the directions for preparing the bar cookies from a Baker Boy Mix, adding two tablespoons of artificial vanilla (ugh! too much) and three tablespoons of chocolate liqueur. The one more odd ingredient: half a cup of chopped "XXX."

I didn't think "XXX" meant confectioner's sugar. *X for the unknown ingredient* whose mousy smell would need masking with lots of vanilla and liqueur.

What more would Stone need to bring a case against the boy? If only we could find him. But how would I explain my possession of this information? Well, I'd work that out later. Meanwhile, I printed out everything and stuffed the pages into an antique atlas of the world's oceans.

No sooner had I put the big, clumsy book back on its special shelf when the phone rang. It was Phillipa. "Cass! Please get over here fast! Lee's taken the children."

"What! Taken? You mean . . . Deidre's? All of them?"

"No. Thank Goddess, Jenny and Baby Anne are safe. But he's got the two boys and Fiona's little girl. It's like a hit from the Pied Piper."

"Holy Mother! Where's Fiona?"

"Outdoors screaming. As far as I can tell, she's completely undone. So unlike her. Dee's on the phone with the police, so I'm calling on my cell. I think Dee's holding herself together by sheer nerve alone. We need you. Maybe you can zero in on where he's taken them."

"See if anyone has a Valium you can pour into Fiona. Who was watching the children when this happened? Fiona or Deidre would never have . . . Even Jenny . . ."

"Deidre's mother-in-law, just for a few hours while Dee ran to the hospital. It seems that Will fell off the Craig mansion roof."

"Will hurt, too? What in the world was he doing there?" I was incredulous at this run of disastrous events.

"Working with the town crew. Trying to remove the catalpa that caved in the roof so that they could cover it with a tarpaulin.

Pryde's trying to save the goods inside. Maybe Lee was watching for a break to grab the kids, and when Dee went flying out to the hospital, he took his chance."

"Did he take them away in the car?" I felt as if my heart had stopped. An earlier vision was surfacing in my consciousness. Some of the details had gone fuzzy. But I remembered the car, the screaming.

"Yes. His mother's green Volkswagen. Rather conspicuous. With the Amber Alert up and running, someone will surely spot that vehicle before he gets out of Plymouth."

"This is a clever boy. He'll be allowing for that and stay off the main roads."

"Come quickly, then."

"We're on our way. Better see if you can find Fiona's pistol and hide it."

"I already looked. The reticule was full of arrowroot cookies, picture books, and child-care pamphlets. Apparently now that she's a parent, Fiona's had the good sense to lock that pistol away somewhere. Just as well. In her present state, she might start shooting up the neighborhood. See you soon, then."

By now Joe, who'd been fixing a fresh pot of coffee in the kitchen, was leaning on my shoulder, listening intently to our conversation. I guess I had been screaming in an excited fashion. His brawny arm around my shoulders made for one secure place in a crazy world, but I couldn't rest there.

A few minutes later, we were hurtling along Route 3A toward Deidre's house. Joe had insisted on taking the wheel of the Jeep, and a good thing, too, since I was in a strange, otherworldly state—beyond agitation, bordering on coma.

"Why was Laura Belle at Deidre's?" Joe asked.

"It's a shared babysitting deal. What I wonder is how Lee wormed his way in there."

"Doesn't matter now."

"Right." That vision I'd seen. The Volkswagen on top of a

slope, water below, children screaming. And something else. What? Where? Who would know?

My hand found the cell phone in my bag. I punched Tip's number.

"Hi, Cass. What's up?"

I told him.

"If people hadn't let that kid slime his way out of trouble so many times, maybe he wouldn't have turned into a monster. We gotta stop that sonofabitch now."

"I knew you'd want to help. Maybe there'll be some tracking down the line, I don't know. Right now he's driving his mother's Volks. Do you think you could meet us at Deidre's? The trouble is, Joe and I are almost there now and can't turn back for you. Is it too far for your bike?"

"Nah. I'll be there in twenty minutes."

We weren't quite prepared for the scene of utter chaos around Deidre's house. Police cars pulled up at all angles, the fire chief's red car on the lawn, off-duty firemen's SUVs, and, of course, all of us.

"M&Ms had Valium. She took two and got Fiona to take one, also. I think it smoothed the edge off her hysteria, that's all," Heather warned me as soon we got in the door. "And then, to make matters worse, a few minutes ago Fiona took off in her Town Car to find Lee and the kids. She's too agitated to dowse them effectively, though. Oh, and she left a message for you."

"What?"

"Ironically, she said *you* should get control of yourself. Now what did she mean by that?"

"I think I have an idea. But tell me, how's Deidre?"

"Cool as ice. I don't know how she does it, but I'm betting there'll be a nervous breakdown coming down the line. Personally, I'm clinging to the idea that we can stop Lee. I won't be able to stand it if those children are harmed." Heather was beginning to sound a little hysterical herself. "Anyway, you'll find Dee in the living room, directing operations."

Joe had been standing on one foot and then the other, listening to all this. "I'll go outside and see what I can find out. Maybe I can help." That glint in his eye said "spoiling for action."

"Okay, but please don't go off searching. We may want to follow some lead ourselves, and I'll need you."

He nodded, then trotted outside to where a cluster of men huddled together, looking at a map.

"Phillipa?" I asked.

"Upstairs with Jenny and Baby Anne. Phil's reading them stories. I have to say this is a side of her I've never seen. Jenny's terribly upset, too. Apparently, M&Ms had just gone to get Baby Anne up from her nap. Jenny was supposed to stay downstairs with the other children but instead she followed to fetch some books. Lee came to the door at that fortuitous moment, with what ploy we don't know, but the children went with him. They didn't even put on their coats. M&Ms looked out the upstairs window and saw the Volks leaving the driveway with three little faces looking out the back window."

"Okay. I'm going to Dee. Tip's going to be here soon on his bike. Tell him to find me. Somehow I've got the wild idea that he's the key."

"Tip is the key?"

"Well, maybe *a* key."

Deidre was sitting cross-legged on the floor in front of the round oak coffee table, the phone in the crook of her neck, while she made notes on a pad of paper. Other pages of neatly printed notes were lined up on the coffee table. "Of course you can arrest them," Deidre was saying in a tone of icy fury. "I demand you arrest those two women. They know where that miserable bastard has taken the children, I'm sure of it. Just let me get my hands on them. I'll have the truth out of them."

She looked up at me, her eyes completely without expression. For a moment, I thought I was looking at one of the Stepford wives. Hoping to break the spell before she cracked in two, I held out my arms. Suddenly she put down the phone with a low cry of such anguish as I hope never to hear again, and she let me hold her. "How's Will?" I whispered. Heather came into the living room, and I motioned her over to us.

"Broken leg, cracked ribs, and concussion. Doesn't have a clue. His buddies are all out on the roads looking for the Volks," Deidre said, sobbing.

"I'm going to try something. Here's Heather, now. I want you to sit with her quietly, no more phone calls, while I go upstairs for a few minutes. I need to concentrate. I can do this, I know I can."

I nodded to Heather, and she took my place holding Deidre. Upstairs, I heard Phillipa's voice reading aloud in the girls' room. Baby Anne was laughing. I closed myself in Deidre's workroom and sat in her rocking chair, surrounded by her handiwork, a phantasmagoria of dolls. They all seemed to be looking at me with beseeching eyes, as if I were Gepetto and could wish them into reality.

I thought, *If you have spirits, join with my spirit now in finding our children*.

A fronds-of-fern candle, one of Heather's creations, was standing on the bookcase with a box of matches beside it. Exactly what I needed! I lit its wick and fixed my eyes on the light in the unthinking way that had often triggered clairvoyant episodes in the past. Always before I had been an unwilling participant, dragged into some fearful knowledge or frightening experience. Now I reached for the source of all-knowing love. I asked to return to the vision I'd had earlier—the car and the screaming children—then I allowed all thought to cease. The images seemed to form slowly, but it may have been only a few moments, because such episodes are as timeless as dreams.

Again I found myself in a woodland setting looking down at an earthen track that sloped toward water. Ocean or lake? It rippled quietly in the sunshine. I could see boats moored below, some of them shining. Half-filled with freezing water. Wooden canoes with hand-hewn surfaces. It was all coming back to me. I tried to look around within the vision for some sign that would reveal where I was, but all I could see was a packed earthen path with dark pines looming overhead. Far at the end of that path, opposite the water, I caught sight of a kind of lean-to hut beside a campfire site, cold and lifeless. At that instant, the green Volks came sputtering up over the hill's crest. This time I could see the driver and the passengers. It was Lee, no mistake, and the three screaming children were our children. The car screeched down the slope, heading toward the water.

I shook myself out of the vision, feeling faint and nauseated. Then I realized that Tip was in the room with me. Had he opened the door without my even hearing him? "Put your head between your knees. I'll get you a glass of water and be right back," he said.

I did as he suggested, and a minute later he was back with a glass in his hand. Sipping the cold water did help, but there was no time to waste. As if in answer to that thought, Joe came bounding up the stairs and joined us, looking at me with a worried expression, from which I gathered that I appeared somewhat wild-eyed. The Sibyl run amok.

"I've seen the car, Lee, and the children, and I have this setting in my mind's eye. I'm going to describe it." The words tumbled out of me with great urgency. I needed to get everyone moving. But where? "Must be in Myles Standish State Forest, maybe somewhere near College Pond. I hope that what I saw has not happened yet and we still have time to stop him."

There was a drawing pad and colored pens on the table. Joe handed me paper and a blue pen. "Give me a green and a brown one, too," I said.

I talked, I drew. When I started to sketch the boats and tried to show how they were hewn, Tip cried out. "I know! I know! That's not College Pond. That's Eel River Pond. It's Plimouth Plantation. Paw and me worked there some summers. Come on—I can take you to that exact spot, where they show how Indians made canoes out of logs."

The three of us raced down the stairs. Heather looked up startled as we clattered by. "Plimouth Plantation, Eel River," I whispered hastily. "Tell Stone to send help—he'll know how to handle things—avoid a tragedy. It won't do to have that whole herd of firemen crashing in there, maybe panicking Lee. But keep Dee here—in case it's bad. Oh, and don't forget to send us some good white light." With that, I ran after Joe and Tip, and we all jumped into the Jeep. Plimouth Plantation was only a few miles down Route 3A, closed for the winter, but that wouldn't stop us.

Chapter Thirty-One

I don't think I took a full deep breath during that whole wild ride. At the speed he was traveling, it took Joe only a few minutes to reach the plantation. A steel gate obstructed the main entrance. *Closed until March 27*, the sign said. *No trespassers. Police take notice.* Without hesitation, Joe rerouted the Jeep off-road around the gate and rammed it through the bushes, following a track that appeared to have been made by past trespassers. Was that Lee's work? Or had resourceful teenagers found their way in here earlier?

"Take the right road at the fork." Tip gave urgent instructions. "Up ahead it's meant to be a footpath, but it's probably wide enough for you to get the Jeep through. Yes, that's it. Now bear left. The hill slopes down to the water where the dugouts are moored. They'll be sunk for the winter, so the wood won't crack—keeps them watertight."

Suddenly we were there, and Tip had been right, as I knew he must be. I was looking at the same scene I'd seen in my vision—the lean-to, the cold fireplace. Joe slammed to a stop at the track to the water, and we jumped out of the Jeep.

As soon as I looked down the slope, I began to scream. The Volks was already in the river. The water was up to the windows.

The children's frightened faces were pressed against the glass, their cries soundless.

At the same instant I was seeing this, Joe was already in motion, running for the water as if his clothes were on fire. Hard on his heels, Tip was shouting something. Without hesitation, Joe jumped into the river and struggled with the door of the Volks. Either it was locked or held tightly closed by the weight of water. Tip, behind him, was waving a dark object. The big, old hammer I keep under the floor mat in the Jeep in case I ever need to break a window myself. When Tip got close enough, he tossed the heavy object ahead of him and Joe grabbed it in midair. Then Joe pulled his jacket off, wrapped it around the hammer, and smashed the window.

I could see the river water pouring into the Volks now. Still screaming, I was no help at all. Joe was still struggling with the door. Now he reached in through the broken glass and unlocked it. He and Tip together pulled it open. The children's voices could be heard, choking and crying, so I knew they would live, praise Goddess. Joe came back out of the car holding Bobby and Laura Belle, one in each arm. He passed the children to Tip and half-waded, half-dove back for Willie. Now that river water was filling it, the Volks was sinking fast.

My feet finally moved, and I rushed down the slope to take the children from Tip, then back to the Jeep to get the blankets I keep there for Scruffy. I would strip the drenched children and wrap them in the dry blankets, still warm from the car.

Lee was standing in front of the Jeep! He was holding a tire iron and grinning at me. The smile didn't reach his eyes; they were like ice.

"Get away from us," I said with all the authority I could muster. "You tried to drown these children, and I'll see you prosecuted for it, and for all those poisonings as well. You're a sick, sick boy."

"I was trying to save the children, but you guys got in the way. I was going to break the windows with this iron."

"You grabbed those children with the intention of killing them," I protested.

"Hey, the kids begged me to take them for a ride. That's not a crime, is it?"

"Yes, it is, Lee. It's called kidnapping."

He raised the iron in a menacing gesture. Bobby screamed, and I half-turned away to protect the children with my body.

I felt rather than saw something rush by me like a streak of blurred colors. I looked back at Lee to see his gloating expression instantly changed to dismay. He dropped the iron and ran for the woods. Tip was running after him. Two boys who had contested with each other in track were now running for their lives, but I couldn't watch. I was in the back of the Jeep wrapping up the children. Joe came running up with Willie. They were both wet right through, but Joe's smile was triumphant. In the distance, we heard the sirens. *More blankets*, I thought. *We need more blankets. And Joe needs to get out of those wet clothes, too.*

"Joe! Willie! Are you all right? Hear that noise, Willie? That's help on the way. Oh, here, Laura Belle, you stay wrapped up tight now, and hold on to Bobby." Laura Belle's huge violet-blue eyes gazed at me fearfully. What further damage would this trauma do to the child's psyche?

Joe was looking around in surprise. "Where's Tip? If he hadn't brought that hammer, I don't know what I would've done."

"Lee," I said. I couldn't seem to talk very well. "Lee was here. Tip chased him into the woods."

"Which way?"

I pointed, as just a minute later, I was pointing out the same route to the three uniformed cops who'd come in the squad car with Stone. One of them, a petite blonde who looked as if the gun at her belt might topple her over, stayed to help me comfort and warm the children while Stone and the other two raced after Tip and Lee. I noticed that Stone outdistanced the rest, his tall, rangy form seeming to melt through the trees effortlessly. For a scholarly type, he sure could sprint.

Leaving the children with the policewoman and Joe, I grabbed the cell out of my bag and called Heather. No answer. I tried Phillipa.

"Oh, Cass, am I glad to hear from you," she cried. "News?"

"We have the children. Other than the fright of their lives and a chilly dip into Eel River Pond, they're all right. We've got them dry and warm right here. Go tell Dee this instant."

"Dee overheard Heather's call to Stone and insisted on following him to the plantation. Heather wouldn't let her drive, of course, so they're both on their way to wherever you ended up. Eel River, you say?"

"Yes. Part of Plimouth Plantation extends to the river. What about Fiona? Have you heard from her? We've got to let her know that Laura Belle is safe."

"Well, that's another problem. Fiona finally gave up roaring around town and drove back here. But when she heard the latest developments, she insisted on racing to the scene to rescue Laura. And, worse, she was waving her pistol. Apparently, it's been locked up in her glove compartment. No one could stop her. Or at least, I couldn't. For a plump little lady, she packs a lot of muscle. So I left M&Ms to stay with Jenny and Anne, and I'm in my car right now, trying to get to Fiona before Fiona gets to Lee."

"Good move. Two ambulances just pulled in, so I've got to go now. *Call* the minute you catch up with Fiona. Talk about a loose cannon on the deck!"

I don't know how Heather managed it, but somehow she'd run red lights and raced recklessly after the ambulances. Right after the paramedics arrived, the Mercedes careened in behind them. Careless of fenders and paint, Heather pulled it into the woods so as not to block their exit. Then Dee was jumping out, crying and screaming.

"They're all right. They're all right," I kept saying as she threw her arms around the two boys and Laura Belle, too. The paramedics were hovering nearby, wanting to evaluate the children. They gave Joe a blanket for himself, but he was too edgy to sit still. I had to hang on to his arm to keep him from running after Stone. "You've done enough now, Joe," I murmured warmly. "It's you who saved them, you know. Now let the others bring in that wretched boy. Oh, I wish Fiona hadn't gone off half-cocked. She should be here with us."

"Fiona's hysterical right now," Heather said. "But basically she's a finder. She knows we're at the plantation, and she'll roll in here any minute now. Isn't it wonderful that the children are safe! What happened?"

I was about to tell her when we heard a gunshot somewhere up near the Visitors' Welcome Center. Then a whoop and a scream from the general direction of the old fort.

"That's it," Joe said. "I'm going after them." He tossed off the blanket and began running toward the fort.

"You and I had better follow that shot," I said to Heather. "That's got to be Fiona." With the ambulances still filling the dirt track, it would be too difficult to get either of our cars out of the odd places where they were parked, but the distance wasn't that far. We ran uphill to the Welcome Center, then on to the fort when we spotted Fiona crouched behind her baby blue Town Car. She seemed to be trying to get a bead on someone at the fort. Heather literally threw herself on Fiona and wrestled away the pistol.

"He's up there. I saw him up there!" Fiona cried out.

"So are Tip and Stone and a couple of cops," I hissed. "What if you'd hit the wrong person? Or even the right person. You'd be going to jail right along with that depraved youth."

"And, besides," Heather chimed in, "we've rushed up here to tell you the best news. All the children are safe! You can go to Laura Belle right now—she's waiting for you just down this road. So come on, you crazy lady. Let's go!"

I gave a kind of sign to Heather to escort Fiona to her little girl and leave me there. Fiona needed no more urging, a bundle of tartan hurling itself down the hill toward the child. Heather handed the pistol to me and went, too, but looked back to say, "Be careful, Cass. Don't go into that fort until you know it's safe. And don't shoot that damned thing."

Fiona's keys were still in her car. I had turned my back on the fort and was hiding the pistol in the trunk under a box of car junk when I felt myself hit hard in the back. I almost fell into the trunk. Then Lee was on top of me, slamming my head against the floor of the trunk. Again and again. I was more than "seeing stars"; my brain was bursting with exploding supernovas.

Yet somehow, although dazed and in pain, I managed to turn myself around to see five guys, including Tip, pounding out of the fort after this one agile kid who was now dancing around with Fiona's pistol. Without a moment's thought, I threw myself forward and tackled the boy's legs. He fell to the ground with a cry of panic. The pistol skittered out of his grip, and we both grabbed for it at once. It was achingly just beyond either grasp. I could feel my fingers barely touching the cold metal. But Lee pushed me out of the way and stretched out his hand just a little farther than mine. Then a foot seemed to come out of nowhere and clamp itself down on Lee's eager hand. I looked up through the agony of quite a few bumps and bruises. It was Joe.

Joe hauled Lee up by his collar and, with admirable restraint, merely pinned his arms and turned him around so that one of the cops could cuff the boy, who now was crying. "I want my mother. I want a lawyer. I was only trying to save those children when this Indian chased me away."

It was probably a good thing that Stone and the officers took Lee away before Fiona got hold of him. With Joe's arm around me and Tip close beside, we watched the cruisers drive away, the boy in the backseat looking stunned and impossibly young. I thought about Lee's mother and grandmother, how they would fight tooth and nail for their darling. I imagined that confrontation could easily spin out of control.

But what I never dreamed was that the Reverend Selwyn Peacedale, the newest millionaire in Plymouth, would insist upon hiring a prominent criminal lawyer in Boston to defend Leonardo Deluca. The famous and infamous Owen Llewellyn, defender of murderers, gangsters, and felons of all description, agreed to take the case.

"Wyn feels a spiritual responsibility in this whole tragic series of events," Patty tried to explain over a cup of tea at the parsonage. I wasn't sure she understood herself. "We prayed over the matter, and Wyn feels God spoke to him."

"Yes?" I urged. What I really wanted to know was God's point of view about all the poor souls who'd been poisoned, some of them fatally, by a greedy kid.

"I don't know exactly, but the gist was that Wyn wouldn't feel able to administer a single penny of that Craig fortune with a good conscience if one of the Craig family, only a child really, and a talented child at that, went to prison for some grisly life term among a lot of hairy, horny older men. Wyn said if Lydia Craig hadn't practically disinherited her own family, none of these terrible things would have happened."

"Wrong! Neither Lee nor anyone else except the firm of Borer, Buckley, and Bangs knew the provisions of the Craig will. When those poisoned brownies showed up at the church social hour, Lee must have thought his mother was still a primary heir."

"Well, you can't be sure what the boy knew," Patty said. She glanced at the door as if to be sure that her husband was still safely tucked away in his study, then continued in a whisper. "Wyn may have mentioned the bequest to someone, what he knew about it at the time, and you know how news travels in Plymouth. Neither one of us is comfortable with the thought of that youngster shut away from the world for most of his young life."

"A terrible prospect, I agree. And it's happening more every day that really young children, even younger than Lee, are committing heinous adult crimes. What can the law possibly do with the boy?"

Chapter Thirty-Two

As it turned out, what the law did was pull in its claws when Owen Llewellyn strolled into the courtroom and melted the stony heart of Judge Lax. The attorney's mellifluous voice caressed every consonant that rolled off his tongue. A big, handsome man with a mane of white hair, he wore a gray Armani suit and sincere blue tie; Llewellyn looked solid and sympathetic, confident of the virtue of his argument as well as of his own personal power. The prosecuting district attorney, Liz Strait, a shrill, nervous young woman with dark hair in a stylishly uneven haircut that condemned her without a trial to the scorn of every Plymouth matron in the courtroom, was no match for the Welsh word-sorcerer.

When search warrants were finally issued, the potted hemlock plant that once had been growing in Bianca Deluca's cellar room was still missing, and every file in Lee's computer had been erased by a special program he'd installed. Stone couldn't use my copies of Lee's incriminating computer notes because, as he informed me sternly, I had virtually stolen them. With little evidence, and that circumstantial, to connect Lee to the poisonings, the D.A. had settled for a charge of attempted murder of the children he tried to drown in Eel River Pond. But the boy was still two weeks short of his sixteenth birthday. So in his first appearance before Judge Lax, Llewellyn succeeded in having Leonardo Deluca's trial moved to juvenile court. The juvenile court judge was Maria Lacrimas, whose bias in favor of youngsters was well known. And since now there would be no jury, the decision would be hers alone.

No one was allowed in the courtroom during a juvenile criminal trial except the attorneys, family members, and witnesses. Fiona's humming spell could not be used to shake the truth out of Lee. But Deidre, Joe, Tip, and I were present as witnesses. Lee looked up from the yellow legal pad on which he was writing notes, and I could tell from the hint of a grin that he had found a way to resist any psychic intrusion.

"Truly a changeling," Deidre murmured.

Behind Lee and Llewellyn, the entire Craig clan was assembled to show familial support. Jean and Arthur Deluca held hands. Bianca Deluca glared at everyone. Arthur Deluca looked bemused, like a man lost in a perplexing dream, while Jean beamed loving trust to their son. Heidi Craig sat at the defense table with Lee, Llywelyn, and Llewellyn's two assistants. With Wyn's deep pockets at the ready, no expense needed to be spared.

Deidre testified to Lee's earlier intrusion into her home, how she had come home and found him trying to poison her children with so-called Maraschino Milk, how she had wrestled him out the door.

"Mrs. Ryan, have you ever been treated for anxiety or depression?" Llewellyn asked sympathetically in his cross-examination.

"No, I have not."

"Are you saying that you've *never* been prescribed medicine for anxiety or insomnia?"

"Oh, perhaps once. After my baby Anne was born."

"So the answer is *yes*, then. You have been treated for anxiety. Did you strike the boy?"

"Not exactly."

"Did you draw blood in any way?"

"Well, just his cheek got scratched."

"But you had no actual evidence of poison? Just what you fancied was the case? In fact, you didn't even lodge a complaint with the police or have the milk analyzed."

"He ran away with the bottles. But I knew, I knew. And that day Lee Deluca threatened my children."

"Oh, come now, Mrs. Ryan. What did he say, exactly, that you construed as a threat?"

"He said 'You shouldn't have marked my face, lady. I play a mean Richard the Third, so watch out.'"

"So you did assault the boy . . . you're admitting that."

"But Richard the Third killed the princes in the tower. That was a direct threat, a reference to my children."

"A threat you never saw fit to report to the authorities? Why do you imagine the boy was trying to harm you or your family?"

"He's a sociopath, that's why. He doesn't need a reason."

"But in what context did he know you, Mrs. Ryan."

"I'd been at his school, asking questions about his record."

Llewellyn turned to the judge with a significant look. "You'd been trying to discredit him at his school, is that it?"

"Not discredit him, no. But he does have a history of—"

"We're not here to discuss the boy's school record, although it's an outstanding one. Mrs. Ryan, are you an alumni of Assumption High School?"

"Yes, I am."

"And are you still a practicing Catholic? Or have you recently joined a witch cult professing satanic beliefs?"

"*Objection!*" Liz Strait finally came to life. "Mrs. Ryan's religious beliefs have nothing to do with her testimony here today."

Judge Lacrimas agreed.

"No more questions for this witness, Your Honor."

M&Ms was called to testify that she'd just gone upstairs for a minute to lift Baby Anne from her crib when Lee Deluca sneaked into the kitchen and lured the two boys and Laura Belle out into his car. "Just like the Pied Piper," she affirmed, glaring at the boy.

Then it was our turn to relate the events we had witnessed at Plimouth Plantation. Tip and Joe testified to the scuffle with Lee and the gun. I described my confrontation with Lee and the tire iron. If looks could slay, the beady-eyed Bianca would have had me dead and buried before Llewellyn sauntered over for his cross-examination.

"Ms. Shipton, what did young Leonardo himself *say* he was trying to do?" the defense attorney asked me.

"He said he was trying to save the children. But—"

"Thank you. And what did he say about the implement he carried?"

"You mean the tire iron? That he was going to break the car windows with it. But that's such a—"

"No more questions for this witness, Your Honor."

Perhaps impressed with Lee Deluca's theatrical skill, so much like his own, Llewellyn allowed his client to testify. The boy's demeanor exuded trustworthiness, kindness, bravery, and every other Boy Scout virtue, as he explained how he'd dropped in to apologize to Mrs. Ryan for scaring her on their earlier encounter. He'd found the children alone and unattended, and when they begged him to take them for a ride in his little green car, he reluctantly agreed, thinking they'd at least be in someone's care. Just for fun, he'd driven into Plimouth Plantation to show the boys the Pilgrim settlement. He'd stopped the car for a moment and got out to check the tire—the steering had been pulling to one side. Perhaps something sharp in the dirt road had caused a leak. He'd picked up the tire iron, thinking he might have to change the tire. Willie had locked the car doors and somehow managed to shift the car into neutral. The Volks had rolled down the hill into the water. Then we—Joe, Tip, and I—had arrived and misunderstood the whole situation. Lee had been about to run into the water and break the car window so that he could rescue the children.

It was a performance worthy of a seasoned Shakespearean actor. By the time he finished speaking, it was late afternoon, and the sun's rays through the courtroom window rested on Lee Deluca's tousled curls like a halo. I did not feel it was going well for our side.

The testimony completed, we all stood up while the judge retired to her chambers; she would deliver her decision at ten the next morning. Meanwhile, Lee was released into the custody of his father and mother.

All of us, including Tip and Patty, who had been in the hallway knitting furiously all during Lee's trial, gathered for a gloomy supper at Heather's, whose conservatory could be pressed into service as a dining room for the multitudes. Captain Jack, always unfazed by the unexpected guest or a horde of them, busied himself cooking up an impromptu feast featuring baked haddock and sourdough bread, like the miracle of the loaves and the fishes. Meanwhile we hung around in disconsolate postures, drinking.

"Patty, why don't you call Wyn to join us," Heather suggested. "It makes me nervous to think of him rooting around in your refrigerator by himself."

"Thank you, dear. Of course, I'll call, but surely we're safe enough now that the Deluca boy is on trial, for heaven's sake," Patty said.

Wyn said he was too tired to be good company. He'd spent the day in prayer, meditation, and a meeting with the architects he'd hired to design Gethsamane's new entrance and addition. He'd just have a peanut butter sandwich and a glass of coffee milk. Then he was going straight to bed.

"Call him back!" I insisted, handing her my cell phone. "What about that milk? Has it been vetted?" Joe put a calming hand on my arm. Was I sounding hysterical?

Patty dropped her workbag instantly and called Wyn right back.

But it was all right. The coffee milk hadn't even been opened. I was definitely getting paranoid.

"Surely the boy won't want to cast suspicion on himself in the middle of his trial," Phillipa pointed out.

"I wouldn't put anything past him," Tip said. "I know that kid from track meets. He's got the idea that he can get away with anything. And he usually does."

"But remember that the Reverend Peacedale is financing his legal eagle," Phillipa added. "No point in killing the heir who's laying the golden egg."

"Yes, I guess you're right," I admitted. "Patty, I'm sorry for alarming you. I just hope Judge Lacrimas sees the light."

"I'll pray that she does." Patty said, holding out her wineglass for a refill as Heather waltzed around the room topping up glasses with two open bottles of a delectable Orvieto. Dick smiled at her indulgently and wielded the bread knife, cutting chunks from a sourdough loaf to accompany the mammoth wheel of Vermont cheddar cheese that was Captain Jack's notion of hors d'oeuvres.

"What an excellent idea," Fiona said. "Let's all pray for that lovely judge, each in her own way. In fact, put down your glasses, ladies. For this, we must hold hands." *Yes, of course,* I thought, and could see the same resolve on my friends' faces. We formed a circle, joined by Patty, and bowed our heads silently for an interval of meditation. Then suddenly Fiona flung up her hands, still hanging on to those she was holding, Deidre's and Patty's, as Phillipa, Heather, and I did the same. Our fervent thoughts flew out into the cosmos and directly, I hoped, to Judge Lacrimas's inner ear.

"That should do it," Fiona said. "Carry on, ladies." Soon we were dining and reveling again, each somehow assured that right would prevail.

We might never know if our thoughts and prayers had a real effect. But however she was moved to see the light, Judge Lacrimas was not taken in by Lee Deluca's deceptive version of events. The facts remained that three small children had been lured away from their home, driven to a deserted tourist park, and nearly drowned in the Deluca car while Lee himself was watching from a safe distance. She found Leonardo Deluca guilty of aggravated assault and sentenced him to two years in a maximum-security juvenile detention training center in Framingham. He would be released when he was eighteen. In addition, Lee was ordered to take part in a new psychiatric program for youngsters who had shown high scholastic achievement and/or artistic promise before they got into trouble with the law.

"And the sessions will be off-campus, so to speak. MacLean Hospital is running the project, which is privately funded. You might call it a 'gifted delinquent' program," Phillipa announced. "I'm disgusted with the way this sociopath is being coddled."

So were we all. We'd gathered at Deidre's to discuss the verdict. Jenny and Willie were in school, but Deidre was kept busy running up and downstairs to tend to Will, home from the hospital, and to get Bobby and Annie into their beds for afternoon naps. Phillipa had offered to make the coffee, which, brewed by her hands, gave a bright-eyed caffeine boost to the afternoon slump. "And that charming lad will seduce all his therapists for sure. So we'd better all watch out when he's released in two years," she predicted.

"Too late, though, for him to murder Wyn and collect that inheritance," I pointed out.

"I wonder how tight security will be when they're schlepping those delinquents over to MacLean twice a week," Phillipa mused.

"Well, one good thing—Arthur's moving his family out of town. No one will say where, but I'll wager it's not far away from the training school," Deidre said. "Still, I don't know if I'll ever feel safe."

"Fiona will know where," Heather said. "Won't you, Fiona?"

Fiona smiled mysteriously. "Don't worry, ladies. I'll see to it that Leonardo never gets near my little darling again."

"Uh oh. Watch it, Fiona," I warned.

"Never mind that, Cass," said Deidre. "Whatever you're going to do, Fiona, include all of us and our families. That depraved kid got off way too easy. No more Ms. Nice Witch, I say."

Chapter Thirty-Three

Honeycomb gave birth to a litter of seven pups on Valentine's Day—and through Valentine's night as well—effectively canceling out the romantic plans any of her attendants might have been entertaining. It was a home birth, in the familiar surroundings of the conservatory, the rest of Heather's canine companions being relegated to their lavish garage kennels. The golden was attended by her personal veterinarian with Heather assisting.

I thought it best to leave Scruffy at home, but I was there for the first five whelps before exhaustion claimed me. Tip had wanted to witness, as he described it, "the miracle of birth," but at the sight of the first pup emerging in its bloodied caul, which the mother immediately licked off, he turned grayish-green and rushed out of the conservatory.

We were all back the next morning, however, this time with Scruffy, to admire the litter. Honeycomb, weary, but proud and poised, accepted our effusive praise as only her duc. She knew she had done something extraordinary. The soft, roly-poly pups blinked their first at the world, nuzzled against their mother, and drank deeply of their new lives.

Picking up an abandoned tennis ball, Scruffy wandered over

nonchantlantly, and looked down with some amazement at this new development. Perhaps he would have dropped the ball into the whelping box for the little buggers to play with, but Honeycomb simply raised her lip, showed her teeth, and growled low and mean. It was clear that she meant business. Scruffy immediately backed away and thereafter remained just beyond the big double doors that led into the conservatory from the main house. *Geez, what got into her! Was it something I did?*

"Honeycomb's really tired now. She'll be in a better humor in a few days," I said, hoping it was true.

All newborns are adorable, even this motley crew. Tip grinned with delight, his quiet chuckle ending in a cough, so like his father's. Under her close supervision, Honeycomb permitted him to sit on the edge of the whelping box and delicately examine each pup. Two had the sleek, wavy coat and silky ears of a golden retriever, except for being sandy in color. The other five sported ears that were perkier, fur that was shaggier, and a squarer jaw than Mom's. One in particular instantly claimed my attention, the spitting image of his old man, already cocky and spunky, not too quick to mind Honeycomb when she was barking her brood into a manageable heap.

"See that one trying to get out of the whelping box?" I said to Heather.

"I know. Chip off the old blockhead, and I'm saving him for you. What are you going to name him? And, more importantly, how is Scruffy going to react?"

"He looks like a 'Raffles' to me. Thief of hearts. Scruffy will just have to cope. What about the rest of the litter?"

"I'm anticipating an easy sell. Tip wants to take a pup down Maine with him this summer, and Patty said she'd be interested."

"*Patty!* How's she going to get that idea past Wyn and Loki?"

"Patty can be a fairly determined woman when she sets her mind to something. And I think hanging around with us has been a consciousness-raising experience as well. Especially Fiona, who is rather like the Wife of Bath in her views on marriage.

Speaking of Fiona, she would just love to take a pup for Laura, but we fear that Omar would never adapt."

"What about Phil?" I suggested.

"Are you kidding? I wouldn't even dare to broach the subject."

"I will. We have eight weeks or so to work on her, right?"

"Oh yes. We won't let the pups go until they're fully weaned."

"Perfect! It will be spring then, well past the vernal equinox. A beautiful season to welcome someone new into the family. We'll have already celebrated Ostara to shake off all the nastiness and negativity of this winter,"

"I like your optimism," Heather said as she busied herself in preparing a tray of mimosas to toast the blessed event. In Heather's view, it was never too early in the morning for champagne.

"Well, I have to admit to a certain frustration with the outcome of the Deluca case. That boy is a murderer, and all he's been tapped for is aggravated assualt," I said.

"The murder evidence was not only circumstantial, it was dubious at best. You know the truth, we know, but nothing could be proved. The Plymouth church poisonings, like so many other crimes, will forever go unsolved. But personally, if I were you, Cass, I'd watch my back with the Deluca boy in the future."

"I think of my continued well-being as proof positive that magic happens."

"Let's get the others. Time to propose a toast. To life and all its glorious complications, even mixed-breed mutts and postponed justice."

"All part of the cosmic cocktail," I agreed.

"Oh, thank Goddess," were Deidre's first words when I answered my kitchen phone.

"Is something wrong, Dee?" In truth, she sounded more triumphant than troubled.

"As the mother of three close-in-age children, I just wanted you to be the *very first* to know that my search for an au pair has paid off, finally. Well, she's not an au pair, exactly. She's a bona fide nanny, and she's affordable. And you know who recommended her? Serena Dove, the doyenne of Saint Rita's Refuge for Women. Serena just happened to see my plea on the Nanny Network. A plea that was being royally ignored, probably because I have this mob of children, practically the Old Woman Who Lived in a Shoe."

"Listen, Dee, are you okay? You sound a little hysterical."

"'Free at last, free at last, Goddess Almighty, free at last.' The children seem to adore her—she has this amazing knack of getting right down on their level." Deidre giggled.

"Wow! Amazing good fortune. But what's so funny?"

"She really is at their level—tiny, round little woman, brown as a berry. Betti Kinsey. Betti with an i."

Bettikins! "Does she carry a teeny-weeny sewing basket?"

Deidre began giggling again. For a minute there, I thought she might not pull out of it. "She just happened to have a basket over her arm when she appeared on my doorstep. It gave me a turn, I'll tell you. And to think that there are still ladies out there who don't believe in magic," she said, chortling.

"Not to throw a bucket of cold water on this love match, but how exactly did she come into Serena Dove's sphere of attention?"

"Some Catholic charity. I didn't get all the details."

"Oh, good. Then they probably did good works together. For a minute there, I was worried that Bettikins might be another abused wife fleeing to Saint Rita's from a homicidal husband."

"You know what I think? I think I conjured this woman out of thin air."

"Yes, I know. When you get to know her better, you'll probably find out she has a Pictish heritage."

"Talk about 'the winter of our discontent,'" Phillipa complained. "Nothing but ice, snow, gloom, and poison. I don't think

I've ever been so thankful to see the willow branches turn yellow and the maple buds redden."

"'If winter comes, can Beltane be far behind?'" Since we were waxing poetic, I paraphrased from my own store of memorized lines. We were sitting on my glassed-in porch, wearing heavy sweaters and gazing out at the waves, hot mugs of coffee warming our fingers and noses. A few sailboats were braving the Atlantic in April, their white sails dazzling in the light of the lowering sun.

From where I was sitting, I could see my own sailor in his navy pea coat, collar turned up, and his jaunty Greek cap set firmly in place as he raked off winter's debris from the perennial herbs. In two days' time, he'd be leaving on another assignment, to join up with *Rainbow Warrior II* on a campaign against pirate fishing in the Pacific. Now he was hurrying to finish some of the heavy cleanup that he deemed to be "man's work," as if ignorant of the fact that I'd done those laborious tasks by myself for all those lonely springtimes before he came into my life.

Scruffy was larking about with a long, trailing branch that winter had trimmed from the white birch. He dropped his prize and looked up at the sound of an approaching car, which he was always the first to detect.

With a riff of soft, celebratory honks of her horn, Heather eased into the driveway and parked the Mercedes. She got out, grinned, and with a flourish, opened the back door of her Mercedes, otherwise known as "the dog car." With a cautious sniff of the air, eight-weeks-old Raffles, a veritable clone of his sire, emerged from the dog carrier and jumped out of the car, looking through the shaggy fur over his eyes with wary bravado. Even his tail had that characteristic briard hook at the end.

Hurrying down the porch stairs, I greeted the little fellow with a dog treat in my hand. I crouched down to his level so that we could exchange kisses, and Raffles chomped up his treat. Feeling a little surer of himself, the pup showed off by peeing on the nearest tree (an art he had not quite mastered yet) and racing around the yard like a wild thing.

Scruffy surveyed this performance with amazed disapproval and his sternest alpha-dog stare. *What's that little baggage doing here? Why isn't he home where he belongs—with his mother?*

Actually, Honeycomb had been giving every evidence of being heartily bored by the whole business of pup-raising. She often left the pups to wander around the conservatory on their own, unless Ishmael appeared. Honeycomb had some sixth sense where Ish was concerned and would chase him remorselessly as he squawked and screamed epithets, green feathers floating through the air, if he ventured anywhere near her pups. But the puppies barked shrilly in Honeycomb's ear, roughhoused and often pulled on her tail, and bit her when they nursed, which they rushed to do every time she lay down to catch a moment's rest. She'd struggle up with an expression of disgust, toss them off, and stalk away. *Enough is enough.*

"This is Raffles," I explained to Scruffy. "It's time for him to leave home, so he's going to live with us and help you in guarding the property."

This scrawny little scamp? He's still wet behind the ears. You got to be kidding, Toots.

"You can teach him how to chase squirrels and crows and UPS men."

Don't know about that. It's very tricky, creeping up on those critters. We briards are famous for our excellent stalking and herding skills.

"Raffles is a briard, too."

Hearing his name, the pup picked up one end of the birch branch, lowered his head, and waggled his rear end. A minute later the two dogs were tug-of-warring around the yard, tussling through piles of soggy old leaves that Joe had collected into a heap. Heather unloaded the wire crate she was loaning me for housebreaking, and we watched the game's progress with indulgent smiles.

"Scruffy is going to really enjoy the company once he gets used to sharing," I said.

"Sure he is, dreamer," Phillipa said, leaning out of the porch door to watch. "But I have to admit, Raffles is a cute little mutt."

Heather and I glanced at each other. Was this a chink in Phillipa's armor? There were still two pups needing homes. "Try talking up the runt," I whispered to Heather "The one that needs special *feeding* and care. And how the poor baby *can't stomach* commercial dog food."

What are friends for if not to con each other into fun new experiences?

Beltane! Surely it was my favorite of all the Sabbats. But, then, I managed to be totally enchanted by whatever Sabbat turned up on the wheel of the year—the drama of Samhain, the hopefulness of Imbolc, the richness of Lammas. Still, Beltane, with its heady mixture of frivolity, creativity, blossoming beauty, and robust sex, had much to recommend it.

We'd decided to celebrate the first of May at Heather's with a traditional Maypole dance during the day. The private Beltane ceremony would be celebrated by starlight and moonlight.

It was a gloriously azure afternoon with a few puffy white clouds like a flock of Summerland sheep. Deidre's children and Laura Belle were invited to dance with us, while Dick manned a hidden CD player playing medieval flute music. The little girls wore Kate Greenaway–style dresses and the boys Greenaway print shirts that Deidre had made. We danced the circle together, each holding a gaily colored ribbon attached to the flower-decorated Maypole. By the ancient, intricate steps of the dance, we wove the ribbons until we were tightly knit together. Then we reversed the steps in the same order to unravel the web.

Our first Maypole—our technique was hardly perfected. As we fell on the soft grass in the highest good humor, exhausted with merry high-stepping, especially we older Maydancers, in a lull that came suddenly upon us, we all heard a sound more welcome than music. It was Laura Belle's voice. She said, "I'm thirsty, Aunt Fifi."

There was laughter to follow, and tears, and hugs, and our hostess pouring glasses of lemonade and woodruff-flavored May wine to toast the miraculous occasion.

The balmy temperatures continued that night; a half moon shone on the ring of stones Heather had laid out on her extensive grounds. Surrounded on three sides by trees, the circle for our celebration was all wonderfully magical.

But to me, the loveliest celebration came later when Joe and I took a midnight walk on the beach, leaving the two disappointed dogs at home, noses pressed at the kitchen window. I'd brought a blanket that we spread between secluded rocks. On Beltane, another sacred tradition, the fertility of earth always must be encouraged by lovers. In New England, on the Plymouth seashore, it might be just a little chilly, but we hardly noticed until much later that night. The moon was long down, but the brilliant constellations above us described their timeless mythic patterns. I felt at that moment that they belonged to us—our own lucky, loving stars.

Epilogue

"The tarot," my friend Phillipa declares, "is a key to ancient wisdom. Each card has a story to tell—about the future and the past." She turns up The Fool, a card of the Major Arcana. "See this youngster walking along the cliff's edge with a merry dog companion? That's you, dear Cass, and your faithful dog, Scruffy. You are gazing into the horizon, not watching your step, careless of danger. Probably leading your friends along the same narrow trail. About to make another leap of faith."

What could I say? It was all so true. Phillipa reads people as well as she reads the tarot.

"But there's much to be said for The Fool," she continues, tapping the deck with her finger, the shining dark wings of her hair falling forward. "She's on the path to adventure. Risky but rewarding. Exciting. Edgy in the true sense of the word. And, always, amazing. There may not be safety and security ahead, but there will be love, laughter, and bad news for bad guys."

Not such a terrible prospect. I'll take it.